COLUMBIA UNIVERSITY STUDIES IN ENGLISH
AND COMPARATIVE LITERATURE

A DICTIONARY OF
SPANISH TERMS IN ENGLISH

A Dictionary of
Spanish Terms in English

With Special Reference to the American Southwest

By

Harold W. Bentley

OCTAGON BOOKS

A DIVISION OF FARRAR, STRAUS AND GIROUX

New York   1973

Reprinted 1973
by special arrangement with Columbia University Press

OCTAGON BOOKS
A DIVISION OF FARRAR, STRAUS & GIROUX, INC.
19 Union Square West
New York, N. Y. 10003

Library of Congress Cataloging in Publication Data

Bentley, Harold Woodmansee, 1899—
    A dictionary of Spanish terms in English.

    Original ed. issued in series: Columbia University studies in English and comparative literature.

    Originally presented as the author's thesis, Columbia.

    Bibliography: p.
    1. English language in the United States—Provincialisms—Southwest, New.   2. English language—Foreign words and phrases—Spanish.   I. Title.   II. Series: Columbia University studies in English and comparative literature.

Printed in USA by
Thomson-Shore, Inc.
Dexter, Michigan

TO

JOSEPH CHARLES BENTLEY

AND THE MEMORY OF

GLADYS WOODMANSEE BENTLEY

ACKNOWLEDGMENTS

The author is grateful and heavily indebted to those who read this work or portions of it in the course of preparation and by their suggestions or criticisms greatly improved it. He would especially thank the following persons: Professor William Witherlee Lawrence, Professor Harry Morgan Ayres, Professor Ashley Horace Thorndike, Professor William Cabell Greet, Doctor Clarence Gohdes and Professor George Philip Krapp of the English Department, Columbia University; in particular, Professor Krapp, under whose direction the study was made, and who gave assistance and counsel on many occasions; also Professor Federico de Onís and Professor Frank Callcott of the Spanish Department, and Professor Louis Herbert Gray of the Department of Oriental Languages.

To Doctor Howard J. Savage, Secretary of the Carnegie Foundation for the Advancement of Teaching, the author owes much. He would also thank Mr. Philip M. Hayden, Assistant Secretary of Columbia University, and Mr. and Mrs. Paul E. Webb.

To the Columbia University Press he is indebted for many favors performed graciously through the Manager, Mr. Charles G. Proffitt, and for constructive editorial guidance by Miss Ida Lynn and Doctor Clarke F. Ansley.

To Miss Ethel Driggs he is indebted for intelligent and tireless assistance in preparing the typescript and finally but not least to his wife, Verna Decker Bentley, for criticisms and encouragement throughout the prolonged endeavor.

CONTENTS

INTRODUCTION

INTRODUCTION

GENERAL CONSIDERATIONS

I. PRESENTATION

Spanish-English contacts in America began when Spanish sailors and British seamen encountered each other on the waters and coasts of the New World. Those contacts have continued to the very present and with increased opportunity for the association of the people speaking the two languages. In view of this condition and of the fact that Spanish and English are both current, widespread, and aggressive languages in the Christian world of today, we may with propriety and the prospect of interesting results ask a number of questions, sociological and linguistic, which bear upon the language situation: What are the chief linguistic results of this association of speeches? At what period during the time under inquiry and where within the territory under consideration have the more important contacts taken place? More specifically, has either of the languages replaced or begun to replace the other as the language of the people within the territory concerned? What bilinguistic phenomena have arisen? Has the grammatical structure of either language been affected and, if so, how and to what extent? To what extent also has one language borrowed words or phrases from the other? How extensively are these used? Do they occur naturally and commonly both in the written and in the spoken language of the people? Do such borrowings represent a permanent and useful part of the vocabulary of the borrowers? What changes, if any, in form and pronunciation have taken place in the items borrowed?

II. Aim of the Study

This study aims to throw some light on the foregoing questions from one point of view, that of the English language. In other words, its chief purpose is to inquire into and to determine as far as possible the Spanish element found today or formerly in the vocabulary of the English language, particularly American English, written and spoken, as a result of its contacts with Spanish-speaking peoples in and about North America from the earliest times of recorded events in North America to the present time. It may be assumed at the outset that in the main these borrowings and influences have been a result of the association of the two languages in the southwestern territory of the United States as at present constituted. For this reason the study resolves itself largely into a consideration of the linguistic situation in that territory along with the historical background necessary for such a study.

A consideration of the facts wherever there have been intimate linguistic contacts, as for instance in the case of Latin in the south of Europe, French and Scandinavian in England or French in Canada, serves to bear out the generalization that among human institutions language is one of the most enduring in its effects and one of the last to yield in the decadence of a system of institutions. Art, science, law, government, and even religion may be replaced with greater ease than language. Appropriate recognition of this is important in a study of the influence of Spanish on English in North America, for Spanish has been extensively used on this continent for nearly four centuries and even now it is the common speech in nearly all of the republics of South America, of Mexico and of the neighboring islands and territories. For a long and important period, also, Spanish was the dominant language throughout the domain now composing a great part of the United States.

Perhaps even more important for the present consideration
is the fact that in many towns and cities of the United
States Spanish is spoken today by a large proportion of the
population and it is heard and generally understood by
nearly all who are native to that region. And although the
Anglo-American civilization is overpowering and in time
may obliterate the Spanish civilization in the southwestern
part of the United States, the Spanish language maintains
at present an important place in the lives of the people of
that region. As pointed out in detail in another place, it
has added not a few popular words to the common vocabulary of the American people.

III. Summary of Spanish-English Contacts in America

To comprehend, even in part, the race and language
contacts in the border territory of Mexico and the United
States and thereby to understand the possibilities of language borrowings and influences, it is helpful to know
something of the historical background and of the present
conditions with respect to population and social relationships. To trace these factors will be attempted in detail
further on in this study. More than three centuries ago,
territory which is now New Mexico and Arizona was first
colonized by Spanish-speaking people. Most of those original Spanish settlers were driven out of the territory or
killed by the native Indians. Within a century, however,
permanent settlements had been established in New Mexico. Until the invasion of the United States Army in 1846
Spanish culture, including of course the Spanish language,
existed—even flourished, in a rough way—without inter-
ference or competition. In the West Indies, in Florida, and
in California, likewise, Spanish life, language, and culture
make up the foundation of civilized society upon which the
English- or Saxo-American later built. In Texas, because

of the Austin and other colonies and grants of land, the intermixing of Spanish and English began early in the nineteenth century. By 1850 the contacts whether political, economic, social, cultural, religious, or linguistic had become intimate in all regions of the country under study.

The number of people of both races who have been affected by these contacts is much greater than is commonly supposed. This is particularly true as regards the Spanish and Mexican elements. When in 1846 American soldiers entered the Southwest by way of the Santa Fe Trail, there were probably not more than 75,000 Spanish-speaking people, including Spaniards, Mexicans, and Indians in all this territory, excluding Texas. Fifty years later the number had almost doubled. Today there are approximately as many Mexicans in the southwestern states of the United States as there are in the corresponding border states of Mexico herself. Many communities in New Mexico and Arizona are almost as Mexican as towns in Mexico. Los Angeles is estimated as the second largest Mexican city in the world and in cities and towns on the borderline the inhabitants are not infrequently divided about evenly, as, for instance, in El Paso, Texas.

Significant for the study of the contacts of these two peoples are, first, the attitude taken toward the Spanish-speaking element by the English-speaking, and, second, the attitude maintained by the Spaniards or Mexicans concerning themselves. These two attitudes vary. While in one section sympathy and interest may predominate and things Spanish be adopted eagerly, in another there may be antipathy and a resultant depreciation or even contempt. The attitude that obtains in a given region will, of course, relate directly to the degree to which one people has influenced the other. Then, too, the feeling has rather generally persisted among the native and immigrant Mexicans in the United States that they are still in their native country and are a part of Mexico. This notion also has its effect. Although the Mexican population in the United States is relatively permanent, there is not much desire for Americanization except as it improves the economic status. American habits, customs, commodities, and language may be taken over for this purpose, but citizenship does not seem so alluring as it is to the prospective American from other foreign countries who goes through the various required steps in anticipation of becoming American. Likewise, the American residing in Mexico rarely considers becoming a Mexican citizen.

As a result of this attitude, race antagonism has existed with varying intensity. It has assumed most undesirable aspects in communities where Americans of low cultural standard have crowded in with the railroad and other modern developments and have assumed an air of superiority towards the native Spanish-speaking people. And yet, notwithstanding this fact, there has been continuous, direct, and often intimate contact between these peoples. Where this is true the influences of the two languages on each other may be expected to be evident and the respective borrowings and mixtures greatest.

IV. Spanish Borrowings from English

The motives prompting English borrowings from Spanish are varied. Absolute necessity is not always the explanation. Picturesqueness and connotations as well as local color are sought after in a great many instances. Spanish borrowings from English, on the other hand, have seldom been made from any other motive than that of necessity. When new commodities, practices, or concepts, not found among Spanish-speaking peoples, have been taken over from the English-speaking races it has been necessary to take over names for the things as well.

Likewise pronunciation and spelling have been adapted. In many instances new Spanish words have been coined with the English borrowing as a root. English "home run" for instance has given the Spanish the word *jonronero*. A *jonronero* is one who makes home runs just as a *zapatero* is one who makes *zapatos* (shoes) or a *panadero* is one who makes *pan* (bread). Again "scraper," an English word for a road-building implement, has produced the Spanish equivalent *escrepa;* from "plug" comes *ploga; ponchar* from "puncture"; *vamos flat* from English "to have a flat tire" although the Spanish, literally translated, means "we go flat." Other adaptions are *llaqui* (jack, a lifting tool); *rieles* (rails); *talla* (railroad tie); *yompa* (jumper, wearing apparel). Examples such as these could easily run into the hundreds and perhaps thousands. Their listing involves a separate and important study in itself. It has been done[1] in part and for restricted sections but as far as I know a comprehensive study has not been made.

English words have been and are being introduced by the scores by those who speak Spanish in America but who are in contact with English-speaking people and the many new phases of Anglo-American life and inventions.

V. English Borrowings from Spanish[2]

The English-in-Spanish phase of the situation is mentioned here merely because this study deals with the other side of the picture. That is, it attempts to explain and illustrate more clearly and completely than has been done heretofore how and why Spanish words were taken into English. Because of the readiness with which English

---

[1] Aurelio M. Espinosa, *New Mexican Spanish;* Manuel Gamio, *The Mexican Immigrant in the United States;* H. E. McKinstry, "The English Language in Mexico," *American Mercury*, Vol. XIX.

[2] Words recognized by Webster as fully adopted into English are printed in roman type.

makes adoptions from other languages it would be expected that a number of words, phrases, and expressions would be taken over as a part of English in general. The reasons are not always determinable. In some instances words have been adopted because there existed no adequate words in English. More often Spanish elements are taken over into English for local color effects, for their richness of connotation, including humor, for picturesqueness, or for descriptive contribution of some kind. Such words as "siesta," "hackamore," "cockroach" (from Spanish *cucaracha*) are illustrative of the first situation. "Rodeo," *savvy, mañana,* and *juzgado* illustrate the second. Many such words have passed through interesting changes of spelling and pronunciation at the hands and tongues of their adopters and some words from Spanish are common in the spoken language, or at least not uncommon, that are not found in print. The business man, for instance, talking to his employees will use with naturalness and effectiveness such words as "pilon," *pagare, factura;* likewise the farmer out directing his laborers or discussing the problems and subjects of his work finds *tiempo, soga,* and "sacaton," falling off his tongue with all the ease of English words; and the ranchman would sorely miss *colear, remuda, caballada,* "hackamore," and "chaps" if they were taken from his vocabulary. It is important to keep in mind that nearly all of these Spanish words are of a popular, rather than a learned, nature.

Some of them apparently never appear in print; others appear in print very rarely. Moreover, it is quite likely that many of them would hardly be recognized in printed form by the people who use them in common parlance. This perhaps is not so illogical as might at first appear inasmuch as the same situation would be true in the case of some of the native Anglo-Saxon words used by the same people.

Practically the entire vocabulary of some of the people in question has been acquired through ear learning and not eye learning. In any case, the average person along the border who uses these Spanish words regularly in his vocabulary if confronted with a printed page on which appeared *tegua, cienega, hectolitro, olla, jaquima,* and *que hubo le* might either fail to recognize them or at least might mispronounce them at the first attempt. If, however, the same words were spelled "taywa," "sinigie," "hec" or "hecktroll-iter," "oyuh," "hackamore," and "cubo," the same person might without hesitation recognize them as part of his vocabulary.

VI. NATURE OF AND CHANGES IN ENGLISH BORROWINGS FROM SPANISH

All phenomena, which relate to the intermixing of Spanish and English, have a place in a study of this sort. For this reason, an attempt has been made in these pages to indicate changes or developments in the forms or meanings of words which have come into English from Spanish. Words, for instance, like "rodeo," "sombrero," "lariat," "coyote," *jefe,* and "junta" have undergone a change in meaning as they have been taken over more completely into English usage. The word "rodeo" may be cited as an example. "Rodeo" means literally a round-up or gathering together of the live stock on a ranch. The actual thing it stands for in Spanish and also in English originally among early border ranchmen is quite different from that for which it stands generally in the minds of Americans today, or in New York City, where the annual rodeo is performed by professionals, men and beasts, at Madison Square Garden. From the process of an annual, or at any event a periodic, inventory of the live stock on a ranch in the West it is coming to stand for a theatrical performance not unlike those of Roman times where man and beast matched skill for the entertainment of their curious fellow beings. On the ranch it was not *'ro:di:o* but *ro:'ðɛ:o*. Although a *ro:'ðɛ:o* was looked upon as somewhat of a celebration or fiesta, it was performed with all the seriousness and earnestness of the cattle trade or any other industry. There was nothing artificial, no sham about the performance, but genuine effort of man pitted, for a very definite purpose, against resistance of cows and horses and calves. Skill in riding, roping, and running was taken for granted and with no applause from the grand stand. There was neither time nor place for tricks and stunts in the actual *ro:'ðɛ:o* business, except after regular duties had been performed. In short a *ro:'ðɛ:o* in the cattle business was, and in a few places still is, a regular affair of gathering, identifying, segregating, marking, and counting the stock: an inventory. Contrast this with the New York citizen's *'ro:di:o*, with its animals prodded artificially to run and buck and cavort about and its professional contestants for prizes all exerting themselves as little as necessary in order to obtain the allotted share of the gate receipts. The tricks and stunts of a theatrical performance, in fact, a vaudeville with old steers, maltreated calves, spiritless nags, and expatriated cowhands as actors signifies the present meaning of rodeo. The earnest *rodeo* of Spanish is in English no longer a *rodeo*, and the term will seldom be heard used in the sense of a round-up; it has come to mean a kind of entertainment following the trail of Ringling or Barnum and Bailey. The change in meaning has taken place since the word entered the English vocabulary.

VII. EFFECT OF ECONOMIC LIFE OF THE PEOPLE ON THE BORROWINGS

As one reads certain literature and accounts relating to the Southwest, he encounters in English context words which are good modern Spanish in common usage among speakers of Spanish but which are seldom used by the present-day American of the same territory. Evidently the status of these words has undergone a change. It is not an unusual phenomenon for words or phrases of one language to be borrowed by another and to have but a short literary or colloquial life in the new environment. As a matter of common philological knowledge, many words borrowed by the English during the Renaissance were not in current use a century later and have never been readopted. The same is true as with regard to Spanish in America. Spanish words in question are in many respects similar to English words of Anglo-Saxon or other origin that, having been current for a time, long or short, have passed into disuse. In English these words can be, and have been, listed in unabridged dictionaries. Some of those from Spanish in America have been listed in the vocabulary section of this inquiry. The number of obsolescent Spanish-English words is thus far comparatively small. It is, however, increasing as the several phases of frontier life in which they were useful disappear. One such phase of American life is that of the cattle industry in the old Southwest.

A. *Cowboy Life and Language*

Of all agents responsible for the incorporation of Spanish words into the English vocabulary in America probably none has been so prolific as that picturesque and romantic figure in the life of America—the western *vaquero*. The cowboy learned the art of the lasso, including broncobusting and steer roping, from the Spanish and Mexican *vaqueros* with whom he worked and associated intimately on the cattle ranches and the ranges along both sides of the border. He found it convenient and sometimes necessary to adopt the nomenclature of its various tools and processes just as today descendants of those Mexicans and Spaniards, under conditions reversed, are finding it convenient to incorporate *besbol, aiscrim* (ice cream), *ploga,* and numerous other words of English origin into their vocabularies as they take up with things American or Anglo-American. Likewise, the cowboy, having adopted the vocation, the paraphernalia, and the words of the Spanish, rode romantically along over the "llanos," "mesas," or mountains on his "bronc," or his "mustang," usually at a "running" walk, singing ballads to his poetic *chiquita* or *querida* or to his prosaic "dobes." His head was shaded by a "sombrero"; his *caballo* was urged on by a "quirt," and his legs were protected by *chaparejos* or more briefly "chaps." He seldom allowed himself to be seen in public or in private without his "lariat" or *reata* or one of its equivalents, the *pita,* or the *mecate.* In an instant he could, if necessary form a loop through the "hondoo" (*honda*) and prepare to "lasso" almost any animate or inanimate object that he might wish to capture. If his horse was not bridle-wise he controlled it by means of a "hackamore," (Spanish *jaquima*) a *bosal* or a *cabresto* rather than a bridle, and if the trip was long or pertained to a "rodeo" he was provided with fresh mounts in the *remuda* or *caballada* which was under the supervision of a "wrangler."

The words indicated are only a few of many Spanish words used by the American rangeman regularly and naturally in his everyday work and conversation.[3]

[3] "The speech of the American cowpunchers, on the other hand, is nearly as much Mexican as English and in common conversation many Spanish words are met, permanently engrafted upon the local tongue and used in preference to their English equivalents. For instance, one rarely hears the word *yes,* it being usually given as the Spanish *si.* The small numerals, *one, two,* etc., are usually spoken as *uno, dos,* etc. A horse is nearly always called *caballo,* a man an *hombre,* a woman a *moharrie* (*mujer*). Even cattle are sometimes called *vacas,* though this is not usual. The cow man of the range clings closely to the designation *cows* for all the horned creatures in his possession. Everyone says *agua* when meaning *water.* The Spanish diminutives are in common use in the English speech of this region, as *chico, chiquito.* The cow-

Now that the cowboy has been civilized almost completely out of a vocation, the question arises whether the words that he unwittingly corralled and branded for the mother tongue will go the way of the vocation itself.

B. *Early Transportation*

Another phase of life in the Southwest which utilized to advantage Spanish terminology was that of early transportation. Before the wagon was introduced and long after it was used on the better roads, before the stage coach, before the train, the automobile, and the airplane, the pack outfit, composed of one pack animal or a pack train, served to carry provisions, supplies, machinery, household goods, ore, wool, and other commodities over valleys and mountains, across terrible *jornadas*. Intercourse between the outposts of civilization and the centres or markets relied on these *atajos* of "burros" or mules. The whole outfit of a pack train is known as the *atajo* (Spanish *hatajo*). The animals whether "burros," "mules," or "horses" make up the

---

boy will speak of the *cavvieyah* or *cavvieyard* (*caballado*) instead of the *horse herd*. One hears *poco tiempo* instead of *pretty soon;* and this expression as coming from a native he will learn all too well, as also the expression *mañana* (to-morrow), which really means *maybe sometime but probably never.*

"There are many descriptive words used in the ranch work which would be strange to the Northern rancher, such as *rincon, salado, rio, mesa,* etc.: and many of the proper names would seem unusual, as applied to the Mexican cow hands, slim, dark, silent fellows, each with a very large hat and a very small cigarette, who answer as Jose, Juan, Pablo, Sanchez, or Antone, and who when they are uncertain answer, as do all their American fellows, with the all convenient reply *Quien sabe!* (kin savvy, as the cowpuncher says).

"The Northern rancher country got most of its customs with its cattle, from the Spanish-American cattle country, and the latter has stamped upon the industry not only its methods but some of its speech. The cowboy's *chaps* are the *chaparejos* of the Spaniard, who invented them. Such words as *latigo, aparejo, broncho* are current all through the Northern mountain and plain region, and are firmly fixed in the vocabulary of the cow country of the entire West."—Emerson Hough, *The Story of the Cowboy*, p. 26.

remuda. While being packed or unpacked they are blinded by means of the *tapaojo.* The pack saddle and accoutrements are universally referred to as the *aparejo,* and are "cinched" on the animals securely by means of one or more "cinches" and *latigos.* A *mozo* or *arriero* is in charge of the *atajo.* Numerous other Spanish words were used by Americans engaged in transportation enterprises *a la Española.*

A third frontier activity which involved the adoption of Spanish terms by English-speaking people is found in the business of colonization, particularly in Texas. Each colonizing enterprise, for instance, was directed by one or more *empresarios.* An *empresario* was one who introduced at least two hundred families into the territory. Letters patent, authority and regulations were defined by means of *cedulas* issued to the colonists through the *alcaldes* usually at the *juntas* of the *ayuntamientos.* According to the colonization laws of 1823 land was parceled out on the basis of family responsibility in portions measured by *varas* (three geometrical feet). A portion of land was described as a league (5,000 *varas*), a *sitio* (a square league), an "hacienda" (five *sitios*), or a "labor" (1,000,000 square *varas*). Taxes or other contributions were paid in "pesos" or "reales" or, if in kind, by "arrobas" or "quintales." Some of these terms are now seldom heard; others have become technical in aspect and are known chiefly to lawyers; others have become obsolete.

No doubt a number of the words once extensively used in these and other phases of frontier life will be adapted to other uses and remain active in the language. A large proportion of them may reasonably be expected to experience the same fate as that of many Spanish words borrowed earlier in Europe by the English for a special purpose.

VIII. FULLY NATURALIZED WORDS

On the other hand, some words taken from the Spanish as a result of contact in and about North America have already become so much a part of the English language that people in general do not recognize them as being of Spanish origin. Many of these, being among the earlier borrowings, have undergone changes in form or in pronunciation that make them difficult of recognition. These changes either of form or pronunciation were not sudden; they were arrived at after other forms had had a vogue. Among the more fully naturalized words may be mentioned "alligator," "avocado," "banana," "barbecue," "canoe," "cockroach," "cocoa," "corral," "creole," "tomato," "tobacco," "mosquito," "mustang," "cannibal," "hammock," "sassafras," and "vanilla."

These words, accepted without limitations as part of the English language, give rise to the question, how many Spanish words actually are in the English language?

IX. DICTIONARY AND BIOLOGICAL LISTS

English speakers, by and large, if confronted with a complete list of the Spanish words and phrases found in the *New English Dictionary* and Webster's *New International Dictionary* together with those used along the southwestern border and those found in English writings in America would undoubtedly be amazed at its length. The Spanish derivation of some of them would be surprising. This would be true in particular of some of the very common words such as "hammock," "corridor," "plaza," "corral," "alligator," "cannibal," etc. To many people it would no doubt appear that the dictionary makers had included words which have no more reason for being included than do thousands of others not found in the list. They might also be surprised not to find words which they had "always supposed" were Spanish but which are really of some other derivation; such words for instance as "tarantula," "gallop," "cayuse," "bandanna," "creosote," and "buffalo." And finally there would be words in the list which are not generally known among speakers of English but which are really in frequent use in the United States. Among such might be "olla," *tequa*, "piloncillo," *pagaré, pelado*, "aparejo." Of all such words in the complete list the number that will become a legitimate, useful, and permanent part of the English vocabulary is perhaps relatively small. Even such words as "quirt," "corral," *remuda, empresario*, and *caliche* which have replaced the English equivalents or forestalled them are losing or may lose their standing in the language as the phases of American life in which they are useful are replaced. It is not highly profitable, although interesting, to speculate as to which will be permanent. Some, having weathered the elimination process, have become well established, like, for example, "alligator," "cockroach," "hammock." "vanilla," A number of others are at present a part of the English vocabulary by virtue of their being needed and used by English speakers or writers in an English context.

Of the complete list totaling thousands of words, relatively few have become sufficiently a part of the English language to justify extended treatment by way of derivation, definition, pronunciation, variant spellings, and illustrations of usage. It is with those few, approximately four hundred, that this study is chiefly concerned. Among them are only a few of the scores of Spanish words listed in dictionaries as biological names of animals, plants, and insects found in Spanish American countries for which there may not exist an English name because there has been no occasion for it. To understand this it should be remembered that when the specimen in question has been discovered by an English-speaking scientist after it has already been known to the natives by an Indian or Spanish name, a scientific name is given to the specimen and the native name is accepted for common purposes of speaking and writing. Seldom does the specimen become of sufficient importance in commerce or in other fields to develop for its name an extended usage in the English language. Words which are notable exceptions to this rule have been included in the study.

X. Borrowings from South America

A relatively important and large number of Spanish words now in the English vocabulary are a result of South American contacts. This being a study of adoptions in North America they are not given the full treatment here that words from North American Spanish contacts receive. For completeness of the lists, and more especially because of the common belief that many of them are of North American sources and may therefore be sought in the vocabulary of this study, they have been inserted in their alphabetical order and followed by the notation that their source is South American. Some of the more commonly known words of South American Spanish and Portuguese (Brazil) origin are "alpaca," "armadillo," "chinchilla," "cocaine," "condor," "cougar," "coumarin," "jaguar," "javelina," "llama," "maté," "pampa," "peccary," "poncho," "puma," "quinine," "tapioca," "tapir," "vicuña."

XI. Spanish Place Names in the United States

Spanish place names in the United States merit an entire chapter or even a treatise. In this study they could not be entirely ignored.[4] An outstanding fact about Spanish place names found in the United States is their number.

---

[4] A list of place names by states will be found in Appendix II.

The exact total is not ascertainable without making a careful investigation but it may be estimated at about two thousand names of cities and towns besides a large number of names for landscape features such as rivers, mountains, etc. California leads with more than four hundred Spanish names of cities and towns alone, New Mexico has more than two hundred and fifty, and Texas has about the same number. Colorado has more than a hundred, and Arizona nearly a hundred. All the one-time Spanish territory might be expected to have a sprinkling of Spanish place names. In the more sparsely settled regions like Nevada, Wyoming, Utah, and even Oregon, Montana, and Idaho the number of names is not large but the percentage is fairly high. It is more surprising to find Spanish place names in almost every part of the United States—Pennsylvania, Ohio, New Jersey, New York, Alabama, Georgia, Tennessee, Mississippi.

An examination of the names in states formerly Mexican territory indicates that there has been no hesitation in combining Spanish words with English to form appropriate names for places. It is noticeable, furthermore, that the tendency to resort to this practice is more pronounced in California and Colorado than it is in New Mexico and Arizona. This is, no doubt, explained by the fact that California and Colorado have been more completely under the influence and control of Americans than have the other states, at least until recently. In California we find listed in the *United States Postal Guide* an "Altaville," a "Sierraville," and a "Vacaville" besides word combinations such as "Buena Park," "Casitas Springs," "Hermosa Beach," "Lomita Park," "Point Arena," "Point Loma," "Point Reyes," etc. In Colorado is a "Niñaview," a "Cuchara Camps" and an "Escalante Forks." In New Mexico we find a "Romeroville," and a "Glenrio."

Of interest also are the changes in spelling of Spanish words due to Anglicizing. In California *chilicote* has become "Chilcoot," *chuchilla* is spelled "Chowchilla," *recua* becomes "Requa" and *Hueco* has become "Waco." Not a few of the names themselves are interesting or amusing when translated. Such for example as "Loco" (crazy), in Texas, Oklahoma and Georgia; "Callaboose" (jail), Kentucky; "Mosca" (fly), Colorado. Again, it is noteworthy that some names recur many times. There are "Mesas" in at least eight states, "Alamos" in six, "Cubas" in six, "Buena Vistas" in eight, "Bonanzas" in four, "Bonitas" in the same number and "El Dorados" in thirteen.

Without thoroughgoing research it is impossible to give the explanation for all these Spanish place names, particularly those found in the East. A brief consideration, however, gives justification for belief that the Mexican War is responsible for some (Buena Vista, Monterey, Molino), that others are in commemoration of early explorers (De Soto, Escalante) and that landscape features account for others (Bonita, Loma, Bella Vista).

Finally, two points should be kept in mind when considering the lists of Spanish place names in the appendix. In the first place there are undoubtedly a fairly large number of Spanish place names that have been omitted. Secondly, a number of those listed although they are Spanish in form and sometimes in meaning may not be taken from Spanish. Some may have been coined, some are probably from American Indian dialects, and others may be Italian or French in direct origin.

XIII. Method of Assembling Materials

In assembling material a list of Spanish words and phrases was first compiled from personal knowledge, and from dictionaries, glossaries, word lists, etc. Then an attempt was made to obtain examples of the usage of these words in an English context. To accomplish this required an examination, at first hand, of the literature of America from the earliest contacts of English-speaking and Spanish-speaking peoples on this continent to modern times. A few words were added to the list during this process. Inasmuch as there are many words used in the spoken language that never get into print it has been impossible to illustrate every word recorded, except by personal testimony. In some instances nothing is lost by this lack of citations. Where necessary for clearness, accurate examples of oral usage have been included. Besides the literary sources mentioned, much material for the study has come from information already recorded in isolated or restricted works and in the various glossaries, word lists, and dictionaries which make a specialty of foreign contributions to the English vocabulary. Perhaps even more important and significant is that material taken from conversations with speakers of both languages, and from personal experiences with the contacts between English and Spanish in the southwestern United States. All words included in the study have been checked against the *New English Dictionary*, Webster's *New International Dictionary*, and Skeat's *Etymological Dictionary*.

HISTORICAL BACKGROUND

I. Spanish-English Contacts

A. *Europe*

The adoption of a single word by one language from another involves intercourse of some kind between the two languages. The contact may be direct and intimate or it may be indirect and distant. It may be in one field such as literature or it may be in many—literature, commerce, politics, science, art. This study does not concern itself to a great extent with the contributions of the Spanish language to the English as they were made independent of the contacts of the speakers of the two languages in and about North America. Yet long before the Spanish-English contacts in America attained linguistic significance the English vocabulary contained many words from the Spanish. The early intercourse of English and Spanish in Europe, which led to the adoption of the words by English speakers, concerns us here only as an introduction to a historical resumé of the background of this study of Spanish-English contacts in and about North America.

It will be recalled then that before the English nation under the first Tudors had recovered from the Wars of the Roses, Spain had emerged from divided weakness to united strength under Ferdinand and Isabella, the former of Castile and the latter of Aragon. And although the late fifteenth century is not the time of initial contacts between the English-speaking and the Spanish-speaking peoples, it is the time when such contacts assumed linguistic importance. The "Catholic sovereigns" encouraged expansion of their domain through exploration and colonization. For a time Spain's only formidable rival in such exploration and colonization was another Catholic country, Portugal, and Portugal, during Spain's internal troubles, had already explored the coasts of Africa and founded an empire there. The rivalry between Portugal and Spain could be, and was, theoretically and simply solved by the Pope, who, as sovereign of all Catholics, had drawn a line down the map from one pole to the other a hundred leagues west of the Azores. All lands discoverable to the west of this arbitrary line he gave to Spain and all lands discoverable to the east of the line he gave to Portugal. This line left the ocean officially free to the two Catholic sea powers, eliminated

Portugal from North America, but gave her a chance at the eastern parts of South America. Thus we have Spanish rather than Portuguese spoken in the Americas except Brazil where Portuguese is the official tongue. With the strengthening, however, of the British under the Henrys (1485–1547), and particularly Elizabeth (1558–1603), England began to have commercial and naval ambitions of her own. These ambitions were exemplified in such spirits as Sir Francis Drake and his adventuring captains on the high seas and Sir Walter Raleigh in the realm of colonial development. The wave of antagonism on the ocean and in the colonial realms between Spanish and English was thus started; it received additional force from the feeling in England toward Catholicism at that time. There resulted a long and, at times, fierce struggle between English and Spanish seamen for right of way on the ocean. From this struggle came also England's challenge of the monopoly Spain and Portugal, chiefly the former, held on colonization in America. England suffered a relapse in the 1550's under the forced policy of the Catholic Mary Tudor, daughter of Henry VIII and Catherine of Aragon, and was fettered wherever possible to give an advantage to Spain. With Mary's marriage to Philip of Spain, which contravened the wishes of her English subjects, England seemed little more than a vassal of the Spanish monarchy. The consequence was restriction of development in greatness at home, on the seas, and in America. It was shortly before or shortly after this time, that the large majority of Spanish words now current, or once current, in the English vocabulary in Europe were introduced.[5] It is quite likely that

[5] "Armada" came into usage about 1550 in the forms *armadoes* and also *armada;* "carbonado" was used about this time and in 1586 by Shakespeare; "cask," a word from Spanish, is recorded first in 1548; "comrade," also used by Shakespeare, appears in print in 1591; "cork" appears about this time as also "hidalgo," "peccadillo," "renegade" and others. The usage of "don"

many more words would have been adopted by the English had the feelings between the two nations been less hostile.

B. *America*

Under Cromwell this hostility next found expression. Cromwell revived English activity on the seas and in the Americas. The place of chief activity in America was in the West Indies and specifically the island of Jamaica. There English colonists and Spanish-speaking people came into intimate and constant contact. It was inevitable that there should be an interchange of words. With this contact, however, we find ourselves out of Europe and in America. And it is the American borrowings with which this study chiefly concerns itself.

English explorers of America had already recorded in their annals a few Spanish names for new things seen during their American travels. "Alligator" had appeared in English context as "largato" and perhaps with other variant spellings; "cockroach" was reported by Captain John Smith as "cacarootch"; "mosquitos" had been discovered as well as "sassafras" and other things with Spanish names. Some of the words had been picked up in the West Indies and others farther north along the coast.

C. *Geographical Delineations in America*

With the exception of the Jamaica colony, English colonization in America started up the northern coast and extended itself southward until it met the Spanish of Florida, Louisiana, and the Antilles. Contacts of importance linguistically aside from those already mentioned did not take place there until about 1700. It is therefore helpful at

---

is questionable until 1568 and "negro" became a much-used English word beginning about 1555. "Junta," "picaroon," and others were adopted shortly after 1600 and "marino" as late as 1780. Shakespeare, as might be expected, used a number of Spanish words. and so did other writers of his day.

ths point to review the historical facts bearing upon the exploration and colonization periods and to fix in the mind a rather clear picture of the conditions in the territory extending from the Rio Grande on the south to an irregular line on the north running across the entire continent. The line would begin at a point on the northern California coast and cross to another point on the northern Florida coast. The line would pass through what is now the middle portion of the states of Idaho and Wyoming, touch Nebraska and Kansas, go through Oklahoma, pass along Arkansas, and run above Louisiana and Florida. To be of value such a picture must not be confusing in detail yet adequate to present the main contacts resulting from the movements of individuals and groups that have taken and are taking part in the great drama of the Southwest. The picture, too, must include all the elements that have contributed to the linguistic situation. For the earlier period this would embrace the mode of travel and transportation of goods, the chief vocations and avocations, the scarcity of white women, the foods, the clothes and the equipment of man and beast, the social and political organizations and all the other factors which contributed to the results as set down in another chapter of this study.

II. Historical Outline by Regions

The purpose of the following few pages is to outline the picture and to fill in some of the details.

From a linguistic point of view except as a background not much is to be gained by dwelling long on the history of the region now making up the states of the Southwest, California and Florida, before the opening of the nineteenth century. Before 1800 contacts in this territory were occasional and few as compared with what took place after serious colonization by the Anglo-Americans began.

A. *Florida*

In the case of Florida,[6] we may without much inconvenience for this study pass briefly over the events from the time when Ponce de Leon first visited there in 1513 to the early years of the nineteenth century when the United States was fast drawing in the lines that gave her formal control in 1821. We thus pass over the tragic story of the expedition of Panfilo de Narvaez in 1527 when five hundred and ninety-six out of six hundred men perished "somewhere in Florida." Among the four survivors was Nuñez Cabeza de Vaca, from whom we later hear. We also pass by the desperate conflicts of Jean Ribaut and his French Lutherans or Huguenots against fanatic Inquisitors under command of Pedro Menendez de Aviles. Nor need we dwell long on the first English-Spanish contacts in Florida which were hostile and in the form of an attack on St. Augustine in 1586 by Sir Francis Drake and another by Captain John Davis in 1665. With these exceptions the contentions in Florida were until near 1700 between the Spanish and French but for fifty years after that date the Spanish of Florida and the English of the Carolinas and Georgia were constantly at each other's throats. Hostilities were abated in 1748 by treaty. In 1763 Florida was ceded to England but was taken back by the treaty of Paris exactly twenty years later. The American war of the Revolution was over by this time and the young republic had already felt growing pains. Louisiana was acquired by the United States in 1803 and Florida, East and West, soon yielded to the concerted efforts of political intrigue and barter, squatter bravado, and the aggressiveness of the Anglo-American race.

[6] Still pronounced *Flo:r í: ða:* by the Spanish blood descendants; itself an abbreviation of *Pascua Florida*, the flowery Easter season, when the region was first seriously explored.

B. *New Mexico*

In New Mexico, which before 1800 included Arizona, Utah, and part of Colorado, let us pause only long enough to mention the courageous treks of Juan Cabeza de Vaca in 1528, of Pedro Mendoza in 1539, of Friar Marcos de Niza and his attendant Estevanico in 1539, and of Vasquez de Coronado who first conquered the Zuñi Indians and established a settlement where the present town of Bernalillo stands. Later, in 1597, Juan de Oñate with a small band made his way up the valley of the Chama River. In 1609 Santa Fe (La Ciudad Real de la Santa Fe de San Francisco) was begun. By 1680 more than 2,000 Spaniards were in the New Mexican territory and were making far but slow progress, as they imagined, toward conquering, civilizing, and Christianizing the native Indians when they were disillusioned through the overwhelming revolt of the Pueblos who were unwilling to overthrow their entire socio-religious system to accommodate themselves to the system the intruders sought to impose upon them. For twelve years the Spaniards contented themselves, in so far as Spaniards of such exploring instincts could content themselves, in the vicinity of our present El Paso. Then under Diego de Vargas they reconquered New Mexico. In 1706 Albuquerque was settled. During the eighteenth century the Spaniards in New Mexico increased from 2,000 souls to approximately 20,000 in 1800. The important centers were at Santa Fe, Albuquerque, and Taos. Independence from Spain was established in 1821, and about this time the contacts with English-speaking whites, from the United States chiefly, which had been increasing since 1800 began to have important bearings—political, commercial, social and linguistic.

C. *California*

Few white men had entered California before Juan Rodriguez Cabrillo had made his way among them in 1542. In 1579 Sir Francis Drake included the California coast in his tour. He gave it the name of New Albion. Sebastian Vizcaino discovered the bay of Monterey in 1602. For nearly one hundred and fifty years thereafter, the richest of all the Mexican territory bordering what is now the United States lay untouched by European foot. At any rate we have no record of any exception to this.

When the Spaniards resumed activities in California it was for the same reason that they had sixty years before taken active steps toward the settlement of Texas. In Texas the ventures of certain Frenchmen from the Louisiana country jarred the Spaniards from their neglect of the Texan territory. In the case of California the Spaniards were stimulated, at least to some extent, by the sniffing of the Russian bear in the direction of that little-known region. By 1759 a number of expeditions of Spanish soldiers, Jesuits, and Dominicans had ventured into California. In that year San Diego was occupied and what is now San Francisco Bay discovered. The missionaries prospered in their new home. They early established the mission system.

Under this system the natives who could be converted and domesticated were taught the trades and economic ways of the Spaniards and encouraged toward a condition of dependence upon the leadership and direction of the monks or Spanish officials. They were indeed virtually slaves. Within fifty years, more than twenty missions were established in California. The civil power rested with a Spanish governor whose headquarters were at Monterey. When, in 1810, the southern part of the Mexican country declared its independence from Spain, the Californian leaders decided to maintain allegiance to the mother country.

But with the coming of independence to Mexico in 1821, California was not slow to take advantage of it. In 1822 the allegiance of California was given to Mexico. Until this time no contacts between English-speaking and Spanish-speaking people took place in California except on the very rare occasions when vessels touched the coast.

During the period of political unrest and internal quarrelling which followed, American scouts and trappers began to drift into the settlements on the Pacific slope. Jedidiah Smith was among the first in 1826. As the influence and power of the missions declined and the political rivalries increased the trend toward republicanism, the few Americans, ever increasing in numbers, played a progressively important part in affairs. The Spanish laws forbidding foreign trade and immigration of foreigners were entirely ignored, and by 1830 foreigners, Russians, Englishmen, and Americans, were already establishing and operating centers in various parts of the California domain. In that year the Hudson's Bay Company found in California a new field for its activities. During the next fifteen years the American population increased to about 700 persons. Some of these intermarried with the better Spanish families and became influential citizens.

The Spanish had long held fears about the designs of foreign schemers, Russian, English, French, but particularly American, concerning the control and possession of California. The activities of ambitious politicans in Washington reflected in various ways made them aware of the readiness with which the United States held herself to leap at the first opportunity for taking the territory. Commodore Jones, in fact, leaped in 1842, and raised the American flag over the capital city of California before the opportunity had really made such an act graceful. The secession instructions of Larkin, the American consul in Monterey, and the "scientific expedition" of Fremont, gave additional cause for alarm. Indeed there was little real surprise when the Bear Flag of independence was raised over California in 1846 and when the United States put an end to the political rivalries of Spanish hidalgos by settling the quarrels in its own way with Commodore Sloat as agent in July, 1846. This was the culmination of a long and determined effort on the part of the United States to acquire by purchase if possible, or by other means if necessary, the territory on the Pacific Ocean side of the North American continent. This had hardly been accomplished when the discovery of gold in the San Francisco foothills caused the everlasting doors of the Rockies to be "rushed" as never doors were rushed before or since. By 1850 nearly 100,000 non-Spaniards were in California and little was left of the Spanish régime except tradition, history, and bits of the Spanish language which had been taken over into English.

D. *Texas*

At the present time there are in the border territory of Texas not fewer than 400,000 Mexican people. This number is equal to the number of people there are in some of the states of the American Union and likewise as many as there are in some states of the United States of Mexico. Although Los Angeles houses more Mexicans than any other city in the United States, Texas far outranks other states in its Mexican populace. It was in Texas, moreover, that the most extensive and intimate associations between the English-speaking and the Spanish-speaking peoples of this continent took place. And although Texas today is not nearly so Mexican in its social and political make-up as New Mexico, or quite so Spanish in its atmosphere, architecture, and traditions as California, linguistic borrowings by English in the Lone Star State have been more numerous than in any other section of the country.

Texas was first traversed by Europeans chiefly because of necessity. Juan Cabeza de Vaca seeking the vague glories that lay somewhere beyond, possibly in New Mexico, passed through Texas in 1528. Likewise Vasquez de Coronado, founder of Bernalillo in New Mexico, tramped across Texan soil twelve years after Cabeza de Vaca. But it was nearly a hundred and fifty years before a permanent settlement was effected in Texas by the invading Spaniards. This was in 1682 at Isleta not far from the present city of El Paso in the very extreme western corner of the state as it is now defined. Isleta was the gathering place for the Spaniards when they were driven out of New Mexico at the time of the Pueblo Indian revolt. About this time, also, certain Frenchmen became interested in this Texas country and ventured out into it. The Spanish were quick to react to any such outside activity by increasing their own development activities. Consequently, before the close of the seventeenth century the establishment of pueblos, presidios, and missions began in earnest.

By 1727 the domain of Texas had become rather clearly outlined, at least in the minds of those who possessed it. It seems to have been named after the Tejas Indians of that region.[7] The hitherto quiet, almost lazy, stream of activity in Texas began to quicken its current very shortly after the purchase of Louisiana by the United States in 1803. The cause is not hard to find—another race of men began to cast eyes, covetous eyes, toward Texas. Immediately there was competition for possession and for power with, of course, the resultant strife and contention. Language contacts then began in earnest between English speaking and Spanish speaking races. The population of Texas for 1805 is generally estimated, not counting the

[7] At that time the "x" and the "j" in Spanish were readily interchangeable and carried the same aspirated sound value.

wilder Indians, at about 7,000 persons of which only a few were Americans, some were French, and nearly all the rest were the gentler Indians and mixed Indian and Spanish. Two thousand of the seven thousand inhabited San Antonio de Bejar and approximately two thousand more were in the only other two towns of importance— Goliad (then La Bahia del Espiritu Santo—the bay of the Holy Ghost) and Nacogdoches. No part of the North American continent was more desolate than the plains of Texas except perhaps the desert regions of Utah, Idaho, and Nevada. The three small towns already mentioned and a few scattered missions and presidios established by the Spaniards constituted the political fabric. Most of the people themselves, of whatever race, were about as wild in their natures and inclinations as the buffaloes and wild horses they preyed upon. Exceptions to this, if there were any, were to be found among some of the better Spanish families who had emigrated from Spain. Agriculture had hardly begun to develop and the chief items of commerce were cattle, horses, and ore. Commercial intercourse was carried on with great difficulty through distant centers like Chihuahua, Monterey, Natchitoches, and New Orleans. The vehicles of transportation were chiefly plodding burros and Mexican mules or horses with occasional ox-drawn carretas. Political power, furthermore, was vested in government officials residing at Chihuahua so that governmental procedure and especially justice were handled in a very loose way. This in sketchy outline was the condition of Texas during the first decade of the nineteenth century.

By the end of the second decade Spanish authorities, sensing the aggressive and determined ventures of the Anglo-Americans as they sought a footing in the Texan territory, put up an excluding wall wherever possible.

They also sought to build up their political and military strength by the encouragement of colonization by citizens and the increase of military posts. The usual disputes over boundary lines between the United States and Mexico and the warlike attitude of both governments initiated the spirit of hatred and distrust that has characterized their relationships ever since. The consequence, then as now, was a mutual dislike between the two peoples. Political and other schemes and ventures by Americans such as those of Philip Nolan and later Aaron Burr gave the occupants of Mexico further cause for suspicion. The boundary problem was temporarily settled by the treaty of 1819. Before this time and even after, because of opposition to the treaty or for other reasons, several attempts had been made by Americans to colonize or take possession of Texas by force. All such attempts had met with failure and sometimes disaster, and had made conditions in the territory much worse than they would otherwise have been.

These attempts had been erratic and superficial. It remained for Moses Austin to inaugurate the first solid movement of Americans into the Mexican Texas. Austin's peaceful activities began with the second decade of the nineteenth century, and, although he died in 1821, his son, Stephen Fuller Austin, took up the difficult work. Stephen Austin proved to be an empresario magnificent, indefatigable in his efforts and dauntless in courage and determination as well as infinitely resourceful. It required a full and repeated exercise of all these qualities to make a successful beginning in the colonization of the Texas territory. At first the terms offered to family heads and other settlers were quite liberal and colonists were attracted in large numbers. It was not long, however, before the Mexicans began to have fears for the results of such an influx. Indirect measures were passed to deter immigration. One of these was the law against slavery which caused much complaint among slave-holding Texans. Comparative peace and prosperity, however, was enjoyed between 1822 and 1828, but from that time until independence was attained there was a constant *lucha* (struggle) between the Spanish-speaking and the English-speaking peoples in Texas. Austin as the leading character in the drama seems to have tried to fulfill his contract of loyalty to Mexico but he was not able, nor would anyone else have been, to avoid what was and has been termed the "irrepressible conflict" between two very different types of people. The definite outcome of this conflict was not indicated until the independence of Texas was established in 1836 and was not completed until the "lone star" was joined with the other state stars in 1845.

Thus, very briefly, were the various units of the expansive region of the South, Southwest and West discovered, claimed and settled by the Spanish-speaking peoples and later yielded to the English-speaking Americans. Political influence of the Spanish was lost immediately; social influence disappeared or is disappearing fast; linguistic influence was felt more slowly but is likewise disappearing more slowly. In fact, it is safe to say that it will never entirely disappear.

III. TRADE AND TRAVEL ROUTES

Having now briefly traced in outline the beginnings of each section of the territory most concerned in this study —Florida, New Mexico, California, and Texas—it will be helpful to a further understanding of the contacts between English and Spanish to consider for the moment the chief trade routes between the early United States and the territory occupied by people speaking the Spanish language. These trade routes were the first cables thrown across the wilderness sea. On them was built the bridge between two civilizations from Europe struggling for supremacy in the New World. Along these routes ventured the daring, the inquisitive, and the acquisitive who initiated the internal contacts between the Spanish and English languages in North America. The routes in question at first resulted from ill-defined attempts to reach the two or three half-known passes that made it possible to get over the great wall of the Rocky Mountains. Slowly but surely as the terrible obstacles were overcome—obstacles of drought, cold, hunger, and Indians—the ill-defined traces deepened into well-defined trails and later wagon roads, four abreast, in deep ruts. Some of the routes traversed a northerly section of the western part of the continent and thus came into little contact with the Spanish inhabitants, although much of the way they were actually in Spanish territory. Others purposely or necessarily were in constant contact with the Spanish of New Mexico or California. The most important of these for this study was the Santa Fe Trail.

A. *The Sante Fe Trail*

This long hard route from one civilization in the eastern United States to another civilization in western North America played an important part in the activities and developments which contributed to linguistic contacts between Spanish and English in the Southwest. The Santa Fe Trail began at various points in the vicinity of the present Kansas City—Fort Leavenworth, Franklin, Westport, Independence, and other places. Within a few miles the various beginnings of the Trail came together and pointed directly west to the big bend in the Arkansas River. Without dividing, the Trail followed the river west, southwest, or northwest as far as the present Fort

Dodge. Here two routes presented themselves to the traveller. One of these took the Cimarron crossing of the river, and traversed the desert to a point near the headwaters of one branch of the Cimarron River. The left fork of the river was then followed for approximately a hundred miles west of McNees Creek, Rabbit Ear Creek, and Rock Creek. On reaching the mountainous region northeast of Las Vegas on the Rio Gallinas the route had joined or been joined by other divisions of the Trail.

The other chief division continued directly westward from the Dodge City point along the Arkansas River to Bent's Fort just beyond where the Picketwire (Purgatoire) River flows into the Arkansas. Here the Trail turned south and southwest almost directly to the New Mexican settlements.

1. *Early explorers—Spanish and French.*—These routes represent the travelled way after the Trail had become fairly well known to Americans and was being used as an avenue of commerce beginning shortly before the 1820's and extending into the '70's and '80's, indeed up to the advent of the railroad. Before this time, however, the route which developed into the Trail must have been traversed by the early Spanish explorers, if not mile by mile at least in its general directions, so that the way from Santa Fe to the Missouri River was known as early as 1540, when Coronado pushed his expedition into Kansas. Again in 1600 Oñate must have traversed much of the Trail country. Another crossing was made by Baca about 1630. Between that time and 1700 the route became fairly well known to the Spaniards. This, it should be remembered, is more than a century before the American "pathfinders," so called, pushed out from the borders of the United States.

Before the days of the Americans, the French trappers

and traders wrote their chapter of activities on the Trail. They might have come to dominate it, had not conflicts between the mother countries in Europe put a sudden end to French hopes and possibilities on the frontiers of North America. Although Frenchmen did not entirely abandon the Trail and its commercial activities, nevertheless, after 1765 they play a minor rôle. Events at that time were shaping for the inevitable breaking over the dike by adventurous Americans. Once more before the American tide reached its height, that is, from about 1770 to 1800, the Spanish were the principal competitors against dangers of the Santa Fe Trail.

2. *Earliest Anglo-American crossings.*—American participation in the activities of the Trail may actually have commenced as early as 1773, when John Peyton seems to have made his first venture into the New Mexico region. In 1804 an American merchant sent some goods over the Trail at great risk and loss. Other adventurous and ill-fated names are encountered in accounts dealing with the Santa Fe of the early nineteenth century.

The most important of these is that of Zebulon M. Pike, who, in 1806, under orders from Governor Wilkinson of Louisiana, organized and began an expedition into the Sante Fe country. It was in and through Pike's journal and writings that a few Spanish words received their first introduction to the English vocabulary. Pike apparently had a way with him that appealed to the Spaniards and New Mexicans, for contrary to the usual treatment afforded American intruders both innocent and otherwise, Pike's reception was genuinely hospitable throughout his long detention in the Spanish territories. He thus had opportunity to become more intimate with the inhabitants and learn more of their ways of living and of their language. Here, as elsewhere, the attitude of English-speakers towards Spanish-speakers has had significant bearings on the extent to which Spanish words have been introduced into English contexts.

Between the time of Pike's first expedition in 1806 and the year 1820 not less than a score of expeditions by Americans set out across the Trail. From a business point of view the results of these expeditions were discouraging. But the men who made them seem to have become fascinated with the country. With few exceptions they either returned for second visits or settled permanently in the Spanish domain. All had tales to relate which incited the curiosity of the home folks and quickened the pulses of both the venturesome and the seekers after gain, among whom stand out prominently the fur traders.

The attitude of the Spanish authorities was at this time one of hostility toward invasion by foreigners and especially Americans, even for commercial and sight-seeing purposes. The dominating Spaniards of the provinces of New Spain were in their greatest glory. They guarded their position jealously. It is natural that they should resent intrusion by a race of people who were, as they knew by tradition and history, the ultimate ruination of the pleasantly despotic and leisurely life dear to their hearts. What appears, therefore, as wanton cruelty on one side of the picture appears as justice when seen from the other side. The names of such trail travellers as McLanahan, Smith, Patterson, McKnight, Philibert Williams and Merriwether, may be those of martyrs of the Trail on one hand or victims of their own follies and ambitions on the other.

3. *Successful commercial ventures.*—According to recorded accounts Merriwether was the last American to be detained in a Spanish prison. In 1821 a great change came over those in power in the New Mexico country. This was

an echo of events taking place farther to the south in Mexico. There Iturbide was cutting the last links of the chain that held the New Spain subject to the Old. The result was a wave of anti-Spanish and pro-American sentiment on the part of those in power. Evidence of this important change of attitude was encountered by the Americans along the Trail quite by chance when the trading expedition of Captain William Becknell, headed for the Rocky Mountains to trade with the Indians, met with a contingent of Mexican troops. To their great relief they were greeted cordially and invited to make Santa Fe their goal. The invitation was accepted with the result that the Becknell expedition of 1821 became the first really successful commercial venture into New Mexico over the Santa Fe Trail.

The expedition returned quickly to Missouri and news of its success immediately spread. Other companies were organized and within a decade travel on the Trail was regular and frequent. Although still attended by great hazards to life and property from Indian attacks and the hostility of nature, relations between Spanish speakers and English speakers were, if not cordial, at least not hostile, and transactions involving the contact of the two languages and the exchange of words and phrases multiplied fast.

4. *Regular commerce on the Trail.*—About this time Senator Benton of Missouri, later to become the father-in-law of John Charles Fremont and lend encouragement and support to that ardent frontiersman, became intensely interested in the possibilities of the Santa Fe Trail and the country it led to. It was through the influence and efforts of Benton that money was appropriated with which a survey of the Trail might be made. The survey itself did little toward improving the travelling conditions on the

Santa Fe Trail, but it was another step toward making it more secure and it gave assurance to those who were interested in developing commerce along its route. Whereas in the earlier days of the Trail merchandise had been transported on pack animals, after the experiment of Becknell wagons grew in favor. The Trail thus developed into a road. As the use of the road increased experience demonstrated that a long caravan single file was not the desirable formation but rather four or five shorter caravans abreast because of the protection thus afforded against Indian attacks. Thus the Trail grew into a road and from a road into a highway.

The intermingling of Spanish-speaking and English-speaking frontiersmen was not limited to the western extremities of the Trail, although there the contacts were naturally much more common and intimate. Along all the distance from Missouri to Santa Fe and thence to California and Chihuahua, Mexican or Spanish and American or English mingled freely. Among the earlier traders and expeditionists of the Trail were prominent Spaniards and Mexicans from Taos, Santa Fe, and Chihuahua. Although their companies were composed chiefly of Spanish-speaking Indians or of Spaniards, invariably a few individuals whose native tongue was English fell in with the caravan. On the other hand, not long after traffic on the Trail began to multiply, a great many of the laborers and helpers and hangers-on of the American outfits were Mexicans or Indians who spoke Spanish. Thus the language of the Trail from Missouri to the coast was made up of both English and Spanish, understood by all.

As the commerce of the prairies assumed a truly important aspect in the eyes of both United States government officials and the government of New Mexico some effort was made to protect the travellers with escorts of troopers.

Although this practice was discontinued when the caravans became large enough to protect themselves or the limited protection proved to be impractical, it did result in an increased use and development of the Trail. Even today parts of the Trail remain hazardous. In the old days, by the time a caravan reached the quaint but glorious haven known as Santa Fe, the travel-worn members were hungry for the repose, the luxuries, the entertainment, and the hospitality that oasis afforded. There was little restraint and aloofness on the part of either nationality. The result was that the Americans joined in the "fandangos" and *bailes* with much "gusto." They were far from blind to the glances of the *señoritas* much to the jealous disgust of the native men; and they found the "tortillas," "frijoles" and "tamales" of the Mexican both nourishing and appetizing after the monotonous diet of the Trail.

This life of romance on the Trail mingled with much of hardship and tragedy and no little bloodshed, but withal general financial gain, increased without a check until 1843. By this time relations between Mexico and the United States had become so strained that General Santa Ana ordered the Trail closed to commercial traffic at its point of entry into Mexican territory. Within six months, however, the order of Santa Ana either had been rescinded or was ignored. Traffic was resumed and continued normally until 1846, when the movement of United States troops as a part of the war maneuvers with Mexico converted the Santa Fe Trail into a military highway.

B. *The Chihuahua Trail*

From Santa Fe the traveller of the first half of the nineteenth century, if he wished to continue his journey, could take one of the several routes or "trails" westward to California or southward into Mexico proper. The Route south into Mexico was known as the "Chihuahua Trail." From the town of Santa Fe the Chihuahua Trail led directly south toward El Paso del Norte on the Rio Grande.

After leaving El Paso the Chihuahua Trail continued due south over desert and sand hills to Carrizal or skirted these obstacles by way of the river route. From Carrizal the Trail led to Gallegos and thence to Chihuahua. Most of those Americans who travelled this Trail earliest from Santa Fe did so as political prisoners against their own wishes. Most of them also were forced to march under hardship. But one of the most noted, Pike, was escorted courteously over the Trail in 1807. Among other well-known travellers of this route were Josiah Gregg in 1839 and Dr. A. Wizlizenus, a German scientist, in 1846. These two as well as Pike have left comparatively accurate and complete descriptions of the Trail itself and of the conditions of society, commerce, and politics along its course. After the trade caravans had become fairly well established along the Santa Fe Trail from Missouri, that is in the 1830's, 40's and later, many of the travelling merchants took their *atajos* of merchandise on "down the trail" to Chihuahua. The Chihuahua Trail was never travelled so frequently and regularly as the main overland route, but conditions on it and the contacts which resulted in every way paralleled and even formed a part of the Santa Fe conditions and contacts.

C. *"Southern Route" or Gila Trail*

Another trail which went south out of Santa Fe was that known as the "Gila" or "Southern" route. This route coincided with the Chihuahua Trail until it reached the elbow of the Rio del Norte just above El Paso. At that point it turned due west toward the head-waters of the Gila River and followed the course of that stream rather persistently to its junction with the Rio Colorado, thence straight west to the Pacific at San Diego and from there up to Los Angeles. Kearney in 1846 made it his route to California from New Mexico.

D. *The Spanish Trail*

Another way to reach Los Angeles from Santa Fe was via the California cut-off and "Spanish Trail." This route led northwest from Santa Fe into the Uncompahgre mountains across the Grand River and also the Green River, through the Wesatch range into Utah, and thence southwest into California. A journey over this route by Jedidiah M. Smith in 1826–27 seems to have been the first American use of the Trail. Fremont followed it most of the way from Utah to California in 1843–44 and soon thereafter it became a much frequented route for emigrants to California.

E. *The Oregon Trail*

A good part of the Oregon Trail passed, during its earlier years, through territory claimed by Mexico. But it lay far enough to the north of the Spanish-speaking centres to eliminate the numerous contacts with the Spanish which took place on other overland routes. Phases of Spanish life, however, were not entirely lacking on the Oregon Trail and accounts written by those who travelled it introduce a few Spanish words into their English contexts.

F. *Pacific Coast Contacts*

The other Spanish-English contacts during the period of exploration and colonization before the Mexican War took place along the Pacific Coast in the two Californias. Trading vessels plying between the North Atlantic coast and the Orient made stops at most of the suitable California ports. It is evident that all these latter trading and colonizing routes resulted in rather minor linguistic effects as compared with those provided on the Santa Fe, Chihuahua, and California routes but they do add to the sum total of contacts between Spanish-speaking and English-speaking peoples in North America before the time of the Mexican War.

IV. THE MEXICAN WAR

The linguistic importance of the Mexican War period is quite out of proportion with the length of time the war lasted. For it was during the conflict that the entire citizenry of the United States was given at least an introduction to many Spanish words and phrases and at most an opportunity to incorporate some of them into the English vocabulary and put them into regular and natural use both in speaking and in writing. Military engagements between Mexican and American troops began in April of 1846. On May 13, the President of the United States signed a bill which had already passed both houses of Congress providing the first emergency men and means for the war.

A. *The "Texas Question" and Newspapers*

The Mexican War, therefore, began officially in May, 1846. Long before this time, however, a paper war had been in progress in the United States over some of the very same points of dispute as precipitated the armed conflict. Chief of these was the question of the annexation of Texas to the Union. From the time this possibility loomed in the northern political sky until after annexation took place in 1845, hardly an important newspaper in the country failed to display "important news from Texas" or "the Texas question" in its headlines at least once a week. Besides frontier news there were frequent and spirited talks and orations on the Texas question in congress and elsewhere. The linguistic significance of all this commotion about the Mexican frontier territory is that the Mexican-Spanish subject was constantly in the American mind and, more directly, there was hardly a dispatch from the border in which did not occur one or more Spanish words. Such usage was appropriate and effective. After the annexation of Texas hostile feelings between the governments of Mexico and the United States were accentuated and hostile feelings make news. Sentiments and maneuvers of the Mexicans were watched with great interest by the politicians and people of the United States chiefly as reported by the newspapers. The question of new territory had become so inextricably bound up with the slave question that it was impossible to mention one without discussing the other. As a result the relation of Americans to Mexicans became important in the relation of Americans to Americans. Mexican affairs received their share of public, private, and newspaper discussion regularly and constantly during the period preceding military engagements between the two countries.

When these engagements began, as would be expected, the newspapers reported every obtainable detail pertaining to movements of the armies. Some editions were made up almost exclusively of Mexican War matters. The use of Spanish words was at times desirable, at times necessary, in the "news." Spanish place names were the reporters' stock in trade. Palo Alto, Matamoras, Monterey, Buena Vista, Rio Grande, Resaca de la Palma, Cerro Gordo, and scores of other Spanish names were read and repeated by Americans with almost daily frequency. It is likely also that most Americans who read the newspapers of that period had some understanding of such words as "alcalde," *pronunciamento*, "adobe," "jacal," "chaparral," "corral," *pedegral*, and scores of others introduced into newspaper reports of military activities and the life at the front. Mexican towns were governed by "alcaldes" and hardly a Mexican town was occupied, passed through or approached without the preliminary and regular confer-

ences and negotiations between American army officers
and Mexican alcaldes with consequent *pronunciamentos*.
In reporting such negotiations no word other than "alcalde" was quite fitting as a title for the Mexican official.
He was more than judge, he was more than mayor. There
was no word in English hence the Spanish *alcalde* met the
need. In describing a squalid Mexican town the houses
could be called "huts made of dried clay bricks" without
much inaccuracy but many of those who wrote descriptions preferred to say "jacals made of adobe." "Jacal"
would likely be pronounced "jækul" by the American
reader unless he were assisted in parenthesis with "pronounced 'harcal' in English as observed in the *New York
Herald*. Illustrations of the natural usage by newspapers
of Spanish words during that period might easily be multiplied.

B. *Soldier Contacts with Mexican Life*

More intimate if not more important even than the
newspaper introduction of Spanish words and phrases to
the American public was the contact of approximately
fifty thousand Americans from all sections of the United
States with Mexican and Spanish people and life. Not all
those who enlisted in the Mexican War were privileged
to ransack the "halls of Montezuma," but very few of
them were denied direct and often intimate contact with
the people of the Montezumas. Furthermore, the Mexican
War did not, as wars sometimes do, represent an outburst
of hatred and enmity between two peoples. It was natural,
therefore, that hostilities were confined pretty much to
the battlefront. In general the United States troops were
considerate of the natives in their community or ranch
life and made a determined effort to convince them that
they, the Americans, were trying to "conquer a peace" for
the American president. The natives were not coerced nor

maltreated unless such treatment was found necessary as a military program. This does not mean that there was a great amount of love for the native Mexicans on the part of the American soldiers and that the military occupation of Mexico took on the aspect of a missionary endeavor. There is sufficient evidence that many of the soldiers held the Mexicans in contempt. This contempt, however, was more often than not tempered with sympathy, and the official attitude of the officers was not one of hostility toward the civilian populace. Mexicans, on the other hand, were not slow to realize the material advantages of having the American army as voluntary guests. This meant a ready sale at high prices for every bit of foodstuff they could produce. Many a Mexican *rancho* which had had no outlet for its poultry products was "huevozed"[8] by the Americans.

Another advantage of American occupation was that it brought comparative peace to the natives and assurance of security from the raiding Comanches or Apaches. The Mexicans, accustomed to the petty or serious internal conflicts and the uncertainty of peace welcomed the brief respite offered by the invading Yankees. National pride yielded to more practical satisfactions. Of course, there are always exceptions to any such generalizations. But on the whole there was sufficient friendliness between the American troops and the Mexican inhabitants to foster a daily intimacy which was important linguistically. The soldiers got glimpses of the domestic phases of Mexican life and naturally became more interested. They were permitted to visit the "bailes" and "fandangos" which the Mexican loved then as now. And the opportunity to dance with an attractive *señorita* or "moharrie" was no doubt

[8] *Huevo* is Spanish for egg. "Huevozed the ranch" is analogous to "vamoosed the ranch."

put down in many a Mexican War diary as a rare treat by the soldier exiled from the women of his own race. From Mexican housewives the American soldiers purchased, when necessary, *tortillas*, "tamales," and "frijoles," often after observing how these native foods were prepared by means of a "metate" or other native implement. And when the commissary exhausted its supply of American liquors the soldiers took a few swallows of the native beverages—"pulque," "mescal," "sotol," and *tequila*.

There is good reason to conclude that as a result of such daily contacts a number of Spanish words were incorporated first-hand into the vocabularies of English-speaking soldiers. Some of them were bound to be retained. But there was also an indirect linguistic result recorded in the writings of the soldiers. The Spanish words used verbally at the front were used in letters written home, in journals and diaries, and occasionally in formal reports. It is from these writings chiefly that we are able to arrive at an estimate of the social and linguistic contacts of the Mexican War.

C. *Indirect Influences*

Another contribution of the Mexican War to the English vocabulary came after the war in that rather large body of fiction, drama, and memoirs written around characters or settings of the war.

V. THE POST-WAR PERIOD

A. *The California Gold Rush*

On the heels of the Mexican War came the California gold excitement and the western stampede of emigrants "with their wash-bowls on their knees." A large part of the hosts that made their way to California or other western states in the late 1840's and the 1850's did so by way of the Santa Fe Trail or the Old Spanish Trail. After being in territory of Spanish and Mexican background for a great part of the way the emigrant found himself planted in a region dominantly Spanish in its recent history, politics, and society. Although the Anglo-Saxon aspects of the society that followed soon dominated the Spanish-American the intimate contact of the English speakers and Spanish speakers had its effect in language.

In Texas and New Mexico during this period Mexican-American elements were intermixing to a greater extent than at any time before. The foundations of the present biracial society were being laid. By the late 1850's the great American controversy which brought about the Civil War had so engrossed the people of the United States that even the popularity of "the Texas question" and "news from California" became secondary in the public mind and in the newspapers. These frontier regions, however, were not entirely ignored and Mexico herself, then in struggle with European imperialism represented by Maximillian of Austria was a live topic in the United States.

B. *Rise of Ranch and Cowboy Life*

The period from 1870 to 1900 in English-Spanish linguistic contacts was chiefly noteworthy for the rise and development of ranch and cowboy life in the west. As noted elsewhere, the *vaquero* vocation and practically everything that goes with it by way of equipment was adopted from the Spanish or Mexicans along the border territory. This meant the introduction of numerous useful or picturesque Spanish words and phrases some of which bid fair to remain permanently as a part of the English vocabulary. The words "cinch" and "corral" are already well popularized.

C. *Mexican-American Capital; Revolutions*

It was during this period—the Porfirio Diaz régime in Mexico—that American capital investments flowed southward over the border. The small merchant and adventurer of 1840 or 1850 from St. Louis or New England on the Santa Fe Trail was replaced by the capitalist of Wall Street. But Spanish-English contacts continued.

This period of economic and social development in the Southwest and Mexico may be said to have extended, for convenience of this study, to 1910. Many American sightseeing writers and writing sight-seers visited the territory south of the Rio Grande and gave to others in the United States the impressions of their travels. In numerous magazine articles, news reports, and books appeared Spanish words in English contexts.

By the time of the revolution of 1910 under Francisco I. Madero, newspaper reporting had been so organized, under the Associated Press, the United Press, and other similar services, that news was distributed ready prepared. Consequently there was less opportunity for the reporter or the newspaper along the southwest border to prepare his copy *a la Española* or *a la Mejicana*. It is for this reason chiefly that present-day newspapers of the Southwest do not contain more Spanish words. National and international news, standardized through a distributing agency, comes to them almost ready for the typesetter.

In spite of this situation, the revolution in Mexico since 1910 has provided occasion for the introduction of a great many Spanish words into news columns. The chief thing, however, that it did toward increasing the number of Spanish words in the American vocabulary was to bring about the social and industrial conditions which resulted in a great influx of laborers from Mexico to the United States.

VI. Recent Influx of Mexicans to the United States

These immigrants when added to the native Spanish-Americans found in the southwestern states, makes a total Mexican population in the United States which cannot but have some language results. What these results will be depends to a great extent on the social and economic status of the Spanish-speaking people in the United States.

A determination of the exact number of Spanish-speaking people in the United States is almost impossible because of the difficulty of registering immigrants along the Mexican border. Manuel Gamio's study (1926–27) of the Mexican immigrant gives a distribution of Mexicans which would not be materially affected by the addition of Spanish-speaking immigrants from the Antilles and from Spain except perhaps in one of two of the larger cities and particularly the city of New York. According to Gamio, there are Mexicans in all states of the Union except the extreme northern states of New England—Maine, Vermont and New Hampshire. The South Atlantic States, the Virginias, the Carolinas, Kentucky, Tennessee, Georgia, Alabama, Mississippi and even Florida, and the North Central states, Montana, the Dakotas, Minnesota, and Wisconsin, have very few. In all the other states except those of the Southwest and California, the Mexican population is not large comparatively speaking, but on the other hand is greater than might ordinarily be expected. In New York, Pennsylvania, Illinois, Nebraska, and Kansas the largeness of their numbers is surprising; and only a little less so is the number in Michigan, Indiana, Ohio, Iowa, and Missouri. The migration of Mexicans to the states located far from the Mexican border has recently resulted from the demand for industrial laborers. Thus far the linguistic significance of their presence in the United

States is not apparent. It is in the states of Texas, New Mexico, Arizona, California, and possibly Colorado that the Spanish-speaking people are sufficiently numerous to provide contacts with English-speaking people frequent and intimate enough to allow the appearance of language influences. Texas in 1900, besides the numerous native Mexican inhabitants, had over 70,000 Mexican settlers. By 1910, when the revolution in Mexico took place the number had grown to 125,000, making Texas one of the important districts of Mexican population. Conditions in Mexico because of the revolution together with the demands of American industries stimulated an even greater influx from Mexico so that in 1920 there were in Texas more than 250,000 Mexicans from across the Rio Grande.

In California and Arizona by 1920 the number of Mexican immigrants was comparable to the figures for Texas although in 1900 there were only about 800 Mexican immigrants in California and 14,000 in Arizona. By 1910 in Arizona the number doubled, and in California quadrupled. In 1920 the figures were over 20,000 for Arizona, and 89,000 for California. In other states bordering those already mentioned increases were smaller numerically but as large, or even larger, proportionally. This statement applies to Colorado, Idaho, Kansas, Louisiana, Oklahoma, Utah, and Wyoming. Since 1920 there has been no slackening of Mexican immigration, and in California, where the race antagonism once aggravated by the influx of Orientals has been tempered, Mexicans have literally flocked in hordes.

A colony of Spanish-speaking people is congregating in New York City in the vicinity of Fifth Avenue and One Hundred and Tenth Street. This colony may provide an interesting sidelight on the subject of Spanish-speaking people in the United States. Individuals from various countries or regions where Spanish is spoken—Spain, Mexico, South America, Cuba, etc.—are represented. The colony is growing and language is the unifying factor. The neighborhood is becoming somewhat Spanish in certain aspects. A Spanish theatre, for one thing, with vaudeville and motion picture performances in Spanish is operating successfully. Many stores, shops and restaurants have signs in Spanish, or in English and Spanish. Such establishments carry merchandise to suit a Spanish-speaking clientele and are often operated, if not owned, by Spanish-speaking individuals. Thus far there seems to have been very little linguistic contact but the phenomenon of a Spanish colony of this sort so far removed from the Spanish provinces of the West and Southwest is unique and may be productive of interesting English-Spanish language influences.

A Mexican colony of a different sort is found at Bethlehem, Pennsylvania, where several hundred Mexican people live under supervision of the Bethlehem Steel Company, for whom most of them work.

A. *Work Done by Mexicans in the United States*

It is important to know something of the activities of all these Mexicans in the United States. Most of them are unskilled laborers and a great percentage of them obtain employment in some branch of agriculture beginning in the spring with ground preparation and cultivation and continuing through the summer and fall with harvesting. In Texas particularly in the southern and western districts, farm and ranch hands are Mexicans. In California the orange and grape crops and the melon and beet fields are dependent on laborers from Mexico. In Arizona the cotton fields and agricultural crops in general gladly utilize the services of Mexican labor. In Colorado, Utah, and Idaho, it is the beet fields chiefly that offer employment. Farther east and north, the Mexican is found more commonly in the various industries and everywhere in the Southwest he is found on the railroad construction gangs and in mine crews. A few of the immigrants acquire land or interest in land or other property and remain in the United States semipermanently. But the great mass of Mexican immigrants are on the move most of the time until they finally return to the various localities in Mexico from which they have come.

Because of this condition the immigrant Mexican is more a problem in the society of the Southwest and California than he is a factor. There is little opportunity and no inclination for race mixture through intermarriage of immigrant Mexicans and Americans. The Mexican obtains a glimpse of American life and way of living and adopts, superficially, the more convenient material advantages. It is never safe to estimate how deeply he is affected until he has returned to his native land and attempted to fit again into his former life and associations.

In return for what the Mexican may adopt and take away from the civilization of the United States it is doubtful whether he gives anything except his labor and a few linguistic contributions. And the latter are so inextricable from the contributions and influence of the Spanish-speaking peoples already natives of the United States that it is not possible to determine just how great or how numerous they are. Certainly the presence of so many people speaking the Spanish language and calling objects by their Spanish names tends to familiarize and to perpetuate those Spanish words in the minds of English-speaking people in the sections of the country affected. There is good reason to believe or assume that numerous words and phrases adopted by the Americans of the colonization days in Texas, California, and other territory formerly Mexican, are kept from obsolescence in the English vocabulary because of the fact that they are being used by the Spanish-speaking people still in those provinces. Indeed this would be true of most of the words listed in the vocabulary section of this study.

B. *Immigrant Mexican and Native Mexican*

In this connection the Spanish-speaking immigrant from Mexico is not so important a factor in the naturalization of Spanish words in the American-English vocabulary as is the Spanish-speaking person born and reared in Texas, New Mexico, or other border states. These natives, although the victims of racial antagonisms and conflicts, are involved in an interesting adaptation of two different standards of civilization. Of necessity most of those born since 1900 have become bilinguists. The public schools prescribe English; the economic struggle exacts it. In those communities where both Spanish-American and Anglo-American children are to be found there is much more intimate social mingling than is the case with the immigrant Mexican children and the Americans. Anglo-American children acquire a familiarity with the Spanish language and with much else that is Spanish. This knowledge comes quite naturally and it is therefore no strain or unnatural exertion for them to incorporate Spanish words and phrases into English context whether spoken or written. Terms of greeting like *que hubo le* and *que hay* (*ke: ai*), of leave taking such as *hasta la vista* and *adios;* neat Spanish words of enquiry like *que tal* and *como;* names of things such as "acequia," *atole,* "burro," "baile," *chamaco, cura, remuda, pagaré,* "pilon"; deft noncommittals like *quien savy,* and *que le hace;* and convenient descriptions such as *grullo, guero, chiquita, muy hombre, panzon,* and *pelado* come so naturally and usefully that it would be unfair linguistically to deny them a place at least in the fringe of the English vocabulary. The place in English assigned to some of them may be admittedly insecure as compared with the places held by borrowings from other languages, particularly those words of long standing in the English vocabulary. Indeed, it is not accurate to consider all these Spanish words as having the same currency in English. Some of them are used often by many Americans; others are used seldom and by few. But this is also true of many native Anglo-Saxon words of the vocabulary. It is also obvious that most of the words of Spanish-American source are young as ages go in the family of words. Time will give them the required maturity for stability or else eliminate them entirely from the ranks of English words.

VII. PRESENT ATTITUDES

Before concluding this chapter attention should be called to the marked change in attitude, official and unofficial, between the citizens of Mexico and those of the United States. The feeling in both countries compares favorably today with that of any time during the history of the relations of the two nations.

For the Mexicans the turn toward better feelings was noticeable shortly after the arrival in Mexico City of the late Dwight W. Morrow as American ambassador. The appointment of a man already a leader in the affairs of his own country and a close personal friend of the president of the United States was a complimentary gesture greatly appreciated by the Mexican people. Appreciation of the gesture was only exceeded by the appreciation of the man which followed as a natural result of his fair dealing and magnanimous actions. When to complimentary gesture and magnanimous actions were added the glamour and idealism of a universally admired hero—Lindbergh—associated with the United States Embassy in Mexico, the deep-seated suspicion and jealousy of the Mexicans began to give way to genuine good will. The Mexican people have always admired the Americans, but admiration could hardly kindle a feeling of friendliness while resentment, suspicion and envy smouldered beneath. Anyone, therefore, close to this almost national feeling regarded it as a near miracle when newspapers reported the citizens of Mexico hailing "Meester Morrow" with spontaneous *vivas* and *"viva* Meester Morrow." Others factors may have had their influence on the present feeling in Mexico but clearly the Morrow régime was the most important.

Causes for the change of feeling in the United States whatever they are, are more subtle than those observed in Mexico. Prohibition in the United States may have placed Mexico in a favorable light as a vacation spot for many who can reach the border resorts and fewer who can spend extended periods in Mexico City or such pleasant places as Cuernavaca. The emergence in Mexico of a few outstanding men with an unusual interest in the development of their country and its people and with power sufficient to maintain control in the face of any and all emergencies, has established confidence abroad not unmixed with admiration. The further fact that some of the leaders have close affiliations with the people of United States, either by marriage or by education, has no doubt contributed favorably toward the situation.

The Morrow ambassadorship also contributed to a better feeling in American circles except among certain fairly covetous individuals who have watched with an impatience approaching imperiousness the easy-going Mexican and his seeming disregard for the economic possibilities of his country. Under the former régimes in the United States these "hundred percenters" have chafed at the restraint that prevented military intervention and "efficient" exploration of bountiful natural resources. Exaggerated reports of Mexico's weaknesses have been responsible in no small degree to the influence of these impatient Americans. An official policy of patience, sympathy, and fair dealing did much to change public opinion in the United States. Another factor, as important as any, which has promoted a sympathetic and friendly interest in Mexico by Americans, is the growing realization that within the borders of the United States all frontiers have been explored. Americans by long tradition have an affection for frontiers, for unexplored and unexploited regions. Good roads, rail and concrete, have eliminated a large part of the lure from the once inaccessible regions of the southwestern United States. In Mexico the lure, the adventure of the old Santa Fe Trail and the tempo of a more natural mode of life still abide. It is these that make Mexico attractive to Americans seeking relief from the strain of a mechanized and hasty way of living.

VIII. CONCLUSION

In concluding this chapter it may be observed that Spanish words, whether hauled into the English language by British seamen in the West India days, picked up on the Santa Fe Trail, lassoed, figuratively speaking, by the vaqueros on the broad mesas, cultivated by the colonists of Texas, bartered by merchants, or come upon by intrepid explorers, are being used by English-speaking people and therefore find justification for being recorded. Their number after all is not large, approximately five hundred, and they are listed in the vocabulary section of this study. Most of them are illustrated in usage by quotations from a variety of writings in which the words appear in English contexts. The writings are given brief consideration in the following pages.

WRITTEN SOURCE MATERIAL

I. LITERATURE OF, OR ABOUT, AMERICA IN WHICH APPEAR SPANISH WORDS

It is neither practicable nor desirable to attempt to discuss every item of literature or other written material that has been examined as a part of this study. Nor was it found simple to classify into clearly defined groupings all material examined. Somewhat by way of compromise, the present chapter considers certain classified groups of representative material assigned to various dates from the earliest to the latest included in the range of this study.

A. *Hakluyt's Voyages*

Any treatment of the Spanish words in English or American literature relating to North America finds both a logical and a chronological beginning in the compilation of travel narratives known as *Hakluyt's Voyages*. These works supply comparatively numerous examples of the earliest recorded usage of Spanish words in the English vocabulary. Hakluyt lived during Shakespeare's time, a period already mentioned as being important for English-Spanish contacts, when the majority of current Spanish words borrowed by English in Europe were taken into the language. Although by profession somewhat of a preacher of the Gospel and by appointment chaplain to the English ambassador to Paris for a time, Hakluyt was by nature a discoverer and an imperialistic son of England, Queen of the Seas. As such he worked tirelessly and lovingly to gather the chronicles which compose his famous collection of *Principal Navigations, Voyages, Traffiques, and Discoveries of the English Nation Made by Sea or Overland to the Remote and Farther Distant Quarters of the Earth at Any Time Within the Compass of These 1500 Years.*

Hakluyt's works are divided roughly into three parts,

It is the third or last part dealing with "the westerne Navigations and Travailes of Ours" that has particular interest for this study. Here occur accounts of "John Cabot a Venitian and his 3 sonnes, to discover & conquer in his [Henrie the Seventh's] name, and under his Banners unknown Regions." Here also are found "3 voyages made by M. John Hawkins now Knight, then Esquire, to Hispaniola and the Gulfe of Mexico" and "the first valiant enterprise of Sir Francis Drake upon Nombre de Dios." It was from the accounts of such explorers and adventurers as Cabot, Hawkins, and Drake that a number of the words now known to all speakers of English first came to be used and were actually introduced into English contexts.

Prominent among the full list of such words are to be found "mosquito" variously spelled. Incidentally the creature for which it stands is usually described with some feeling. Likewise the antecedents of our present word "canoe" are found there in *canoa* and *canow*. "Tobacco," already written as we write it today, is found in Hakluyt and "cocoa" in its original spelling of *cacao*. These words and others introduced at about the same time, became generally known to speakers of English during the eighteenth century. In the nineteenth, conditions, as already recounted, shaped themselves for fresh borrowings.

B. *From Hakluyt to American Period*

From the time of the early explorations of such adventurers as Drake and Hawkins, as recounted in *Hakluyt's Voyages*, to the opening years of the nineteenth century is a long but not an unwarranted stride. During the seventeenth and eighteenth centuries in various descriptions and narrations with America as a background, use is made of Spanish words in English contexts but not in a way comparable to that which took place in the sixteenth and the nineteenth century periods. True, literary men, following the precedent of the Elizabethans, were not backward in using new terms from American sources during this interim. Travelers, adventurers, and colonizers first put the words into print and others at home in England accepted them with evident gusto and helped to give them common currency. Under these circumstances not a great many new words were introduced during this period but those already current, such as "alligator," "banana," "cockroach," "canoe," and "vanilla" quickly acquired the standing in the English vocabulary which time and usage have strengthened.

C. *New American Frontiers*

It was, however, the new American frontiers "beyond the Mississippi" in the early and middle years of the nineteenth century that provided fresh occasion for Spanish words to figure prominently and effectively in narratives and descriptions. Beckoned on by the lure of adventure or of gain, English and American travelers, forerunners of the modern tourists, made their way painfully yet almost religiously through the frontier borders of the United States and across the desert barriers and terrible *jornadas* into Mexico. Their accounts provided the English-reading public both in the United States and in England with descriptions and accounts of Mexican life and activities. Mexican, that is, Spanish, words were used much or little according to the wishes, temperaments, or knowledge of the writers.

1. *Earliest writers.*—Zebulon Pike, beginning with his apprenticeship in the wastes of Minnesota where he first saw "mustangs" and continuing through fascinating experiences in the Santa Fe country and Mexico, introduced new words into his journals. Among the more common Spanish words found in Pike's journals are "siesta," "reboso," "fandango," *alacran*, "pinole," "rancho,"

"ranch," and "hacienda." Visitors to the Texas colonies, likewise, added local color to their accounts by using Spanish names and descriptive terms. An instance of this is found in the writings of an anonymous author who had purchased land from the Galveston Bay and Texas Co., and who who seems to have visited Texas in the year 1834 in the interest of a land speculation enterprise. This writer reflects to a fair degree American usage of Spanish words. His "musquito grass" and "musquito tree"; his *empresarios* and "mustangs;" his "lazo," "lazoed" and "lazooing;" his *calabozas, ayuntamientos,* "alcaldes," and *guias* are all typical and commonly-used Spanish words or adaptations of that period. Charles Latrobe, as an English "rambler in Mexico" in 1836 and previously, incorporates into his narrative context a large number of Spanish and Mexican native words. He is more accurate, however, in his use than in his spelling. Josiah Gregg, in a work that as time passes is more appreciated for its accuracy and thoroughness, seldom uses in his *Commerce of the Prairies; or, Sante Fe Trader,* an English word for a native object where the Spanish name will serve. Citations from his work as found in this study or in any other of similar nature indicate the frequency with which Gregg made use of Spanish words. The reader unacquainted with the extent to which such words are or were actually used by Americans on the frontier might readily conclude that Gregg inserts an unnaturally large number of them into his accounts. On the contrary, it is doubtful whether any writer of that period reflects more accurately the actual usage on the prairies in his day.

Other early travelers in the West and in the Spanish territory, whose written reports or narratives helped to familiarize the American- and English-reading public with Spanish-American words were Parker in his *A Trip to the*

West and Texas in 1836, Bingley in 1821, Kendall in his report of the Texan Sante Fe Expedition in 1847, Ingersol in *Knocking Round the Rockies* in 1874 and many others.

2. *Non-Spanish frontier writers.*—In Pattie's *Early Personal Narrative* are found examples of the usage of those on the American frontier but not always of the Spanish frontier. The number of Spanish words used by any one writer diminishes as the distance from the Spanish frontier increases, yet a few words are found in the writings of practically all. They are invariably the terms that have become most common. Zack T. Sutley, for instance, who spent the greater part of his life on the frontier, although a Pennsylvanian by birth, uses hardly more than half a dozen Spanish words in his account of *The Last Frontier.* Among them are "ranchman," "mesquite," "canyon"— all commonly known.

The significance of actual geographical contact of the speakers of English with the speakers of Spanish in regard to the words that one people will borrow from another is indicated by this removal of the frontiersmen from the territories in which the Spanish were prominent; no farther north than the main course of the Oregon Trail contact was almost negligible. This lack of contact is reflected linguistically in the works of such a writer as Francis Parkman in his *Oregon Trail* in which hardly a word of Spanish is found except the inevitable "corral." For "sombrero" Parkman uses "broad-brimmed hat." Not even the popular "lasso" is found in Parkman. He prefers the English "noose." He does introduce a Frenchified "lariat" in the form of "lariette." Likewise, Ezra Meeker uses very few if any Spanish in his accounts of the West.

In the writings of the more noted frontiersmen such as Crockett, Kit Carson, Cody, Fremont, and Custer very little Spanish is found. With the exception of Fremont none of them left much in the way of first-hand written documents from which to get an estimate of the number and kind of Spanish words used by these men. Fremont's journals do contain a few of the commoner Spanish words such as "canyon," "corral," "mustang," but not so many as one might expect in view of Fremont's long years of contact and experience in Spanish regions.

3. *Early California writers.*— A number of other writers might be considered appropriately as frontiersmen because of their first-hand experiences in the Far West. Their writings are in part the writings of frontiersmen. Among them is Richard H. Dana with his *Two Years Before The Mast* published in 1840 as an expansion of notes taken in a brief journal between August 14, 1834 and September 20, 1836. This was one of the more important literary efforts which incorporated Spanish words freely and naturally into the English context. The very great popularity of Dana's sea story did much to familiarize the English-speaking public with Spanish names of many things then extant in Spanish California. The early reader of this account got a fairly definite idea of the meaning of Spanish terms like "alcalde," "creole," "lasso," *quien sabe*, "rancho," *paseo, presidio*, "padre," "fandango," *pulqueria, calabozo*, and "siesta." This work is still widely read. It is also used in school reading courses and is issued with footnotes to inform the pupil precisely what a "ranchero" or a "real" is if he should have any doubts after reading the context.

This work of Dana contrasts, as regards Spanish usage, with those works of Washington Irving which deal with frontier themes. Irving was one of the first literary writers in America to introduce Spanish words into English context. Although he was thoroughly imbued with the Spanish spirit and had already written on romantic old Spanish subjects, he uses surprisingly few of the Spanish words common to the western regions about which he writes. Dana or Bret Harte writing on the same subjects would have used scores of Spanish words. Irving uses very few. But Irving was not a frontiersman and seemingly was not acquainted with even the more commonly used terms of the westerner. Like Parkman he uses "noose" rather than "lasso" or "lariat." His horses of two colors are not "pinto" but "piebald" and a "caviar" (*caballada*) of horses passes with him as a "supernumerary of horses." For the usual "sombrero" we find in Irving "broad-brimmed hats;" for "chaps" or *chaparejos*, "leather leggings," and even "adobes" are "sun-dried bricks" to Irving. Irving's contacts were primarily with Spain, not with the frontier.[9]

Bret Harte, although he spent the first years of his life in the East and his later years in Europe, was for a time an important frontiersman from a literary and linguistic standpoint. Bret Harte went to California when he was nineteen years old. There he "knocked about" long enough to acquire a first-hand and intimate experience with the life of a newly-settled country before getting into newspaper activities. As assistant on the editorial staff of the *Northern California* and of the *Golden Era* he was instrumental in promoting that local and Spanish atmosphere which later became so characteristic of the *Overland Monthly* of which he was editor. In Bret Harte's own writings as well as the writings of others that appeared in the *Overland Monthly* Spanish words were common and used with naturalness and effectiveness.

Among those who collaborated with Bret Harte for a time was Samuel L. Clemens. Although nearly thirty

[9] Irving made one trip west in 1832 as far as St. Louis. His letters written during the trip indicate that for him it was a genuine frontier expedition. Charles Latrobe was with him part of the way and traveled on into the Southwest and Mexico. Latrobe's accounts are replete with Spanish terms.

years old before going to the Far West, Clemens possessed a background that adapted him to become a naturalized frontiersman without difficulty. First at Carson City and Virginia City, Nevada, on the *Enterprise* and later in San Francisco on the *Golden Era* and the *Alta California* he made his beginnings. When Clemens writes of local themes Spanish words are invariably to be found in the context. His chief works, however, do not center upon the regions where Spanish was prominent and therefore the total amount of Spanish found in his better-known writings is not large.

C. *The Mexican War Period*

Another leading literary figure some of whose writings enter the circle of this study, particularly in connection with the borrowings or influences during the Mexican War period, was James Russell Lowell. The popularity of the *Biglow Papers* and the fact that a writer of the literary status of Lowell adopted the Spanish words to fit his subject are more significant than is the number of words found in his writings for the number is not large.

Among them are "seenoreetas," "fandango," "Rio Grandy," "chapparal," *el vomito*, "Eldorado," "siesta," "pinto." The peculiar spelling adopted by Lowell in the case of certain words is interesting and significant only when it indicates the pronunciation of the Spanish words by speakers of English. Lowell, for instance, when he spells "señorita," "seenoreeta," is giving the word its eye-learned pronunciation, i.e., the anglicized sounding, as well as being jocose.

The Spanish words found in the writings of Lowell are merely an echo in the East of the commonness of such words in the writings of the Southwest during the Mexican War period. No type of writing in which Spanish words are found except accounts of travels in the Spanish territories, is so replete with borrowed words and phrases as the writings of those at or near the front where there was more or less intimate association with the native speakers of Spanish. In the diaries of the soldiers and reports of the officers it was convenient and often necessary to use Spanish names of things that were common in the lives of the Americans engaged in the controversy. Words like *mocho* or "chiquitos" or "huevosed" might be used infrequently while others in a class with "corral," "ranch," "alcalde," and *pronunciamento* occur on nearly every page of some of the journals. Stories and accounts printed by the newspapers of the United States were generally eyewitness, or purported eyewitness, reports from the battle fronts or occupied territories. If the *New York Herald* may be taken as typical of eastern papers, the following words observed on its pages indicate to some extent the Spanish words that Americans were reading during the Mexican War period: "alcalde," *paisano, paseo, caviliado,* "vomito," also spelled "vomitto," *puro, moderado,* "rancheros," *guerilleros, buenas noches,* "rancho," "chaparral," also spelled "chapporal," *montezuma,* "arroba," "pueblo," *vivas, pronunciamiento* "fandango," *proclama, bando,* "lazo," *tierra caliente,* "padre," *segarrito* (cigarito), "jacal" (pronounced harcals, *sic*) "musqueet (*sic*) tree," "alamo," "plaza," "adobe," "hacienda," "arroyo," *sapadores,* "ranches," *vacara* (cow driver, *sic*), "sierra," *tierra, templada,* "rancheros," *laguna,* "corral," "mustang," *ayuntamiento, agiotistas.*

As noted elsewhere the period of campaigning against Mexico by United States troops was preceded and followed by years of agitation, or of reconciliation, during which things Spanish, including words, were kept before readers of American and English newspapers. The Mexican War gave rise to its share of fictional writing with or without historical background in which some of the characters, or the setting, or both, were Spanish or Mexican. In these writings the commoner Spanish words usually occur. All things considered, therefore, the Mexican War period was clearly one of great importance for the familiarization and adoption of Spanish words in English.

D. *Cowboy-Life Writings*

Beginning before the Mexican War period, running through it, and continuing after it, was to be found the cowboy life in the great open country of the West and Southwest. It is doubtful whether any phase of life distinctive to North America has been more largely exploited by writers, good, bad, prominent, and unknown, than the life and activities of the American *vaquero*. The activities of the cowboy, actual and imaginary, provide motives, themes, plots, characters, and action for almost any type of writing—narrative, descriptive, biographical, historical, poetic, fictional—whether long or short. Even today, when the cowboy has become almost extinct, a prolific family of story magazines, not to mention scores of novels, thrive on the literary materials he created. Some of the writings to which reference may be made in an effort to find recorded evidence of the extent to which Spanish words became a part of the language of cowboy life are or were produced by the cowboys themselves in songs or doggerel verses. Occasionally, also, a cowboy has turned writer and made use of his knowledge and experience. More commonly, however, the writings of cowboy life come to us from adopted sons of the West or others who have gained their knowledge comparatively late in life and then chiefly through observation rather than first-hand experience. In many instances the results are gratifying and the recorded language is reasonably accurate. Where the author in question has acquired the spirit and ways of the cowboy it is difficult to distinguish his productions from those of a native son.

Such a one was Frederick Remington, who, although trained in the art schools of Yale and Columbia, journeyed west for his health in early middle age and became one of the best depicters, in both drawings and writings, of the cowboy. His articles in *Harper's New Monthly Magazine* in the early nineties, for example, are representative both of the spirit and admiration of cowboy life and of the effective use he made of Spanish words. "Patron," "hacienda," "sierra," "patio," "ranch," "arroyo," *vaquero*, "lobo," "serape," "burro," *riata, criada, rebozo,* "bronco," *lagunas*, "metates," "lariats," "rodeo," *baile, tequela, torero, barrancas, cincha,* "mesa," "adobe," *chaparras, ramada, casa, tequas, peone, poco tiempo, compadre, tortillas, adios, mañana,* are encountered in Remington's writings.

In the same class with the writings of Remington in some respects but contrasting with them in others is *The Virginian* by Owen Wister, published in 1902 and enthusiastically reviewed in the October, 1902, issue of the *Critic. The Virginian* belongs distinctly to the long list of cowboy literature and as such could not have been written with effect without the introduction of at least some Spanish names for cowboy paraphernalia. Without regard for the literary quality of the story, one can readily conclude that it was not written by one familiar with the Spanish language, particularly as it is found among those native to the cow country of the West and the Southwest. A comparison, for instance, of the work with one by Philip Ashton Rollins, Andy Adams, or Will James shows a significant difference. For the limited number of Spanish words found in Wister's book, however, much publicity was achieved because of the popularity of the story.

Other writers on cowboy life, or the cowboys themselves, who seem to write as they have observed rather than as they themselves have done, but who have used Spanish words rather freely in their contexts, include Emerson Hough, Stewart Edward White, Philip Ashton Rollins, Douglas Branch. Other writers, such as Professor J. Frank Dobie of the University of Texas, combine experience with observation and the gift of expression, and portray accurate pictures of the lives and activities of the old-time and modern *vaqueros*. And finally there are the cowboys themselves who have turned to authorship. Among the earlier was Andy Adams who, in works like *Reed Anthony, Cowman*, and *The Log of a Cowboy*, makes full use of Spanish words. More recent is Will James, who in his *Sand, Smoky*, and more particularly in his *Lone Cowboy*, and *The Drifting Cowboy*, illustrates accurately the run of cowboy words. In the collections of cowboy songs gathered by John A. Lomax, *Songs of the Cattle Trail and Cow Camp*, and *Cowboy Songs and Other Frontier Ballads*, one finds a number of Spanish words representative for compositions of that sort. Among such words encountered are: "quirt," "lariat," "maguey," "cholla," "corral," "dally," "dally welter," *remuda*, "cinch," "chap," *adios*, "sombrero" and others. Practically all are strictly terms used in the cattle industry.

E. *Other Fiction Based on the Spanish Territory*

In addition to the cowboy writings, which naturally use the setting of the West or the Southwest, there are other writings which, for lack of a better heading are termed "fiction with Spanish, Mexican, or southwestern background, theme or characters." Prominent in fiction of this class are the stories of rough border life as C. W. Webber's *The Prairie Scout: a Romance of Border Life*, published in 1852, when border and Mexican affairs were prominent in the minds and thought of all Americans. Few writers before or since have used more Spanish words accurately and effectively than Webber. Yet half a century later we find in the writings of Mary Austin how spontaneously a naturalized daughter of the Southwest uses Spanish. If Miss Austin were a native-born Southwesterner, her works might be cited as examples of how and how much the native uses Spanish in his writings. Although born and schooled in the Middle West Mary Austin would pass admirably as a native of the Spanish territory. In her writings, which include *Land of Little Rain*, *The Ford*, and *Lost Borders*, Spanish words are used profusely but not affectedly.

Like Mary Austin, Harold Bell Wright adopted the West. Although not all of his writings nor even the bulk of them concern the country or the people of the Southwest, nevertheless Wright seems to have acquired accurately the colloquial vernacular of the type of person in the Southwest who uses Spanish mixed with his English. Examples are to be found in his *Mine with the Iron Door*. In contrast to Austin and Wright as regards the lack of affectation in the use of Spanish, one may turn to Stellman, in whose *Port O' Gold* a large number of Spanish words and phrases are employed for the too obvious purpose of creating and maintaining atmosphere.

Although three phases of American civilization—frontier life, cowboy life, and peculiarities resulting from geographical isolation—have practically disappeared, they will continue for a long time to be a source for fiction writers. They provide, on the one hand, endless material of historical romance for such stories as Gertrude Atherton's *Splendid Idle Forties* and *Before the Gringo Came* and, on the other, alluring settings, characters, or plots for books on the order of *Death Comes for the Archbishop* by Willa Cather, and *Cimarron*[10] by Edna Ferber, in both of which occurs a

[10] *Cimarron* is a Spanish word signifying wild, uncivilized, or untamed. It is applied to a river in Arkansas near New Mexico and to a particular district in that part of the country.

fairly large number of Spanish words representative of the Spanish that may be expected in the average writing of this sort. These springs of sound material will be much used by the Wild West magazines.

F. *Wild West Magazines*

It is difficult to determine the extent to which the magazines that feature Wild West stories, cowboy life, Mexican bandits, mining brawls, and the like are influential in introducing and riveting certain words from Spanish into the main body of English. An examination of these magazines, such as those issued by Fiction House, shows that, with one exception, they lead all other writings in English in the use of Spanish words. That exception is, of course, those writings which concern affairs or travels in Mexico or other countries where Spanish is the official language. The chief reason for the use of so many Spanish words and terms in the exciting magazine stories and articles is, of course, to add more color, more atmosphere, more romance. The practice of almost invariably having a Mexican or "greaser" as villain has become trite. But regardless of triteness the concocters of such adventures have failed to find a convenient substitute and the unfortunate "Mex" continues to hold his villainous rôle. Consequently there must be some Spanish words and phrases to accompany him. Such words as *caballo, vamoos,* "sombrero," "rancho," "gringo," "lariat," "quirt," *vaquero,* "bronco" and of course *calaboose, caramba,* and *quien sabe* are commonly found. Western story magazines are widely read by less sophisticated America. They cannot be read without a resultant familiarity with the Spanish words that are used so repeatedly. It is not surprising, therefore, to hear a native New Yorker who has read these stories call back to a companion in friendly leave taking, "Adios, I'll see you mañana." True, the pronunciation of the words is the result of reading and

not of oral use and is therefore faulty, but there is seldom
occasion for pronunciation.

1. *Lariat: a detailed analysis.*—Of these Western-life,
cowboy-life, "real-life" story magazines, *Lariat*, published
by the Real Adventures Publishing Company, Incorporated, in New York City, is typical. *Lariat Story Magazine*
is a magazine of original fiction; the characters named and
happenings described are entirely imaginary. They are
composed by authors who are, or purport to be, "real cowboys." The language and the vocabulary, therefore, it
might be assumed, are those typical of genuine cowboys in
the Southwest. *Lariat*, along with other Fiction House
publications, is sold at nearly all news stands in most of
the larger cities of the United States. An examination of
representative examples of these Western-story magazines
indicates that Spanish words and phrases occur in almost
every story that appears in them. Furthermore the words
and phrases used are in the main true to form and indicative of a fairly accurate knowledge of Spanish on the part
of the contributors.

Lariat, which is hardly more prolific in Spanish than the
other members of this magazine family, may be taken as a
fair example for more detailed examination. A single issue,
that of April, 1931, purchased at a news stand in New York
City, lists the following stories or articles in its table of
contents: "The Black Maverick," "Smokeroo" (no doubt
analogous to *Buckeroo*), "The Mex Notcher," "Rodeo Records," "The Corral." On the first page appear two Spanish
words, on the second eight, on the third four. The number
runs on at about this rate throughout the magazine to a
total of 376 words, by count. Pages with a total absence of
Spanish words are few. Some words occur rather frequently as would be expected. The more common words in
their order are "ranch," 41 times, *hombre*, 31, "canyon,"

23, "corral," 22, "bronco," 19, "rodeo," 14, *savvy* and "mesa," 12 times each; "mesquite," 9, *señor*, 8, *adios*, "arroyo" and "stampede," 6 times each, "burro," "coyote," "lariat," *puerto* and "sombrero," 5 times each.

G. *Scholarly Writings Based on the Spanish Territory*

Poles apart from the sensational fiction of the Wild West "true story" stuff yet drawing on the same source material —the Spanish Southwest and West—is a body of writings often sponsored by, or centered at, the various universities in the West. These writings are in most instances scholarly, albeit sometimes popularized, essays or dissertations resulting from research, often into entirely newly discovered documents or other original material. The object of these productions is not that of fiction, which aims to entertain by commercializing the "matter of Spain in America," but that of the scholar who aims to extend actual knowledge and appreciation of the beginnings of modern civilization in America and the lives of the pioneers of that civilization. In the front ranks, both as scholar and also as utilizer of Spanish words in English context, is Professor Herbert E. Bolton of the University of California, who is sufficiently familiar with Spanish to make use of Spanish words with no evidence of forcing. Where an English word might be found but would probably not be quite so expressive as the Spanish, Professor Bolton does not hesitate to use the Spanish. A French phrase, however, seems to be preferred over the Spanish when the latter could well have been used, in the sentence, "Something sinister was brewing, and Spain must be on the qui vive," in the foreword to his *Crespi*. Other works of this kind such as *The Book of Texas* by Professor H. Y. Benedict and J. A. Lomax, *Historic Towns*, edited by Powell, and *Spanish Alta California* by A. J. Denis, illustrate the extensive, practical and effective use of Spanish words. In the latter work, for instance, are found the following words used once or many times: "adobe," "cedulas," *farallones, adios, cosas bastantes delicadas, jacales,* "juntas," "fiesta," "madroña," "padre," *presidio,* "peso," "rancherias," "pueblo," "panocha," *pelota,* "presidente," "plaza," *reata, vaqueros, vivas.* Younger scholars with bilingual equipment, following in the footsteps of these writers, inject an even greater amount of Spanish into their works. Such a one is James E. Stiff who uses Spanish words naturally and frequently.

Outside college centers, this type of writing in which Spanish words appear prominently is well typified by the writings of Charles F. Lummis, a Massachusetts man who for a time was affiliated with the *Los Angeles Times* and later moved to the Southwest for his health. His works, accurate as to content, carry with them the native atmosphere of the Southwest. They have had wide circulation and along with other similar writings have played their part in establishing a number of Spanish words in the American vocabulary. *Coronado's Children* by J. Frank Dobie, selected by a book-of-the-month club, has a bearing on the question of the adoption of Spanish words by English-speaking people. Dobie is a contemporary writer of the Southwest who makes liberal use of Spanish in his English contexts.

H. *Formal Works on History, Economics, etc.*

More formal in aspect and content than the foregoing type of writing but just as much committed by nature to the use of Spanish words is that body of historical or other literature which deals seriously with the facts pertaining to the former Spanish provinces now a part of the United States. This type of writing is growing in importance. Curricular requirements of schools and colleges specify more persistently the need, and the economic or industrial interests of Americans create a demand for it. A text or reference book such as J. Russell Smith's *North America*, which is widely used in colleges, is an example. As such books increase in numbers they may be expected to contribute to the borrowings of Spanish from English. They will never be so numerous as the historical accounts, but they are appearing at a fairly rapid rate, at times in a more popular form. Examples are *The Santa Fe Trail* by R. L. Duffus, and *Coronado's Children*, already mentioned. Less popular but no less important are the writings of such historians as Hubert Howe Bancroft and the official reports of army or other pioneer scouts and surveyors sent by the United States government into the Mexican border regions to study the land, the fauna and the flora. Several of these accounts have been read with profit in connection with this study, among them the reports of Captains Emory and Ferguson and the survey for a Pacific Railroad. In all of these are accurate examples of the use of various Spanish words known widely among the English-speaking population of the territories under study. The present tendency is toward an increasing interest in the whole "Spanish matter" of the West and Southwest. It is safe to say therefore that the amount of writing about the life of the region will greatly increase, and unless such writing ceases to incorporate as much Spanish phrasing "as the traffic will bear," readers will increasingly encounter Spanish words in English context.

I. *Children's Books*

The increased interest in things Mexican and Spanish-American is shown by the appearance, each publication season, of a number of children's books with Spanish or Mexican themes, background and characters. The widely-advertised and delightfully-told story of *The Painted Pig*, by Elizabeth Morrow, was one of several tales that made their appearance on the children's book shelves during

1929 and 1930.[11] These books give many American children an early introduction to a number of Spanish words.

J. *Radio Programs*

Furthermore, with the popularization of the radio, another factor for adoptions has entered the field. Radio programs featuring Spanish songs, Spanish or Mexican characters, and border life are increasing in popularity and number. Such programs are liberally tinctured with Spanish words and phrases. For instance, the program of "The Scapoose Kid" given over station WOR on January 11, 1931, made use of many Spanish words in both songs and dialogues. Among the words were "tamale," "corral," *bonita, señorita,* "sombrero," *bueno, tortillas,* "enchiladas," "chile," *vamoose,* "hidalgo," "picador," *mañana, hasta mañana, adios, pronto,* "mustang," "pulque-juice," "frijoles." Here are about twenty words all of which were probably understood by most auditors. The ultimate importance of the radio in the borrowing of Spanish words cannot be predicted, but speculation is not entirely useless. In any case, the radio presents to a great multitude of people another opportunity for the ear-learning of Spanish words that otherwise would not be heard.

K. *Motion Pictures*

The "movies" have long featured characters and scenes of the Mexican border and the Southwest. For galloping action, romantic heroism and manly adventure no other medium or setting surpasses, and few equal, that of the frontier and cattle country in screen possibilities. As a result young America knows its bronco-busting, "shootin'-iron," Mexican-killing heroes by name, by looks, and by language. But the silent drama, so-called, offered compara-

---

[10] See also *Cowboy Tommy* by Sanford Tousey—"A picture-story book to introduce every small boy to the Old West."

tively little of linguistic importance, except the perpetuation of traditional Spanish topics and atmosphere, until the introduction of the speaking voice, synchronized with motion, known as the "talkies." Written scenario lines read hurriedly between flashes of action are far behind the spoken word when the introduction of Spanish words into English vocabularies is concerned. Indeed it is no exaggerated estimate to suppose that the "talkies" will become an important contact point between Spanish and English. Productions such as the one entitled "Under a Texas Moon" and another "The Gay Caballero" make use of many Spanish words and phrases repeatedly; often with good effect. In the latter production, for instance, the following Spanish terms were noted: *bien, muy bien, adios,* "coyote," "peons," "gringo,," *vamos,* "pesos," "fiesta," *señor, quien es, si señor, hombre,* "bad hombre," *vaqueros,* "hacienda," *diablo,* "ranch," *manos arriba todos* (hands up, everybody), *señorita,* besides many proper names. It should be noted, however, that the pronunciation of Spanish words is distinctly Anglicized by the majority of motion picture actors.

L. *Contemporary Newspapers and Periodicals*

The use of Spanish words in contemporary newspapers, as well as newspapers of eighty and a hundred years ago, is of some importance. Since the eighteen fifties and sixties the number of Spanish words has materially decreased in the columns of newspapers published in territory formerly Spanish, as for instance in California, Texas and New Mexico. On the other hand Spanish words that have become rather generally known to American speakers of English may be encountered at any time in almost any newspaper of the country. Whereas formerly news stories dealing with Spanish or Mexican themes, local color, or background were written by a resident of the place in question and sent directly to the newspaper, today all such news stories are distributed on a "wholesale" basis by the Associated Press, or other similar news gathering agencies to their constituencies. This change has been responsible for the elimination of many Spanish words that would otherwise have been used. Today the casual reader of a New York newspaper will not be aware of many Spanish words in the columns he scans daily. But careful search will show that they creep in regularly and to good advantage in the run of news articles and occasionally in a flock. Let a dehorned beef steer break loose from a New York City abbatoir and your news reporter brings to the fore his Spanish cowboy vocabulary with effect and an evident delight. The steer becomes a *toro* and the excited motorcycle policeman who gives chase is a *vaquero* on a "mustang" which he urges on by "spurring it in the accelerator and kicking it in the clutch" and "although his equipment does not include a lariat" he finally gets the stampeded *toro* in the "corral" and rides off on his "bronco . . . puffing and snorting and all in a lather." The reporter is well aware that his readers will not only understand but enjoy the fun more if the account is dressed in *vaquero* style. Such "flocking" of Spanish words is comparatively rare, that is, as rare as the occasion allows; yet the casual appearance of Spanish words in the regular run of news accounts is not uncommon. Among those observed in New York City dailies the following are typical: A *New York Times* subheadline "Flier's Report of Party on Mesa Fails on Later Investigation." Another heading reads "Armed '*Vigilantes*' Seek Bandit Trio." Still other words encountered in the same newspaper were "bronco," "corralled," "arroyos," "barracuda," "fiesta," "siesta," *loma*, "bronco-busting," "junta," "bronck," "ranchman" and "Lobo Canyon." In the *Herald Tribune* will be found about the same run of

Spanish words as is found in the *Times*. On one occasion this newspaper ran a headline, "Ranchman off for Europe," while the *Daily News* on the same date said "Cowman flies for Europe." Other contemporary papers in which were observed Spanish words were the *United States Daily* and the *Provo* (Utah) *Herald*. English newspapers in Arizona and Texas and New Mexico do not have as much Spanish in them as might be expected although they have more than do those of any other section of the United States. Particularly prominent in the papers of the Southwest are the Spanish place names, while the various combinations of the word "ranch" are almost infinite— "rancher," "ranchman," "ranchwoman," "ranching," "ranched," "cattle ranch," "sheep ranch," "chicken ranch," "rabbit ranch," etc. The fact that in nearly every town of any considerable size there is a newspaper printed in Spanish, may account partially for the lack of Spanish words in the English papers.

Weekly and monthly periodicals other than those already discussed under "Wild West Stories" admit Spanish words rather sparsely except in articles dealing with Spanish or Mexican themes.

M. *Writings Far Removed from Spanish Contacts*

Other Spanish terms occur in the private correspondence between English-speaking persons in the border territory and persons situated in various parts of the United States. This type of usage would be important if it were wider in extent and thus influenced the speech of more people.

Finally one may expect to find Spanish words from Spanish-American contacts bobbing up in almost any kind of written speech in the United States even though such writings be far removed from direct contacts with the ex-Spanish regions. In *Middletown* by Lynd one comes upon the phrase, "It's a cinch"; in David Seabury's *Growing*

Into Life may be found the Spanish borrowing *vamoosed*
Stuart Chase in *The Nemesis of American Business* finds
use for "serape," "sombrero" and "machete."

N. *Conclusion*

In summarizing the appearance of Spanish words and
phrases in American literature and writings in America it
may be pointed out that such words made their first appearance in the journals and reports of explorers and adventurers plying along the American coasts and the West
Indies. The Spanish words thus introduced continued in
use during the seventeenth and eighteenth centuries, and
some of them became definitely a part of the vocabulary of
the English language. Again, with the expansion of the
United States into the Spanish frontiers of America extensive and effective use of Spanish words was made by
speakers of English. This did not take place to any great
extent until after the second decade of the nineteenth century as indicated by the fact that writers before that time
use English terms like "estate for cattle," "broad-brimmed
hats," "sun-dried mud bricks," and "noose," rather than
the Spanish equivalents, "hacienda," "sombrero," "adobe"
and "lariat"—which had almost completely replaced them
by the middle of the century. By that time speech among
the cowboys and others in the border regions had become a
convenient and picturesque bilingual mixture.

The use of Spanish in earlier writings of this period
gives evidence of a certain unnaturalness or affectation as
compared with its use by those who were born and reared
in the border atmosphere, and whose feeling for the
Spanish came naturally. But even among such writers
Spanish words are not used to any great extent except
where the subject matter is distinctly Spanish. As the
frontier and cowboy life which sponsored and called for
Spanish in English speech is displaced many one-time

commonly-used Spanish words are fading into obsolescence. Yet a few new acquaintances have also become widely and generally known and used, and promise to remain permanently in the American vocabulary. In fact the Spanish-English contacts in the Southwest are not so much diminishing as changing and extending. Increased interest by Americans in things and affairs Mexican and Spanish-American in general, has resulted in an increased amount of English speech, written and oral, in which appear Spanish words.

It is well to note, in addition, that where Spanish words have been adopted in English writings in America it has not been in formal literary contexts but almost exclusively in writings of a more simple, popular, and personal nature such as diaries, journals, personal accounts of frontier adventures and fiction based on such matter.

PHONETIC SYMBOLS

These symbols sometimes indicate approximate pronunciation* rather than minute degrees of sound value.† The continuant, intervocalic consonants g and b, for instance, which occur in *aguardiente* and *lobo* respectively, and elsewhere, are not distinguished here, by separate symbols, from stops g and b. Likewise the a in *padre* and the a in *mal* are not differentiated.

* "The Spanish of America is fundamentally . . . that of Spain . . . The following . . . differences, however, should be . . . noted: (1) In American-Spanish (also in Andalucia) c (before e or i) and z are not pronounced as interdental θ, but as a simple dental s, not unlike English s. (2) In American-Spanish, Spanish palatal *ll*, *l*, is generally pronounced as a y sound, continuant y, or semi-explosive y. This pronunciation of *ll* is also widespread in Andalucia and in some parts of New Castile. (3) In American-Spanish (and in Andalucia) s is pronounced as a dental s, similar to English s, while in standard Spanish it is an alveolar. The three sounds above are . . . nowhere considered as dialectical or vulgar . . . The American and Andalusian pronunciation of these consonants is well known in Castile and hardly noticed when heard."—*A Primer of Spanish Pronunciation*, by Tomás and Espinosa.

† For continental Spanish pronunciation see T. Navarro Tomás *Pronunciacion Española*.

The symbol *a:* is used for both. The unstressed *a* is often represented by the symbol ə.

Finer distinctions are numerous. The pronunciation of Englished Spanish words varies according to the speaker's knowledge of Spanish. *Adios*, for example, would be *a:* ð*i:* ó*:s* to one having a fairly intimate knowledge of Spanish; *a: di:* ó*:s* to one with limited knowledge of Spanish; and *æ di:* ó*:s* to one with no knowledge of Spanish.

For list of phonetic symbols see page 84.

VOCABULARY

PHONETIC SYMBOLS*

a: as in the first element of the diphthong in hide.†

e: as *a* in mate.

ε as in set.

i: as the vowel in meek.

ɪ as the vowel in inch.

u: as in boot.

æ as in sat.

ə slack, unstressed vowel, as *a* in about.

aɪ as in hide.

ʃ as *sh* in shape.

dz as *j* in jump.

ŋ as *ng* in bring.

rr Spanish trilled r.

ð as *th* in this.‡

θ as in thin.

j as *y* in yes.

h as in her.

z as in zigzag.

lj for Castilian *ll*.

ʌ as vowel in buff.

* For discussion of these symbols see p. 81.

† The *a* sound in the diphthong *aɪ* is of a quality between the *a* in father and the *æ* in sat. This sound is quite near the sound of Spanish *a* in *padre*.

‡ The Spanish *d* after a vowel is neither English *d* (a stop) nor *th* but the symbol ð is safer than *d* as a representation of the Spanish sound.

VOCABULARY

acequia English modifications[1] **asequia, cequia, zequia** (*Spanish*, a: sé: ki:a:; *English, the same and* sé: ki: ə; *also* ə se: kwía) A canal or ditch for irrigation purposes or for the water supply of pueblo or village. During the nineteenth century the term *acequia* was widely used in the Southwest. It is not so common today but is generally known.

1848 Emory, W. H., *Notes of a Military Reconnoissance*, p. 81: The outlines of the zequias by which the soil was irrigated, were sometimes quite distinct. *Ibid.*, p. 89: The remains of an old zequia crossed our trail . . .

1863 Fergusson, D., *Report to Congress*, p. 18: . . . population 800; water from river in acequias . . . no grass within a mile . . .

1899 Remington, Frederick, *Pony Tracks:* Presently we saw . . . the plastered gate of an acequia and the blue water of the tank.

1922 Bogan, B. M., *The Ceremonial Dances of the Yaqui Indians*, p. 25: . . . a statue of the saint is carried to the nearest river, spring or acequia and there piously laved . . .

1925 Burns, W. N., *The Saga of Billy the Kid*, p. 106: At last [the] saloon keeper . . . dipped up water in his hat from an asequia and took it to the dying man.

n.d. *College Song*, University of New Mexico: When the 'cequia waters flow.

acequia madre (*Spanish, see* ACEQUIA *plus* má: ðre: *English, the same and or* mǽ dri:) A main canal or ditch. Literally the "mother" canal. In the Southwest where irrigation is necessary it is common of late to hear the *acequia madre* spoken of as the "canal" while lateral outlets or those conducting water to private fields or other private plots are termed "ditches." Each property owner may be responsible for his own ditch but the canal or *acequia madre* is a community responsibility.

1844 Gregg, Josiah, *Commerce of the Prairies*, p. 151: . . . each

---

[1] In the case of words the spelling of which has been modified, the modified forms are recorded with cross references to the Spanish forms under which treatment is found.

farmer has his day for irrigation; and at no other time is he permitted to extract water from the *acequia madre. Ibid.*, p. 151: One *acequia madre* (mother ditch) suffices generally to convey water for the irrigation.

adelantado (*Spanish*, a: ðe: lan tá: ðo:; *English, the same and* æ di: læn tǽ do: *or* ðo:) Past participle of *adelantar* "to go forward" "to advance"; by extension, a forward person or one who is audacious or venturesome. A military and political governor of a frontier province. In the early years of the Southwest the *adelantado* acted as the highest court of justice in time of peace and captain general in time of war. Occurrence, however, of the word in the writings on the Spanish Southwest is limited.

1844 Gregg, Josiah, *Commerce of the Prairies*, p. 118: This adventurer . . . stipulates for some extraordinary provisions . . . with titles of Adelantado and the rank of Captain-general . . .

1904 Bourne, E. G., *Spain, in America*, p. 162: He [De Soto] returned to Spain and was rewarded with the office of adelantado of Florida . . .

a dio (*Spanish*, a: ði:ó:; *English, the same*) From *adios*. An exclamation; an oath; an expression of surprise or doubt. Commonly used in bantering or light conversation by those who have an intimate contact with Spanish along the border.[2]

adios (*Spanish*, a: ði:ó:s; *English, the same*; a: di: ó:s; *and* æ di: ó:s) An expression of friendly leave-taking equivalent to the English phrases "goodbye," "so long," or "I'll see you later." Literally the speaker commends to the care of God the one to whom he speaks. *Adios* is commonly made use of in the border region and is heard in light conversation in other parts of the United States. It is heard in U. S. army parlance and has been adopted also by radio announcers.

1856 (1926) Carson, Kit, in his own story by Mr. and Mrs. Peters: Doctor, Compadre, adios. (Said to be his last words.)

1859 Reid, Samuel, *Scouting Expedition*, p. 93: . . . we took the hat from the man and giving him a dollar, bade him adios.

1886 McLane, Hiram H., *Irene Viesca*, p. 53: And now adios, with more anon, but from where, quien sabe?

---

[2] The number of citations, or lack of citations, recorded may, but does not necessarily, indicate the frequency with which a word is used.

1889 Ripley, McHatton E., *From Flag to Flag*, p. 275: The kind old priest in the village . . . called to bid him adios . . .

1913 Kyne, Peter B., *The Long Chance:* Dan, old friend, adios. *Ibid.:* And now I must toddle along. Adios.

1922 Rollins, Philip Ashton, *The Cowboy and His Interpreters*, p. 71: Except for an occasional *adios* the universal parting salutation was "so long."

1930 Recorded conversation of a native New Yorker on March 29th: Adios, I'll see you mañana.

adobe English modifications **dobe, dobie, dob, adaubi, doby, adabe, dogie** (*Spanish*, a: ðó: be:; *English*, ə dó: bi:; dó: bi:; *and* do:b) The word occurs frequently in spoken and written forms and is usually spelled *adobe* rather than *dobie* or *doby*. The contracted form, however, will hardly disappear from spoken English. Two forms, therefore, may persist contemporaneously. 1. An oblong, mud brick, approximately eighteen by six by ten inches in dimensions, made from clay that adheres compactly when mixed with water. The clay for *adobes* may be mixed by hand implements or by a rude *dobe* mixing mill operated by horse, mule, or burro power hitched to the end of the long, horizontal pole of the mill. When the clay is sufficiently mixed it is cast into wooden moulds. The wet *dobies* are arranged in rows in an open space in the hot sun and allowed to dry and bake. There is no burning by fire. *Adobes* are used almost exclusively for building purposes in Mexican settlements along the border whether it be for houses for wall or for ovens and the like. 2. An *adobe* house, the name of a part standing for the whole. 3. Clay soil that has hardened by application of water; i.e., puddled. 4. Marbles made of clay and painted various colors are known among American boys as *dobies*. 5. Nickname for a thing of inferior quality. 6. The Mexican silver dollar is sometimes referred to as a *dobie*. 7. A "scrubby" or anaemic calf or other animal. The cowboys' "dogies," as applied to cattle, is probably an adaptation of *dobies*.

1845 Stapp, William P., *Prisoners of Perote*, p. 112: . . . miserable villages, built of adobes, here and there checker the roadside . . .

1847 Ruxton, George F., *Adventures in Mexico and the Rocky Mountains*, p. 12: The city is well planned, surrounded by an adobe wall.

1856 Weber, *A Tale of the South Border*, p. 288: . . . the indignant Texans reduced her rancho . . . to ashes, and left no "doby upon another . . ."

1862 Hewitt, R. H., *Across the Plains*, p. 113: Kearney City . . . familiarly called dobie town . . . was a small forlorn burg.

1893 Lummis, C. F., *The Penitent Brothers*, p. 88: Squatting with back against *dobe* walls the men rolled cigarettes from corn-husks . . .

1911 Thomas, Augustus, *Arizona*, p. 5: The dobie house . . . lay sprawling off to the northwest.

1912 Hough, Emerson, *The Story of the Cowboy*, p. 136: A "dogy" or "doby" yearling (a scrubby calf that has not wintered well) . . .

1922 Rollins, Philip Ashton, *The Cowboy and His Interpreters*, p. 217: This . . . provoked much discussion of stock that "had not wintered well" and of . . . "dobes" these last being calves that were scrubby and anaemic . . .

1926 Cather, Willa, *Death Comes for the Archbishop*, p. 101: . . . there was not a handful of soil . . . held in by an adobe wall . . .

1927 Lawrence, David H., *Corasmin and the Parrots*, p. 9: . . . one rather crumbly adobe house built round two sides of a garden patio . . .

1929 Brown, K. Stanley, *Young Architects*, p. 129: A low adobe house surrounding a grassy patio.

aguardiente English modifications **aguardient, aguardente** (*Spanish*, á: gwar ði:én te:; *English, practically the same except that final* e: *becomes* i:) Brandy; liquor; alcoholic drinks in general; literally "burning water." The word occurs frequently in early writings but is not commonly used in spoken English today. More specific names such as "mescal," "pulque," etc., are employed.

1836 Latrobe, Charles J., *Travels in Mexico*, p. 71: He forthwith departed . . . bought himself a bottle of aguardient and got tipsy.

1848 Emory, W. H., *Notes of a Military Reconnoissance*, p. 83: The attraction was the aguardiente. *Ibid.*, p. 86: Aguardient (brandy) is known among their chief men only . . .

1923 Smith, Wallace, *The Little Tigress*, p. 58: Fierro picked up the stone flask of aguardiente.

ajo (*Spanish*, á: ho: *English, the same*) Desert lily (*hesperocallis undulatus*). A true lily, with narrow, ribbony, crinkle-edged leaves lying flat at the base of the straight flower-stem, which is about 2 feet high. Flowers 3 or 4 inches in diameter, fragrant, white with green veining on back of petals, several to a stem. Blooms in mid-spring.

alacran English modification **alicran** (*Spanish*, a: la: krán; *English*, æl ə krǽn) A scorpion. The word is seldom used in English even in the most Spanish sections along the border. English "scorpion" is preferred. *Alacran* does, however, occur in writings descriptive of the state of Durango in old Mexico, where the insect seems to have been abundant at one time.

1836 Latrobe, Charles Joseph, *Travels in Mexico*, p. 182: The alacran of Durango is the most venomous and hundreds of children are killed by them in that province.

1841 Kendall, George Wilkins, *Narrative Texas Expeditions*, p. 114: . . . While travelling through . . . Durango were we regaled with . . . stories of the swarms of poisonous alicrans which infest the capital.

1844 Gregg, Josiah, *Commerce of the Prairies:* A society in Durango pays a reward . . . for every alacran (or scorpion) that is brought to them.

1856 Hughes, Doniphan, *Expeditions*, p. 128: . . . The soldiers while in Durango would sometimes shake their blankets, toss . . . the lizards and alacrans, exclaiming angrily, "damn the scorpion family!"

alameda (*Spanish*, a: la: mé: ða:; *English, the same and* æl ə mí: ðə *or* də) A site covered by *alamos* or poplar trees; applied also to a street, walk, or drive lined by *alamos* or other trees.

1923 Smith, Wallace, *The Little Tigress*, p. 160: It was the memmory of this that reminded me of him just a little while ago at the *alameda*.

1931 (Apr.) *Lariat,* p. 24: But he moved out of the far end of the *Alameda* . . .

alamo (*Spanish*, á: la: mo:; *English*, ǽl ə mo:) Cotton-wood tree *populus monilifera, ocudentalis:* also poplar. The prevalence of the *alamo* as a native tree in the Southwest and the familiarity of the word to those who live in that region make it likely that the word will continue to be used but it will scarcely displace the English "cotton-wood tree." Alamo, as the place besieged by Santa Ana's army in 1836, is famous in the history of Texas. There are several other places in the United States called "Alamo" or with names in which the word appears. New Mexico has an Alamo and an Alamogordo (big cottonwood); Colorado has an Alamo and an Alamosa; California has an Alamo and an Alameda. Michigan and Tennessee each has a place named Alamo.

1853–54 House of Representatives. *Ex. Doc.*, No. 91, vol. IV, p. 10: The alamos grow to a good large size and are quite abundant.

alcalde (*Spanish*, a:l ká:l de:; *English* æl kǽl di:) The chief civil officer of a township or village, often combining administrative and judicial authority, prerogatives and functions. In the Southwest the *alcalde* was mayor, judge and sometimes police or sheriff combined. The law in many places was pretty much in his hands. In fact not infrequently the word or will of the *alcalde* became an autocratic substitute for law and the administration of justice. *Alcalde* was used throughout the Spanish territory of America and only recently has been replaced in parts of New Mexico. It is sometimes confused with Spanish *alcaide* meaning the officer charged with the defense of a fort or castle. *Alcalde* occurs frequently in writings about the Spanish Southwest.

1834 Parker, *A Visit to Texas*, p. 217: There is now . . . an ayuntamiento or council, an alcalde, or chief civil officer . . .

1856; 1926 Peters, *Kit Carson's Own Story of His Life*, p. 53: I arrived safely at Taos, gave the letter to the Alcalde and he forwarded them to Santa Fe.

1918 White, Stewart Edward., *The Forty-Niners*, p. 47: In those days all trials (except military) took place before officials called alcaldes who acknowledged no higher authority than the governor.

alfalfa See the *New English Dictionary*.

alfilerilla English modification **alfilaria** (*Spanish*, á:l fi: le: rí: jə; *English*, ǽl fil ə rí:ə) Diminutive of *alfiler*, pin: pin grass (*erodium cicularium*) a geraniaceous herb with "flat rosettes of greenish laciniate leaves . . . pinkish flowers, long fruits."

1908 Carnegie Institution of Washington, *Publication* No. 99, p. 70: Finding its way about, across the mesas and over the hill slopes, is the alfilerilla . . .

alforjas English modifications **alforge, alforche, alforki, alforka** (*Spanish*, a:l fór ha:s; *English*, ǽl fór hǝʒ) Leather bags made in pairs and usually in a form to fit across the rear or front of a saddle. *Alforjas*, is, in fact, commonly interpreted as "saddlebags." But it has been used also to designate a leather container not of saddle-bag nature. *Alforjas* is not nearly so commonly used, even by those whose borrowings from Spanish are most extensive, as is the English "saddle-bags."

1847 Ruxton, George F., *Travels in Mexico and the Rocky Mountains*, p. 67: No sooner does a stranger enter a meson than to it flock venders of saddles, bridles, bits . . . alforjas . . .

1922 Rollins, Philip Ashton, *The Cowboy and His Interpreters*, p. 154: . . . all or part of the parcels might have been stuffed into the alforjas, which were wide leathern or canvas gats . . . hanging from the saddle's top.

al fresco (*Spanish*, a:l fré:s ko:; *English, the same and* ǽl frés ko:) In the open air or cool air. This phrase, in so far as its usage in the Southwest is concerned, is probably borrowed from the Spanish.

1853 Paxton, Philip, *A Stray Yankee in Texas:* This same camp was an extemporaneous affair, a kind of al fresco home, formed by setting up a few crotches to sustain a rude roof.

1880 Cody, William F., *Heroes of the Plains* [Crockett section]: . . . they were making a spread on the grass preparatory to enjoying an al fresco or open air feast . . .

alligator See the *New English Dictionary.*

alligator pear See the *New English Dictionary* under *avocado.*

alpaca South American borrowing.[3]

Americano (*Spanish*, a: me:r i: ká: no:; *English, the same and* ǝ mɛr i kǽn o:) An American; that is, a citizen of the United States. This word is used often along the border although rarely as compared with the English "American."

1919 Chase, J. Smeaton, *California Desert Trails*, p. 80: . . . sweets of greater charm, because *americano*, are offered in paper bags or lace-frilled boxes at the store.

---

[3] Words borrowed from South-American Spanish are listed in order to account for them.

1923 Smith, Wallace, *The Little Tigress*, p. 195: It is a fact, that the blue-eyed, tawny-mustached *Americano* of fiction often as not turns out to be an affable cut-throat.

amigo (*Spanish*, a: mí: go:; *English*, ə mí: go; *or* gə) Friend; good fellow; companion. *Amigo* is commonly used by Americans in the Southwest.
1854 Mayer, Brantz, *Adventures of an African Slaver*, p. 33: *Amigo*, you take a joke too seriously.
1931 *Lariat*, April, p. 122: So long, amigo.

ancheta (*Spanish*, a:n ché: ta:; *English*, æn chét ə) A venture with merchandise consigned to a frontier province. It was probably used frequently during the colonizing period of southwestern United States. Words used by Gregg are with few exceptions those in common use during his time.
1844 Gregg, Josiah, *Commerce of the Prairies*, p. 83: The Officer . . . was expecting an *ancheta* of goods.

andale (*Spanish*, á:n da: le:; *English*, ǽn də li:) Third person singular indicative also imperative of Spanish *andar* to "move," "walk," etc., plus *le* meaning you. *Andale* is common in colloquial usage and means "hurry" or "hurry up." It is often combined with the Spanish word *pronto* as *andale pronto*. Americans native to the Southwest use the word or the phrase as naturally, at least in colloquial language, as they do an English phrase or word of the same meaning. A mother sending a child or servant on an errand might be expected to conclude her instructions with "Now, *andale*" or "Now, *andale pronto*." (See also *pronto*.)

apache (*Spanish*, a: pá: che:; *English*, ə pǽ chi:) From American Indian *apachn*, man. *Apache* has been extended in meaning from the name of an Indian tribe of North America to include a person of wild, unruly or mean disposition. This is true of the Spanish usage as well as of the English. In this sense *apache* is often used in the phrase "wild apache." An unruly youth might be termed a "wild apache" and such expressions as "they ran like wild apaches" are commonly heard.
1931, *Lariat*, April, p. 28: . . . staked out in Apache-fashion, on an ant-hill to be eaten alive . . .

aparejo (*Spanish*, a: pa: ré: ho:; *English*, ə pə ré: ho: *or* ǽ pə ré: ho:) A pack saddle. It differs greatly, however, in its construction from the simple American saddle. The *aparejo* is a combined saddle and pad. Two large bags of leather or woven hemp fibre, each of a size to cover one side of the horse or mule from hip to shoulder, are stuffed with straw or other appropriate light-weight padding to a thickness varying from two to six inches. These bags are fastened together at the top of the animal's back. The pack saddle thus made is kept in place by means of a cinch about the animal's belly and a crupper strap under the tail or about the shank and often about the chest. *Aparejo* has been completely naturalized and is commonly used for naming the pack horse apparel in question. The United States army, in fact, has its official army *aparejo*.

1844 Gregg, Josiah, *Commerce of the Prairies*, p. 180: It is necessary too for the aparejo to be firmly bound on to prevent its slipping and chafing the mule's back . . .

1847 Ruxton, George F., *Adventures in Mexico and the Rocky Mountains*, p. 49: A big beast of a mule . . . disarranged the aparejo. *Ibid.*, p. 51: . . . the afternoon was devoted to cleaning mules and horses and arranging aparejos.

1874 Ingersoll, Ernest, *Knocking Round the Rockies*, p. 27: By this time the saddles and aparejos (California pack-saddles) have been repaired and distributed.

1889 Ripley, McHatton E., *From Flag to Flag*, p. 238: . . . he traded his interest (in the little patch of family land) for a horse with aparejo (saddle, etc.).

1906 Edwards, William S., *On the Mexican Highlands*, p. 118: Then a halt is made . . . the animals cooled . . . then later, the saddles and *aparejos* are taken off . . .

1922 Rollins, Philip Ashton, *The Cowboy*, p. 153: The West employed two types of pack-saddle, respectively designated as the "cross-buck saddle" and the "aparejo."

armadillo South American borrowing.

arrastra English modification **arastra** (*Spanish*, a: rrá:s tra:; *English*, ə ráes trə) A rude mill used for crushing ore. The *arrastra* is operated by horse power attached to a horizontal bar which turns a heavy wheel within a circular bin. The word occurs rather frequently in accounts of the early activities in the Southwest. Modern machinery having replaced the crude ore-crushing *arrastra*, the word will no doubt disappear, at least from spoken English.

1836 Parker, *A Trip to the West and Texas*, p. 266: Upstream
you catch the growl of the arrastra.
1863 Fergusson, Major D., *Report to Congress:* There are seven
arrastras at work at the pozo reducing silver.
1867 Richardson, *Beyond the Mississippi*, p. 307: The arastra
is the most primitive invention for crushing quartz.

arriero (*Spanish*, a: rri:é: ro:; *English* ə ri: ér o:) A muleteer or
mule driver. *Arriero* occurs often in descriptive and narrative
writings of the early exploration and colonization periods of the
Southwest.
1836 Latrobe, Joseph Charles, *The Rambler in Mexico*, p. 49:
The *arriero* is the carrier of New Spain . . .
1847 Ruxton, George F., *Adventures in Mexico and the Rocky
Mountains*, p. 59: . . . amongst soldiers and arrieros, we passed
a flea bug-ridden night.

arroba (*Spanish*, a: rró: ba:; *English*, ə ró: bə) A measure of 25
pounds or thirty-two pints. Its chief use is in connection with
dealings in flour or other produce in communities where the
Mexican units of measure are or have been used and understood.
It is not uncommon to hear an American in such communities
speak of "an *arroba* of flour."
1840 Turnbull, David, *Travels in the West*, p. 126: The agricultural produce is stated as follows:—Of white or clayed sugar
8,091,837 arrobas of 25 pounds each . . . of arobas of coffee
2,883,528; of arobas of wax . . .
1930 Lyman, George D., *John Marsh, Pioneer*, p. 205: . . . a
cowhide represented two dollars, and tallow fifty cents the
arroba.

arroyo English modifications **aroya, arroya** (*Spanish*, a: rró: jo:;
English, ə ró: jo: *or* jə) The gorge or ravine cut by water running
in the lower parts of a particular region. This ravine may have,
near its source, steep mountainous sides. Here it is a "cañon."
After heavy rains or during the "rainy season" of the year an
arroyo may have in it a large volume of water, even a torrent.
This gradually diminishes as the rains subside until the wash, or
bed, is entirely dry. Thus it remains during the greater part of
the year. The terms "cañon" and *arroyo* loosely used are interchangeable. On the other hand a "gully" or "swale" might be
termed a small *arroyo* never a small cañon. The word *arroyo* as

used in Spain means a stream of water, whether in a ravine or down the street gutter. The Spanish-American usage on the other hand is the same as the English usage, and, of course, father to it.

1847 Ruxton, George F., *Adventures in the Rocky Mountains and Mexico*, p. 96: . . . the lowing of cattle resounded from the banks of the arroyo . . . *Ibid*. p. 120: . . . I fancied I could discern an arroyo with running water.

1854 Emory, W. H., *Report of a Military Reconnoissance*, p. 63: Many deep arroyos have paid tribute to the Gila, but in none have we yet found water.

1912? Cozzens, S.W., *The Young Trail Hunters*, p. 172: Jerry exclaimed, "There they be again . . ." pointing to the mouth of a small aroya . . .

1912 Hough, Emerson, *The Story of the Cowboy*, p. 262: . . . coming up from the arroyo, is the figure of a horseman . . .

1914 Harte, Francis Bret, *The Mystery of the Hacienda:* Down the arroyo, out across the mead, By heath and hollow, sped the maid.

1917 McClellan, George B., *Mexican War Diary* (Jan. 14), p. 46: . . . bridged two wet arroyos and encamped about sunset by a little stream.

1926 Cather, Willa, *Death Comes For The Archbishop*, p. 167: Down the middle of the arroyo flowed a rushing stream . . . *Ibid.*, p. 162: . . . he wrung more pesos out of Arroyo Seco and Questa than out of his own arroyo.

1927 Bolton, H. E., *Fray Juan Crespi*, XXI: He had 25 leather-jacket soldiers . . . to open roads through mountains and across arroyos.

1929 *New York Times*, June 6: . . . there is the possibility of arroyos raging with water . . .

atajo See HATAJO.

atole English modification **atola** (*Spanish*, a: tó: le:; *English*, ə tó: li:) From American Indian *atolli*. A thick gruel-like beverage made of water and wheat or corn flour, and a little sweetened. *Atole* as a food is used rarely by Americans but is a common item in the meal of a Mexican. The word *atole*, like many such Spanish borrowings of a specialized nature, is used for lack of an English word and is well known among Americans who have Mexican contacts.

1845 Stapp, William P., *Prisoners of Perote*, p. 87: In the morning, we received a pint of . . . *atola*, which is nothing more than corn gruel, sweetened with a little sugar . . .

1912? Cozzens, S. W., *The Young Trail Hunters*, p. 38: . . . each man provided with three days' rations, which consisted of about a quart of atole and a piece of jerked beef . . .

1919 Chase, J. Smeaton, *California Desert Trails*, p. 79: . . . and the fruit, which is small and hard . . . when ground entered into the composition of the all-embracing *atole*.

1927 Bolton, Herbert E., *Fray Juan Crespi*, p. 5: When this failed they had to get along with only a little atole . . .

avocado See the *New English Dictionary*.

ayuntamiento English modification **auguntamiento** (*Spanish*, a: jú:n ta: mi:én to:; *English, the same*) The administrative body of a municipality formed by the alcalde and the counsellors. *Ayutamiento* occurs frequently in writings concerned with the settlement and government of the early Southwest and was fairly well naturalized at one time. Its use in current spoken English is diminishing.

1891 Blackmar, Frank W., *Spanish Institutions in the Southwest*, p. 188: Every town, of at least one thousand souls, had to establish an ayuntamiento.

1928 Stiff, James E., *The Spanish Element in Southwest Fiction*: Most of his [Bret Harte's] information was obtained through disjointed memoranda, the proceedings of auguntamientos . . . early departmental juntas . . .

azotea (*Spanish*, á: so: té:ə *English*, ǽ ʒo: té: ə) The flat, platform-like roof of a house built in the Spanish style. The *azotea* is used as an open-air retreat at various times particularly for coolness in the evenings. It is also used for general household purposes such as the drying of fruits, threshing of small quantities of grain or seeds, drying of clothes, etc. In the absence of a suitable English word *azotea* will doubtless maintain a place in the English of the Southwest where it is widely used at present.

1844 Gregg, Josiah, *Commerce on the Prairies*, p. 102: I perceived the *azotea* of the parochial church occupied by armed men.

1873 Wallace, Lew, *The Fair God*, p. 272: . . . he raised his glance to the *azoteas*. *Ibid.*, p. 297: The sun poured a brilliance over the flowers, dwarfed palm, trailing vines with which the *azoteas* was provided.

baile English modification **baille** (*Spanish,* bai le:; *English, the same and* bai li:) A dance; used colloquially in the Southwest particularly when referring to a dance under Mexican or mixed auspices. *Baile* thus used adds local color. Its use is common and effective enough to retain the word in American speech.

1892 (Oct. 14) *Galveston News:* In Santa Cruz, a woman of Matamoras attended the baile, and got up to dance.

1912 Hough, Emerson, *The Story of the Cowboy,* p. 253: In the Southwest such a dance was called a baille [sic] and among the women attending it were sure to be some dark-eyed señoritas . . .

1928 Stiff, James E., *The Spanish Element in Southwest Fiction,* p. 69: They must always have the inevitable fight which breaks up the bailes, when the Americans and the more numerous Mexicans attend.

1932 Coolidge, Dane, *Fighting Men of the West,* p. 228: Then he announced a *baile,* with free mezcal for all, and everybody came.

baile chango (*Spanish,* bái le: chá:ɲ go:; *English,* bái li: chǽɲ go: *or* cha:ɲ go:) A juvenile slang expression. Boys use the term to describe any queer or fantastic dancing motions or contortions as in "He went through a regular *baile chango*" or "He did a *baile chango* on his head." It is also occasionally used as a cry for combatants, as in wrestling, cock fighting, games, etc., to engage in contest. In this sense the word *baile* has had a vogue in Europe. The phrase *baile chango* would be translated freely as "dance, monkey, dance." It may have been acquired from travelling entertainers, one or two persons, who usually have as a main feature a monkey trained to do tricks and dance.

bajada (*Spanish,* ba: há: ða:; *English, the same and* bə hǽ ðə). From Spanish *bajar* "to go down," "to lower." A down grade in the road or trail; a dugway; a sharp descent. The term is commonly used in New Mexico, Arizona and parts of Texas and California.

1919 Chase, J. Smeaton, *California Desert Trails,* p. 259: I came up with him just as we emerged upon the sloping bajada, which is the feature of almost every desert canon mouth. *Ibid.,* 104: Hardly will one find a desert landscape in which the *bajada* is not a feature.

1931 Austin, Mary, *Starry Adventure*, p. 105: There was a *bajada* just as you came out past the cienaga that dropped by way of zig-zags . . .

bamanos See VAMOS.

banana See the *New English Dictionary*.

bandido (*Spanish*, ba:n dí: ðo:; *English*, bæn dí: ðo:, *occasionally* bæn dí: do:) A bandit; an outlaw. Along the border this term is in frequent colloquial use. *Bandido*, however, usually refers to a Mexican outlaw whereas "bandit" in the same region is used for both American and Mexican. In English writing in general it seems that *bandido* or its plural *bandidos* is not so frequently used as the borrowing from Italian, *banditti*.

1898 Lummis, Charles F., *The Awakening of a Nation*, p. 4: By every country road—even into the very heart of cities—the *bandido* robbed and murdered.

1928 Dobie, J. Frank, *A Vaquero of the Brush Country*, p. 60: One issue alone of the Galveston Daily News . . . reported the following items from the lower country all pertaining to bandidos. *Ibid.*, p. ix: It will often cut the sign of bandidos from below the Rio Grande . . .

barbacoa English modifications **barbecue, barbeque, Bar-B-Q** (*Spanish*, bar ba: có:a:; *English*, bár bə u:) Probably from a native Haitian word. The meanings of *barbacoa*, as translated from Alemany (nos. 1–9), all have to do with Spanish-American usage. 1. A rude bed of woven fibre or other material supported above the ground by a framework of sticks. 2. In Chile a woven mat which serves as a door for rude dwellings. 3. A rough structure used by boys who keep watch over the cornfields. 4. A small house built atop of trees or stakes driven in the ground. 5. A mat or wattle on the roof of houses where grain, fruit, etc., are stored. 6. Upright sticks used for climbing plants. 7. A small bed. 8. In Mexico and Salvador, green sticks over an opening like a gridiron used by the Indians to broil meat. 9. Meat cooked by means of the apparatus described in number eight. 10. In English a *barbecue* usually signifies an out-of-doors program-feast often in celebration of some special event such as election returns, athletic victories and the like. The serving of *barbecued* meat is the distinctive feature of such a function. Meat is *barbecued* about as follows: Into a large hole in the ground, which resembles an ordinary grave pit, are put a quantity of stones or bricks that have been thoroughly heated. The *barbecue* animal is cut into quarters, or smaller portions, wrapped in cloth (preferably clean and white) that has been soaked in water or other liquid, and placed on the hot stones within the pit possibly three to five feet below the surface of the ground. Over the meat other hot stones are placed and sometimes a hot fire is built in the pit. The meat is thus steamed and broiled for several hours and has, when thoroughly cooked, a delicate and delicious flavor. No little skill is required to determine when the meat has been cooked sufficiently. Places where *barbecues* are common social events usually recognize certain persons as the official *barbecuers* because of their skill and success in deciding on the right time to remove the meat from the pit-oven for serving. The *barbecue* function is often held in the open air near the pit. The serving is usually quite informal. 11. Automobile tourists through the Middle West and East are familiar with the advertisements and signs along the way, calling attention to sandwiches of *barbequed* meat. The signboard usually reads "Bar-B-Q." The meat at these places is seldom, if ever, genuine *barbecue*. In the other sense, that of a platform or mat for storing and drying of grain, the word has not been adopted by English except as a technical term in written descriptions.

1840 Turnbull, David, *Travels in the West*, p. 307: . . . barbecues, where the coffee is laid out to dry . . . a single Barbecue, laid down with tiles or plaster, is considered sufficient for a whole estate.

1903 O. Henry, *Heart of the West*, p. 112: The day . . . was to be further signalized on the American side by a cattlemen's convention . . . an old settlers' barbecue and picnic.

1929 *San Antonio Express*, June 6: The gathering is sponsored by negro preachers and others, and will be in the nature of a barbecue picnic.

barbecue See BARBACOA.

barracon English modification **barracoon** (*Spanish* ba: rr a: kó:n; *English* bæ rə kú:n) A warehouse; slave quarters; a rude shelter. *Barracon* is of chief interest because of the possibility that English "coon" as applied to negroes was derived from it. Evidence of this is not complete but, nevertheless, is given here. *Barracon* the augmentative of *barraca*, "a building in which are deposited hides, wool, and other produce destined for shipment" (*Diccionario de la Academia Real*), or "a rustic habitation," was early applied by the Spanish to rude structures and pens used to shelter and house slaves destined for shipment to the slave market. Americans, and Englishmen before them, spelled Spanish *barracon* with a double "o," thus *barracoon*. By analogy to a number of words in common English use, among them "pantaloon" from *pantalon*, "picaroon" from *picaron*, "pitacoon" from *pitacon*, the English spelling "barracoon" of Spanish *barracon* might be expected. Likewise in each case where the spelling changes from single to double "o" the pronunciation has changed from "o:" to "u:." Spanish *barracon*, pronounced ba: ra:kó:n, might, therefore, without violence to linguistic ways, become English "barracoon," pronounced bæ rə kú:n. At this point, where there is an unbridged gap, we may resort to analogy. If *barracudo* or *barracouta*, names of sea fish, are commonly shortened to *cuda* and *couta* respectively, why should not *barracoon* be shortened to *coon*?

1868 *Overland Magazine*, Vol. I, F. C. Cremony, "A Cruise on a Slaver": A barracoon is the place where those wretched captives are kept until opportunity serves to dispose of them.

1889 Ripley, McHatton E., *From Flag to Flag*, p. 172: The insurgent rebels . . . began to quiet down, gradually strolling to the veranda of their own barracoon . . . *Ibid.*, p. 281: Chinese and negroes fled to their respective barracoons and fastened themselves in.

barracuda (*Spanish*, ba: rra: kú: ða:; *English, the same*) A large fish found in the vicinity of Florida. It is sometimes called a *cuda* or *couta*.

1929 *New York Times*, March 8: The battle with the barracuda took place off the municipal beach in plain sight of dozens of bathers . . .

barranca (*Spanish*, ba: rrá:n ka:-o:; *English*, bə ræn kə;-o) A rugged fissure cut in a landscape by the action of running water; a steep and irregular incline or side of a mountain. The occurrence of *barranca* or *barranco* in writings of the early West is frequent. The word is often heard also in colloquial language among English-speaking people along the border.

1836 Latrobe, Charles Joseph, *The Rambler in Mexico*, p. 90:
. . . One of the gentlemen . . . was precipitated in the darkness
into a profound barranca . . .

1852 *Humboldt's Travels* tr. by Ross, p. 50: The . . . torrent, or
barranco, in the rainy season forms fine cascades.

1919 Chase, J. Smeaton, *California Desert Trails*, p. 256: Two
hours brought us to the edge of the badlands in the form of a
deep, abrupt *barranca* . . .

basto (*Spanish*, bá: sto:; *English, the same and* bǽ sto:) The
leather lining of a saddle; i.e., that part known as the "skirt" or
sometimes as the *sudadero*. The word is a technical term restricted to those engaged in the saddle industry and to cattlemen. *Basto* was used by Elizabethans to signify "enough." This
is the usual signification of the word *basta* or *bastante* in Spanish.
1922 Rollins, Philip Ashton, *The Cowboy*, p. 125: Usually the
under-surface of the bastos was smooth.

bisagre (*Spanish*, bi: sá: gre:; *English*, bi sǽg ri:) A plant of
the cactus family. Fleshy parts of the plant are sometimes sliced
and candied into Mexican sugar. The word is not extensively
used by English speaking people.

bonanza (*Spanish*, bo: ná:n sa:; *English*, bon ǽn ʒə) *Bonanza* in
Spanish originally signified good weather on the ocean. It still
has this meaning in Spain but in Mexico has come to mean a
vein of rich ore in a mine. In this sense *bonanza* is among the
Spanish words most generally adopted by English speakers in
America. It has been common for fifty years throughout America. It may be considered as fully naturalized in American English. By extension *bonanza* is applied to an unusually promising
or profitable enterprise of any kind.
1847 Ruxton, Geroge F., *Travels in Mexico and the Rocky Mountains*, p. 78: The famous black vein of Sombrerete yielded the
greatest bonanzas of any mine on the continent of America.
1912 Stevenson, R. L., *Silverado Squatters*, p. 27: . . . those vir-
tuous Bonanzas, where the soil has sublimated under sun and
stars.
1919 Chase, J. Smeaton, *California Desert Trails*, p. 41: This is
the bonanza of the thrifty desert bees: now or never they must
restock those rows of empty golden honey-pots in the rocky
cranny of the hillside . . .

1929 *Private Correspondence:* I want you to share in a bonanza.
1930 Ferber, Edna, *Cimarron*, p. 130: Arkansas Grat had pursued his profession in the bonanza days of Denver.

borracho English modification **borrachio** (*Spanish*, bo: rrá: cho:; *English*, bor ǽ cho:) One who drinks habitually; a drunkard. The *New English Dictionary* records it as derived from *borracha*, a leather bag for holding wine. Since the nineteenth century it does not appear to have been used in English and has also become obsolete in Spanish in this sense. In the sense of a drunkard one hears it along the border in such expressions as "I was disturbed during the night by two *borrachos*," or "Two *borrachos* were fighting."
1836 Latrobe, Charles Joseph, *The Rambler in Mexico*, p. 70: . . . when you have said that he was a *borrachio* you have recorded all the positive evil in his character . . .
1929 Castro, Adolphe de, *Portrait of Ambrose Bierce*, p. 338: I saw him . . . despised . . . by the scum that gathered there; who grinned at the viejo borracho . . .

bosque (*Spanish*, bó:s ke:; *English, the same and* bó:s ki:) In Spanish the word means literally a wood or forest. It is used in this sense in English but also signifies a clump, or grove, of trees. Its occurrence is not common either in written or spoken English.
1931 Austin, Mary, *Starry Adventure*, p. 109: . . . a bird stirred in the *bosque* close to the house, with a low, cool note.

bozal (*Spanish*, bo: sá:l; *English*, bo: sǽl) A nose-loop or rude halter; frequently used at one time in the Southwest. In Spain the word means a muzzle for dogs or a blab for calves. In Cuba it has been used to designate a slave.
1844 Gregg, Josiah, *Commerce on the Prairies*, p. 184: . . . the head of the animal is turned towards his subduer, who seldom fails to throw a bozal around the nose . . .
1922 Rollins, Philip Ashton, *The Cowboy*: The reins were attached to the bosal, and their pulling operated to shut off the horse's wind. English ranchmen occasionally called the bosal a *Cavezon*. The bosal stayed in position through being attached both to the bridle's cheek-pieces and also to a looped cord commonly made of braided horse-hair, and passing from the bosal's front.

1930 James, Will, *Lone Cowboy*, p. 329: . . . they was busy . . .
making different work from rawhide, like quirts and bosals . . .

bravado (*Spanish*, bra: vá: ðo:; *English*, brə vé: do: *or* brə vá:
do:) Bluster; affectation of hardihood; arrogance, or defiance, or
menace; boastful behavior; courage. Although this word has
evidently been used by English writers in Europe since about
1590, it is possible that it was borrowed independently in America. Its use in colloquial English in America is not uncommon.
1848 Parkman, Francis, *Oregon Trail*, Vol. II, p. 23: The attempt was made in mere sport and bravado.
1856 Webber, C. W., *A Tale of the South Border*, p. 102: He
thought it was a bravado feat, and determined not to be laid
in the shade.
1903 Torrence, Ridgley, *El Dorado*, p. 69: Once inside, however,
his manner becomes one of bold and insolent bravado.
1917 McClellan, George B., *The Mexican War Diary*, edited by
Wm. Starr Meyers, p. 72: At first we thought it a bravado,
then a reveille, then a parley—so we stopped firing to await
the result.

bravo (*Spanish*, brá: vo:; *English*, brá: vo:; bré: vo:; bræ vo:)
1. An exclamation of approval or encouragement particularly on
the occasion of some public performance or competition. The
word is used by the Spanish-speaking people and by the English-
speaking people along the border who have had first-hand contact with the Mexicans. It is probable, however, that if the word
is established in the general English vocabulary it is from the
Italian. 2. The word also signifies a bandit or villain.
1836 Latrobe, Charles Joseph, *The Rambler in Mexico:* A . . .
countenance roughened with the signs of long addiction to a
life of passion and adventure . . . indicated the bravo *soi distant* Monsieur le Marquis de Maison Rouge.
1929 *Encyclopaedia Britannica*, 14th edition, p. 603: The court
then secured a bravo named Col. H. L. Luttrell to stand
against Wilkes . . .

brazada English modification **brasada** (*Spanish*, bra: sá: ða:;
English, the same and brə sæ ðə) From *brazo*, arm or branch. A
term applied in parts of Texas to a region densely covered with
thickets, i.e., brush country.

1929 Dobie, J. Frank, *A Vaquero of the Brush Country*, p. 204:
The Brasada is still a *brasada*, the openings in it fewer and
smaller. *Ibid.*, p. 229: In short, the Brasada was a strategic
point for stealing and smuggling.

bronco English modifications **broncho, bronc, braunk** (*Spanish*,
bro:n ko:; *English*, bra:n ko: or bra: nk) An unbroken or untamed horse; a wild horse; a native wild pony of the western and
southwestern plains. The Spanish signification of the word *bronc*
is "rough" or "wild." The English use of the word in the West
and Southwest, where it was borrowed, implies the original
meaning. Citations from the early accounts of travellers and others in the West and in California indicate that the word *bronco*
has often been used to signify "a native wild pony of California."
More accurately a horse is a *bronco* until it has been taught the
use of its working paraphernalia whether as a mount or a draft
horse. It remains a *bronco* or *bronc* in the mind of the horseman
or owner until it has attained that reliability which is not characteristic of wild, unbroken horses. Again in the proper sense of
the word a wild pony, even from California, is no longer a *bronco*
when it has become thoroughly gentled and trained. The advanced
age at which native wild horses are captured and enlisted
into man's service, together with the ingrained "bronconess"
of the creatures accounts for the not uncommon fact that
they remain pretty much in the *bronco* state for the remaining
part of their lives. Where this is true it is no doubt as much for
accuracy as for picturesqueness that they are termed *broncos*
long after initiation in service. The term has been rather generally accepted by speakers of English and evidently serves a useful place in the vocabulary. The practice of spelling the word
broncho is widespread. It may have originated because of analogy
to such English words as "broncho pneumonia."
1850? Anonymous, *Life in the Rocky Mountains*, p. 41: I left in
a buggy drawn by light broncos . . .
1899 (Sept.) Hubbard, Elbert, *The Philistine:* Just a boy is our
Teddy, with his thirst for rough riding and broncho busting.
1909 Rye, Edgar, *Quirt and Spurs*, p. 51: As soon as some outfit
gives me a lift back where I can catch onto a bronc again.
1918 Adams, Henry, *The Education of Henry Adams*, p. 260:
One seldom can see much education in the buck of a broncho.
1931 *Lariat*, April, p. 44: . . . go on an' ride my braunk.

broncobuster A rider of broncos; a horse breaker or tamer; a cowboy whose specialty it is to introduce an unbroken or un-ridden horse to the saddle, quirt, spurs, hackamore and bridle. The *broncobuster* may perform only the introductory part of the breaking or he may continue the process and complete it. The first course usually consists of a sufficient number of "ridings" to convince the horse that an effort to dislodge the rider by buck-ing is futile. After that the "bronco" can well be turned over to another rider for further gentling and training. It was not un-common for the *broncobuster* to belabor the horse rather merci-lessly with quirt and spur during the first ridings in order to "get all the buck out of his system" and convince him of the desir-ability of yielding; in other words break the creature's spirit for a time. A horse thus treated by a careless or brutal *buster* usually came out of the first few ridings rather swelled and skinned about the head and neck and probably under the belly, but, as the *buster* might explain, with great respect for horsehair nose piece, quirt and man. The more extended riding by *broncobusters* usually lasts two weeks or longer for each horse during which time the "bronco" is ridden and put through progressive steps of rudi-mentary training each day. When the "buck has all been taken out," it is taught several fundamentals—the principle of double-rein guiding, to stand without being tied when its rider dis-mounts, to allow its ears to be touched during the process of putting on the hackamore and fake bridle. It is then considered ready for graduation by the *broncobuster*. A professional *buster* might have from two to a dozen broncos in training at one time all of which must be put through the daily drill.

1916 Benedict, H. Y. and Lomax, J. A., *Book of Texas*, p. 176: The aristocrats were the ropers and bronco busters. *Ibid.*, p. 187: Bronco-busting is not what it was and roping cougars has gone out of fashion.

1926 Branch, Douglas, *The Cowboy and His Interpreters*, p. 44: No western story writer has cared to describe horsebreaking as it was often practiced . . . with the professional bronco buster beating the horse with a quirt about the head . . . while two cowboys assisted by quirting its flanks . . .

buckeroo See VAQUERO.

buena salud (*Spanish*, bwé: na: sa: lú:ð [ð *is sometimes omitted*]; *English, the same*) A term of friendly greeting signifying literally "good health" but practically synonymous with "greetings!" It is sometimes abbreviated to *salud*.

1925 Burns, W. N., *The Saga of Billy the Kid*, p. 45: Step up, boys, this is on me. Buena Salud!

burro English modification **boorow** (*Spanish*, bú: rro:; *English, similar to Spanish, and* bʌ́ ro:) A donkey; ass. In the southwestern part of the United States *burro* is used naturally and almost exclusively in the place of donkey and this usage was undoubtedly adopted as a result of the Spanish-American contact. When written it is rarely italicized, a fact which indicates a rather complete naturalization. Although in general the word is restricted in use to the western and southwestern part of America, it is used and understood elsewhere and will undoubtedly remain active in the vocabulary.

1874 Ingersoll, Ernest, *Knocking Round the Rockies*, p. 27: . . . it [pack saddle] still bestrides the lacerated spines of unfortunate burros, but generally it has yielded to the California stuffed aparejo.

1909 Austin, Mary, *Lost Borders*, p. 26: He bought a couple of pack-burros and a camp kit.

1916 Benedict, H. Y., and Loma, *Book of Texas*, p. 193: The burro, little brother to the mule, consorts chiefly with the Mexicans but is much less numerous.

1917 McClellan, George B., *The Mexican War Diary*, p. 28: . . . the little burro jogged along with him, occasionally stopping to gather a bite of grass.

1926 Cather, Willa, *Death Comes for the Archbishop*, p. 102: . . . the mule trail down the other side, [is] the only path by which a burro can ascend the mesa . . .

1928 Dobie, J. Frank, *A Vaquero of the Brush Country*, p. 42: When the full history of trail driving is written it will have to include the trailing of mustang horses, buros, razorbacks, and turkeys.

1930 Lee, Bourk, *Death Valley:* My fool boorows thought them white heaps was snow.

burro load This term because of the extensive use of the "burro" in Mexican regions as a means of transportation has found a place alongside "bushel," "peck," or "ton" as a unit of measure chiefly in connection with wood hauling and selling. Wood for burning purposes in small quantities is often bought by the *burro-load*.

burro trail A pathway made by the repeated tramping of burro trains over certain routes, especially in the mountains.

burro train A drove of pack burros used for transporting merchandise, wood, ore, etc. A train usually consists of from six to fifty burros with pack saddles or aparejos and finds its chief usefulness in transporting merchandise through rugged country not traversed by train, automobile, or wagon, particularly through mountains. Burros are sure-footed, enduring and easily managed. They require little care and feed, even in barren country, and thus serve where horses would soon die. See also PACK-BURRO.

burro-weed "A stiff, brittle, rounded, gray bush (*Franseria dumosa*), common on and near the base of desert mountains. Leaves small, gray-green; flowers yellowish, in close spikes. The plant has a strong somewhat turpentiny smell. Blooms in mid-spring." Also a weed (*Dondia moquini*) of the goosefoot family. 1919 Chase, J. Smeaton, *California Desert Trails*, p. 89: Encelia and burro-weed made up the bulk of the plants . . .

caballada English modifications **caballado, cavvieyard, cavayer, cavvayah, cavallada, caballad, cavayard, cavoy** (*Spanish,* ka: ba: já: ða: *and* ka: ba: ljá: ða:; *English, the same and* kæ vi: ár) The "string" or drove of horses, that is, supply of mounts, maintained by a ranching outfit, particularly on a special expedition, such as a round-up or an exploring trip. In the *caballada* each *vaquero* or riding member of the outfit has from one to a score of mounts all of which he uses during the grind of a rodeo or a horse chase. The horses of the *caballada* not in use are kept at grazing or rest by a *mozo* or other "hand" of the outfit but in ready access to the field of action for immediate availability. This word is also used in a more generalized sense to include the supply of broken, i.e., tamed, horses, of a ranch or village or expedition either exploring or military or even colonizing. The usage of the term includes not only horses, from which the word is derived, i.e., *caballo* but also mules. It is not used to describe wild, untamed animals. As long as the life of the American frontier involves the use of horses and "outfits" for riding purposes *caballada* will have a legitimate and useful place in the language of America. Long after such life has disappeared the word no doubt will appear in written form. No other English word is quite adequate. The Spanish word *remuda*, on the other hand, is used synonymously and as extensively as *caballada*. In fact, *remuda* is more commonly used in spoken English than is *caballada*. See also RE MUDA.

1841 McCalla, W. L., *Adventures in Texas*, p. 57: . . . a party of these daring Indians had . . . taken off about fifty or sixty horses from the neighbourhood, forty of which were from one caballado . . .

1846 Kendall, George W., *Texan Santa Fe Expedition*, p. 917: Nothing can exceed the grandeur of the scene when a large cavallada, or drove of horses, takes a "scare."

1859 Reid, Samuel, *Scouting Expedition*, p. 100: Cavallada of 500 mules.

1886 McLane, H. H., *Irene Viesca*, p. 79: They took a large caballada of horses and mules belonging to the Gauchipins.

1912 Hough, Emerson, *The Story of the Cowboy:* These might go into the cavvieyard of some outfit bound up the trail . . .

1922 Hough, Emerson, *The Covered Wagon*, p. 8: I'm leading yonder caballad of our neighbors, with a bunch of Illinois and Indian wagons.

1925 Burns, W. N., *The Saga of Billy the Kid*, p. 88: The *cavoy* is running about eight miles from the camp.

1927 Bolton, H. E., *Fray Juan Crespi, xxiv:* In the rear came the friendly Indians driving the caballada.

caballero (*Spanish*, ka: ba: jé: ro:; *English, the same and* kæ bɔl jéro or kæ bɔl ɛro) Literally a cavalier; a knight or gentleman. These words, however, carry a meaning or connotation that is often lacking when the word *caballero* is used in the Southwest, particularly in spoken English. When used in the sense of cavalier, *caballero* is usually modified by an adjective such as "real," "gay," or "grand." Otherwise it means a gentleman. When used in the plural, *caballeros*, it is practically synonymous with "gentlemen" as used when referring or speaking to a group of men. It is not often used to denote a horseman or a rider either in Spanish or English. The phrase *muy caballero* is occasionally heard as signifying the essence of gentlemanliness. In fiction *caballero* is more often used to signify the cavalier idea.

1902 Atherton, Gertrude, *Splendid Idle Forties*, p. 60: The old men and the caballeros wore the black coats and white trousers . . .

1926 Cather, Willa, *Death Comes for the Archbishop*, p. 66: But you are a caballero . . .

caballo (*Spanish*, ka: bá: jo:; *English*, kə bái o: *and* kə vǽl o:) A horse. This word is generally understood by Americans in the Southwest but is not taken seriously as a part of the English vocabulary. It is occasionally heard in light conversation. One may hear such expressions as "get on your *caballo* and let's go" or "how much for the *caballo*"? It is also repeated often in the story of the man who had lost his horse and upon meeting a stranger whom he could not determine as Mexican or American asked, "Say mister, *señor*, did you see my *caballo*, horse, going down the *camino*, road, with a *soga*, rope, around his *pescuezo*, neck?"
1903 O. Henry, *Heart of the West*, p. 38: . . . throw a pot of coffee together while I attend to the caballo . . .

cabaña (*Spanish*, ka: bá:n ja; *English*, *the same and* kə bǽn ja). A rustic habitation, a cottage, cabin or hut, a "jacal." Used for local color.
1932 Wilson, Edmund, *The American Jitters*, p. 228: Surely that pretty little peppermint cabaña must be the home of Mickey the Mouse.
1932 *Herald Tribune* (N. Y.) June 16. $95 Rents seashore Cabana-Bungalet entire season . . .

cabestro English modifications **cabresto, cabarista** (*Spanish*, ka: bé: stro:; *English*, kə bé stro: kə bré sto:) A rope halter. The *kə bres to:* pronunciation is most common in the Southwest. The word is used to distinguish an improvised rope headgear, or the horsehair rope halter, from the leather manufactured halter. Although the usefulness of the word is continually being restricted by the changing conditions it is still widely used. An interesting possible connection between this word and the English "capstan" of unknown derivation is given in the *New English Dictionary*.
1848 Emory, W. H. *Notes of a Military Reconnoissance*, p. 387: . . . we soon conquered them with the aid of the "lazo" or cabresto, as it is often called—a rope of hair or plaited hide . . .
1859 Reid, Samuel, *Scouting Expedition*, p. 34: We then untied our cabaristas or Mexican halters which are about some twenty or thirty feet long . . . *Ibid.*, p. 118: *Cabestros* [is used].

cabron (*Spanish*, ka: bró:n; *English*, kə br:ón) Masculine augmentative of *cabra*, goat. Although the term literally means "a big goat" and therefore often not taken seriously by Americans who use it, *cabron* is, in the mind of the Mexican, as strong as English "fool" or even "damn fool."

1931 Austin, Mary, *Starry Adventure*, p. 310: As if in reference to her you would admit even the impulse to pound the guts out of that filthy *cabron*.

cacique See Webster's *New International Dictionary*.

cafeteria (*Spanish*, ká: fe: te: ría:; *English* kæ fə tér jə). Note the shifted accent. A self-service eating establishment. Webster derives the word from American-Spanish *cafeteria*, a coffee shop. This derivation is questionable inasmuch as *cafeteria* signifying a restaurant is not in common use in Spanish and is not usually listed in Spanish dictionaries. *Cafetera* is a coffeepot or a woman who makes and serves coffee; *cafetero* is a man who makes or sells coffee and also the coffee tree. In Cuba *cafeteria* is a place where coffee (not the drink) is sold at retail. The adoption, therefore, may have come from that source. It has been suggested that the word may have been coined by some enterprising restaurant keeper, probably in Los Angeles, who used the French *cafetière* as a model. Certainly the word does not appear in writings about the Spanish territory of the Southwest, neither is it used commonly among either Spanish-speaking people of that region or English-speaking before 1900. Other words analogous to *cafeteria* have been coined in English. Among them are "lunchery," "bakeria," "basketeria," "cleaneria," even "roadateria." Perhaps it is the suffix only that has been borrowed from Spanish. Another word with the "ia" ending taken from Spanish is *pulqueria*.

calabozo English modifications **calaboose, calabozo, calaboz, calaboza, calabooza** (*Spanish*, ka: la: bó: so:, *or* ka: la: bó: θo: *English*, kǽ lə bu:s *or* kæ lə bó: zə) A jail; a prison; a place for the detention of culprits, slaves, or prisoners. The word *calabozo* in Spanish signifies an underground compartment or room; a dungeon—"*un lugar fuerte . . . por delitos graves.*" The word was much used in writings about slaves in the South and at present is one of the accepted Spanish words in the Southwest. The earliest recorded use of *calaboose* in English is that mentioned by

Tucker in his *Americanisms*, where he says that in 1797 it appeared in Fra Bailey's *Journal of Tours*. The written examples found, indicate by the form of spelling the Spanish pronunciation rather than the French. Cody spells the word *calabozo* exactly as it is spelled in Spanish; Lummis spells it *calaboz;* Ruxton spells it *calaboza;* Struble, writing of a visit to Texas in 1834, spells the word *calaboza;* and Willa Cather, writing of the early occupants of California uses the Spanish form *calabozo* as did Cody. Rye is the only exception with his *calaboose* spelling. Rye was an Englishman and may have heard the word before visiting America. Whatever the early pronunciation, it has completely given way to the *calaboose* form, at least in spoken English. It is fully naturalized and extensively used in popular English.

1834 Struble, George F., *A Visit to Texas*, p. 132: The refractory lieutenant having been seized and thrown into the calaboza . . .

1846 Emory, W. H., *Notes of a Military Reconnoissance*, p. 113: . . . it was my singular fate . . . to be quartered in the calaboose, a miserable hut of one room . . .

1847 Melville, Herman, *Omoo*, p. 120: Calabooza! Calabooza! Beretance! Cried our conductor, pointing to the building.
Ruxton, Geroge F., *Adventures in Mexico and the Rocky Mountains*, p. 136: My mozo . . .when I arrived had already lodged him in the calaboza . . .

1889 Lummis, Charles F., *"Lo" Who Is Not Poor*, p. 45: Not uncommonly a governor has to be thrown for a few days into the calaboz before he will accept the high office to which he has just been elected.

1909 Rye, Edgar, *Quirt and Spur*, p. 32: That fellow will soon be playing checkers with his nose through the bars of the calaboose.

1911 Cody, Sherwin, *Heroes of the Plains:* . . . they were occasionally threatened with imprisonment in the calabozo of St. Louis.

1925 Burns, W. N., *The Saga of Billy the Kid*, p. 195: Billy was locked up in the Fort Sumner Calaboose . . .

1926 Cather, Willa, *Death Comes for the Archbishop*, p. 74: There was no calabozo in Mora, so Scales was put into an empty stable, under guard.

calaboose See CALABOZO.

caliche (*Spanish*, ka: lĭ: che:; *English* kə lĭ: chi:) From Spanish *cal* which means "lime." Applied to the calcareous deposits found near the surface of the soil in some parts of Texas, Arizona and the Southwest in general. A chemical analysis according to Mac-Dougal shows the presence of calcium carbonate, about 77 per cent, magnesium carbonate about 2 per cent, calcium silicate about 5½ per cent, aluminum silicate 7 per cent and ferric oxide about 2 per cent with some moisture. The composition no doubt varies but any calcareous soil of approximately the composition given above is termed *caliche* in the Southwest. The word is in common use and is not considered technical.

1908 MacDougal, Daniel T., *Botanical Features of North American Deserts:* Caliche forms practically a continuous sheet, a foot or two under the surface, from 3 to 15 feet or more in thickness.

1929 *San Antonio Express*, June 2: Truck load after truck load of crushed rock, followed by *caliche* gravel, was dumped into ruts in order to make them passable.

camino real (*Spanish*, ca: mí: no: re: ál:; *English*, ri: ǽl) Literally the word means "royal road." In Spanish and southwestern English it is used to signify the main highway and implies a highway built by the state or the king. "Where is the *camino real?*" in Spanish, is equivalent to "Where is the main road?" in English. During frontier days the *camino real* was the connecting highway between centers of population. It was a vital factor in the lives of early settlers and colonizers in the southwestern territory. With the building of numerous highways by state and federal governments and the building of railroads the old *camino real* has lost its economic importance and proportionately its importance in the English vocabulary of the border region. It is still heard in light conversation and encountered in the writings both old and modern concerning the Spanish territory. Its picturesque characteristics still appeal.

1840 Turnbull, David, *Travels in the West*, p. 176: In travelling along the neglected highway or camino real . . . I thought I had observed . . . indications of coal.

1844 Gregg, Josiah, *Commerce of the Prairies*, p. 91: . . . after a few days' march we found ourselves once more in the *camino real* that led from Chihuahua to Zacatecas.

1846 Kendall, George Wilkins, *Texan Santa Fe Expedition*, p.

271: After having obtained directions as to our course towards the camino real, or principal road, we proceeded on our way . . . .

1903 North, A. W., *The Mother of California*, p. 64: He journeyed up the Peninsula by El Camino Real, and was accorded a kindly reception.

1931 Birney, Hoffman, *Zealots of Zion*, p. 49; No Chisholm Trail or Camino Real crossed Utah and her frontiers knew no Taos or Tombstone.

camisa (*Spanish,* ka: mí: sa:; *English* kə mí: sə) A shirt. Its use is not common.

1912? Cozzens, S. W., *An Apache Princess*, p. 196: Senseless, half-clad in a coarsely made camisa . . .

campomoche (*Spanish,* ká:m po: mó: che:; *English,* kǽm pə mó: chi:) An insect, *Mantis religiosa*, with six legs, two of which appear to be situated high on the creature's long neck and resemble the arms of a human being. The head is pivoted on the neck and the full, lacy wings "resemble the long coat-tails of the clerical garment" of a clergyman. This feature and the manner in which the insect holds its forelegs have gained for it the title of "the praying insect" and "the praying *mantis.*" It is also known in parts of Texas as the "devil's horse." The *campomoche* is usually light green in color, resembling the foliage it inhabits. Many ranchers believe that because of the color of the *campomoche* cattle often unwittingly eat it, with fatal results. A smaller insect with a stick-like body and either green or gray in color is also known as a *campomoche.*

1919 Chase, J. Smeaton, *California Desert Trails:* It was here that I first identified an insect of bad reputation, the *campomoche.*

campo santo (*Spanish,* ká:m po: sá:n to:; *English, the same, and* kǽm po: sǽn to:) A graveyard; cemetery. The literal meaning of the phrase is "holy field" or "sacred field." Its use among English-speaking people is not common, although it is generally understood and it does occur fairly often in writings with a Spanish setting or influence.

1836 Parker, *A Trip to the West and Texas*, p. 272: Then all the graves in the campo santo are brave with tapers . . .

1900 Anonymous, *To California Over the Santa Fe Trail*, p. 184:

The Mission Dolores, founded in 1776, is still preserved with
its little campo santo of the dead.
1927 Bolton, Herbert E., *Fray Juan Crespi*, p. XIVII: His body
    still rests in the campo santo of the presidial church . . .

Canada A country of North America. The name is Spanish in
appearance at least. John Timbs in *Notabilia*, London, 1872,
suggests that *Canada* was derived from *Capo da Nada* either because of the utter barrenness of the country or because early
Spanish explorers thought they could find a passage to India by
way of Canada. Neither theory seems likely.

cañada (*Spanish*, ka:n já: ðɑ:; *English, the same and* kæn jǽ
duh, *or* kæn jǽ ðɑ). From Spanish *caño* signifying a tube or funnel. A valley or dale. *Cañada* occurs more frequently in written
than in spoken English. Most valleys (excepting very broad ones)
and most defiles, as well as deep ravines or gorges, are throughout
the Cordilleran region of the United States called "cañons" or
"arroyos" rathern than *cañadas* although these terms are all
broadly synonymous.
1836 Latrobe, Charles Joseph, *The Rambler in Mexico*, p. 64:
    We considered the scenery of the Cañada superior to any we
    had ever seen . . .
n.d. Taylor, Bayard, *El Dorado*, p. XIII: Descending a long
    cañada in the mountains . . .

canaigre (*Spanish*, ka: naí gre:; *English, the same and* kɑ né:
gri:) From Spanish *caña* (cane) and *agre*, an old form of *agrio*
(sour). A tall weed of Texas and Northern Mexico, belonging to
the dock family (*Rumex hymenosepalus*). The root of this plant
is very rich in tannic acid. It is dug out of the ground, dried and
used in tanneries where more convenient tanning agents are
scarce or not available. In English it is commonly known as
"sour dock."

canoe See the *New English Dictionary*.

cañon English modifications **kanyon, canyon** (*Spanish*, ka:n
jó:n; *English* kǽn jɔn) *Cañon* is the augmentative of *caño* in
Spanish and means therefore a large tube, funnel, or cane. How
this term came to be applied generally to the landscape phenomenon known otherwise in English as a "gorge," "ravine," or
"gulch" is largely a matter of conjecture. The explorer Fremont

gives in his journal the commonly accepted explanation. Speaking of the sides of the gorge he says that they "frequently approach each other as closely overhead as to form a kind of tunnel over the stream." Of dictionary definitions that of Webster's *New International Dictionary* is the most accurate "a deep valley, with high steep slopes," although even here the deepness of the valley is always relative. The *New English Dictionary* definition is inaccurate in that it requires a stream of water at the bottom of the gorge, having in mind, no doubt, the Grand Canyon of the Colorado. *Cañon* is used extensively and commonly by the natives of Mexico in referring to the same phenomenon to which Americans refer when they use the word. Of all words taken into American English from the Spanish it is doubtful whether any is more completely naturalized than *cañon*. The accent has been shifted from the last to the first syllable and the spelling alternates between *cañon* and *canyon*. Although the words "ravine" and "gorge" are usually listed as synonyms, to a person native to the western part of the United States, they hardly convey the same idea as the word *canyon*.

1805; 1866 Bulfinch, Thomas, *Oregon and Eldorado or Romance of the Rivers*, p. 160: To the chasms of this nature the name of cañons has been applied, borrowed from the Spaniards of Mexico.

1846 Kendall, George W., *Texan Santa Fe Expedition*, p. 230: . . . the canons are in perfect keeping with the prairie.

1856 Fremont, James C., *Exploring Expeditions to the Rocky Mountains*, p. 243: We were approaching a ridge, through which the river passes by a place called "Cañon," (pronounced Kanyon) . . .

1926 Cather, Willa, *Death Comes for the Archbishop*, p. 154: It was . . . surrounded by canyons . . .

cantina (*Spanish*, ka:n tí: na:; *English, the same and* kæn ti: nə) A saloon or *pulqueria*. Used commonly along the border.

1923 Smith, Wallace, *The Little Tigress*, p. 153: In a few steps they were at the cantina called the Spring of Golden Dreams.

1932 Coolidge, D., *Fighting Men of the West*, p. 274: . . . that night the whole gang went down to the cantina, where they drank mezcal straight from the bottle.

cañutillo (*Spanish*, ka:n ju: tí: jo:; *English*, kæn ju: tí: o:) Diminutive of *caño*, tube or pipe; literally a small tube or pipe.

"A shrub (*ephedra*, several species) 2 to 3 feet high, entirely composed of straight, smooth, dark-green stems without leaves. Flowers inconspicuous." "Cañutillo" is the name of a small farming community in western Texas near El Paso.

capitan (*Spanish*, ka: pi: tá:n; *English, the same and* kæ pɪ tǽn) Literally "captain." Once commonly used on the Spanish American frontiers to designate the leader of an Indian or Mexican band or tribe.
1919 Chase, J. Smeaton, *California Desert Trails*, p. 173: Arrived at Toro, I sought an interview with the capitan.
1929 Dobie, J. Frank, *A Vaquero of the Brush Country*, p. 62: The chief, or *capitan*, asked him to join the band, but he refused.

caporal (*Spanish*, ka: po: rrá:l; *English*, kæ pə rǽl) The manager or assistant manager of a cattle ranch; a ranch boss; an overseer or person in charge.
1929 Dohie, J. Frank, *A Vaquero of the Brush Country*, p. 125: . . . his *caporal* (straw boss), jealous and drunk, pointed a gun through the window . . . and shot him dead. *Ibid.*, p. 151: I discharged all but four hands, appointed one of them, Dick Hudson, as *caporal*, and prepared to go . . . to meet the boss.

carcel (*Spanish*, kár se:l; *English, the same*) A prison (see also English "carcelage" and "carceral"). This word is heard occasionally along the border by English-speaking people and is encountered no more frequently in writings of this region.
1840 Turnbull, David, *Travels in the West*, p. 57: . . . the survivor, for safe keeping merely, was sent to the carcel . . .
1930 Duffus, R. L., *The Santa Fe Trail*, p. 66: The old *carcel* in which he had been confined was still standing . . .

carisima (*Spanish*, ka rí: si: ma: *with or without* mi: a:; *English, the same and* kar ɪs ím ə) *Carisima* is the intensified form of *cara*, Spanish for dear. The nearest English equivalent is "dearest" or "my dearest." The word is used not uncommonly by Americans of the Southwest particularly in light conversation on the appropriate subject. One hears "she is his *carisima*" or "he is visiting with his *carisima*." The word or the phrase is used for variety or local color and will no doubt continue to hold its place with English speakers who are familiar with Spanish and in a mood to seek such connotation as the word may bear.

1927 Denis, A. J., *Spanish Alta California:* "To California—
carisima mia—coming into the union, a sovereign state, never
a territory . . .

carreta (*Spanish*, ka: rré: ta:; *English, the same and* kə rét ə) A
rude two-wheeled cart, the wheels of which are of wood and
solid, without spokes. The *carreta* as made by Mexicans and
Indians in the Southwest was often constructed without the use
of nails or other metal. It was the earliest form of draft transportation and was usually drawn by two or more oxen. *Carretas* are
seldom seen in the Southwest today but are common in Mexico.
1883 Sweet and Knox, *On a Mexican Mustang Through Texas*,
p. 367: All the goods that were sold in San Antonio were
hauled up from the coast on uncouth vehicles called *carretas*.
1923 Wilson, Harold G., *Early Transportation in Arizona:* On
these creaky, wobbly carretas, fruit panoche, and zarapes were
brought from Mexico.

carrizo (*Spanish*, ka: rrí: so:; *English, the same*) "A reed-like
grass or cane [*Phragmites communis*], up to ten feet high, with
long, narrow leaves, found in damp places on the open desert."
1919 Chase, J. Smeaton, *California Desert Trails*, p. 75: Bows
were made of the screwbean mesquit, *Prosopis pubescens*, or of
willow, and light hunting arrows of arrowweed, *Pluchea sericea*
or of carrizo, *Phragmites communis*, with points of mesquit
hardened by fire.

casa grande (*Spanish*, ká: sa: grá:n de:; *English, the same and*
kǽ sə: grǽn di:) Literally "a large house" but in the Spanish
American ranch and hacienda life it denotes far more. The *casa
grande* is, in fact, the hub of the universe for the few or many
peons and laborers connected with a hacienda. It is the headquarters and domicile of the *dueño* or the *patron* of the hacienda.
In the case of the larger haciendas it is constructed of stone or
adobe like other buildings of the ranch but is invariably painted
white or whitewashed. A veranda usually extends across the
entire front side. As long as there are haciendas to write or talk
about there will be a demand for the term *casa grande*.
1926 Cather, Willa, *Death Comes for the Archbishop*, p. 53: The
casa grande was long and low with glass windows.
1930 Lyman, George D., *John Marsh, Pioneer*, p. 210: Of the
three buildings found there, the largest, called the casa
grande, was occupied by . . . a sailor . . .

cedula See Webster's *New International Dictionary*.

cequia See ACEQUIA.

chamaco (*Spanish*, cha: má: ko:; *English, the same and* chə mǽ ko:) A small boy, youngster, or "kid." It is used only in familiar, colloquial conversation in such an expression as "The family consisted of the father, the mother and two *chamacos*," or "He was a mere *chamaco* when he left here." *Chamaco* will undoubtedly never gain widespread usage in the United States but is common along the border among those who have a ready knowledge of Spanish.

chamisal (*Spanish*, cha: mi: sá:l; *English* cha: mi sǽl) An area or region covered by the shrub known as *chamiso*. By extension the term *chamisal* is often applied to any dense shrubbery and in this sense is practically synonymous with *chaparral*.
1853 House of Representatives. Ex. Doc. 91: Traveling . . . is rendered very trying by . . . patches of dense masses of shrubbery known as the *chemizal*.

chamiso (*Spanish*, cha: mí: so:; *English, the same and* chə mí: so:) A shrub (*adenostoma, fasticulatu* and *sparsifolium*) or shrubbery. One variety is sometimes called "red shank" and is a tall, fragrant shrub with reddish bark and a rather fine foliage. The *chamiso* is found in various parts of the Southwest and extensively in parts of California. When it grows in dense thickets the region affected is known as a *chamisal*.

chaparejos English modifications **shaps, chaps, chaparreras, chaparajos, chapararas** (*Spanish*, cha: pa: ré: ra:s *or* cha: pa: ré: ho:s *English*, 'ʃǽps *or* ʃǽ pə ré: ho:s) Leather leggings, hip high and fastened about the waist by means of a heavy leather belt. *Chaps* might be described as leather trousers with the seat and crotch cut out. *Chaps* are worn by cowboys and bronco busters, if not for decoration, as protection against scratching of mesquite or other such woody growth on the range, biting by vicious animals, bruises, and other injurious contacts, as well as for protection against inclement weather. The style and decoration of *chaps* vary with the taste, whim, or purse of the wearer. Plain heavy cowhide is most common. Leather with the hair left on is not uncommon. The hair may be on the inside of the *chaps* but more commonly is on the outside. In the case of *chaps* made of goatskin the hair is abundant, wavy, and may be black or white. These latter are properly known as *chivarras*.

1899 Hubbard, Elbert, *The Philistine*, (*Sept.*), p. 126: To promote him [Roosevelt] further would be to invite him to swing his chapararas astride the neck of Freedom . . .

1903 North, A. W., *The Mother of California*, p. 129: . . . *rancheros* protect their legs from the cacti by wearing their immense flaring *chaparejos*.

1912 Hough, Emerson, *The Story of the Cowboy*, p. 99: The heavy "chaps" protect the leg . . .

1922 Rollins, Philip Ashton, *The Story of the Cowboy*, p. 116: . . . more conspicuous were the "chaparejos," universally called "chaps."

1926 Branch, Douglas, *The Cowboy and His Interpreters*, p. 23: Those same cowboys might keep their chaps on always . . .

1930 James, Will, *Lone Cowboy*, p. 264: Some folks wonder why cowboys wear shaps.

chaparral See Webster's *New International Dictionary*.

chaparral fox Occasionally applied to a sneak or a sly tricky person.

chapo (*Spanish*, chá: po:; *English*, *the same and* chǽ po:) Short or chubby; often used as a proper name or nickname. Incidentally, it is a favorite name among Americans for small saddle horses. As an adjective it is used in such an expression as "He is a little *chapo* fellow." Although the word is not uncommon in spoken English in the Southwest, it was not found in the writings examined for the present study. *Chapo* is listed in Spanish dictionaries as a game of billiards.

1929 Lomax, John A., *Cowboy Songs* . . . p. 300: Little brown Chapo bore the cowboy o'er the far away frontier.

chapolin (*Spanish*, cha: po: lí:n; *English* chǽ po lí:n) Literally "a grasshopper"; used derisively by extension to apply to a person of a mean or petty disposition.

chaps See CHAPAREJOS.

charco (*Spanish*, cha:r ko:; *English*, *the same*) A pool, a puddle, a spring. *Charco* was at one time quite commonly used in the Southwest.

1903 O. Henry, *Heart of the West*, p. 153: But when he staggered
   to his feet his first move was to find his soap and towel and
   start for the *charco*.

charro (*Spanish*, chá: rro:; *English, the same and* chá ro:) A
horseman or one skilled in horsemanship. *Charro* is commonly
used in English contexts when referring to the suit which has
become the more or less official national costume, the *charro* suit.
It consists of a large grey, black, or brown felt sombrero decorated with silver or gold embroidery, a short jacket, also embroidered, over a soft shirt with a colored necktie; trousers that
fit snugly and flare at the bottom and are trimmed with braid
and ornamented with buttons. The suit may be made of soft-
tanned leather, buckskin, or of cloth. A beautiful vari-colored
zarape is usually worn with the costume. The riding appůrte-
nances, saddle, bridle, spurs, etc., of the *charro* are elaborately
decorated to harmonize with the *charro* costume. The "rurales"
(*q.v.*) adopted the *charro* suit. Otherwise, however, its use in
Mexico is decreasing except for parade or other similar functions.
1898 Lummis, Charles F., *The Awakening of a Nation*, p. 20:
   Yet Leon is a prosperous and contented city, full of little and
   big manufactures of yarn . . . and the beautiful *charro* suits of
   velvety kid-skin.

chia "A small plant (*Salvia columbarieæ*) a foot or so high, usually with a single stiff stem rising from a few deeply-cut leaves
and bearing one or more clusters of small purple flowers closely
grouped in rings. Blooms in mid-spring."
1919 Chase, J. Smeaton, *California Desert Trails*, p. 78: The
   nourishing properties of *chia* seed should be better known.

chicharron English modifications **chicherones, chikerones**
(*Spanish*, chí: cha: rr ó:n; *English*, chí: chɔ ró:n) Cracklings; that
is, the crisp particles of fat, especially hog fat, from which the
lard has been drained away by boiling. *Chicharrones* are relished
as a food by the poorer Mexicans but are eaten by Americans
also. The designation *chicharrones* is more commonly used by
some Americans along the border than is the English "cracklings."
1856 Webber, C. W., *Tale of the South Border*, p. 48: . . . chicharrones are cracklings, and are one of the greatest delicacies
   the Mexicans know! When they kill a hog, they cut him up in

small pieces; boil them for the lard until they are crisp; then strain and let 'em get cold, and they wouldn't give a handful of them for all the *figur-eed* [sic] sweetnin' doings they have at a ball in New Orleans. *Ibid.*, p. 109: Everyone—men, women, and children—holding in one hand a tin cup . . . and in the other a tortilla and chickerones.

chicle See Webster's *New International Dictionary.*

chico (*Spanish*, chí: ko:; *English, the same*) "Small" or "small one." *Chico* is frequently used by Americans as a nickname or pet name. Often it is given to a boy and is carried with him to manhood. Inconsistency sometimes results thereby in that a very large man may be known as *chico*. The common greasewood of the western United States (*Sarcobatus vermiculatus*) is known in some localities as *chico*.

chigre English modification; **chigoe**, jigger (*Spanish*, chí: gre:; *English*, chí: go:; dzí gr) A species of flea (*Sarcopsylla penetrans*). The female burrows under the skin of man or animal and when distended with eggs causes great discomfort to her host and sometimes death.

chile or **chili** (*Spanish*, chí: le:; *English*, chí li:) From American Indian *chilli*. Mexican peppers (*Capsicum frutescens*). There are several varieties. *Chile* as a condiment is used sparingly by Americans but is one of the chief items of food in the diet of the Mexican populace. A meal is seldom served in Mexico without it and in some instances *chile* with either beans or tortillas constitutes the entire meal or even daily menu. In the green state *chile* is known as *chile verde*. The *chile pods* are also harvested and dried, whereupon they assume a red or reddish color and the fiery element seems to be greatly concentrated. *Chile* in this form is known as *chile colorado*. Americans who accustom themselves to the eating of *chile* often complain of the flatness in taste of American cookery.

1836 Parker, *A Trip to the West and Texas*, p. 271: You will have for a holiday dinner . . . soup with meat balls and chile in it, chicken with chile, rice with chile, fried beans with more chile . . .

1844 Emory, W. H., *Notes of a Military Reconnoissance*, p. 40: Chile the Mexicans consider the chef-d'oevre of the cuisine . . .

1856 Webber, G. W., *A Tale of the South Border*, p. 41: Our
    frontier meal of beef . . . seasoned to ·scalding heat with
    "chili" . . .
1926 Cather, Willa, *Death Comes for the Archbishop*, p. 107: . . .
    the Indians . . . were satisfied with beans and squashes and
    chili . . . *Ibid.*, p. 208: I have learned to like chili colorado and
    mutton . . .

chile-eater (See CHILE for pronunciation). Low caste, i.e., "low-
brow." Commonly used colloquially in New Mexico, Arizona and
Texas.

chilito (*Spanish*, chi: lí: to:; *English, the same and* chɪ lí:to:)
Diminutive of *chile*, pepper. A small variety of cactus (probably
Mamillaria tetrancistrus) known otherwise as pin-cushion cactus,
strawberry cactus and fish-hook cactus. It bears a small red fruit
which closely resembles a red chile in shape.

chinche English modifications, **chinch, chinch bug** (*Spanish*, chí:n
che:; *English, the same; also* chín chi: and chɪnch) Small bugs
of several species. 1. A poultry pest 2. A bed-bug. 3. A louse. 4. A
grain pest (Webster) probably *Blissus leucopterus*.
1846 Kendall, George W., *Texan Santa Fe Expedition*, p. 316:
    Had his room not been completely overrun by chinches, it
    would have been very comfortable.
1903 North, S. W., *The Mother of California*, p. 114: Fortu-
    nately, the "pestivorous" little chinche and the jigger . . . do
    not infest the Peninsula.

chinchilla South American borrowing.

chinch weed "A low, small, rounded plant, (*Pectis papposa*)
vividly green, with bright yellow flowers. It has a strong, rather
unpleasant smell. Blooms throughout summer."

chingar (*Spanish*, chi:ŋ gá:r; *English* chɪŋ gár) To harm, injure,
worry, persecute. The usage of the word in Spanish sometimes
has a decidedly vulgar signification which is not carried over into
English. By Americans it is used most commonly in indirect quotations. Revolutionists or bandits might be spoken of as "coming
this way to *chingar* us." The use of *chingar* is restricted.

chiquito (*Spanish*, chi: kí: to:; *English, same; also* chə: kí: to:)
Diminutive of *chico*, small. A term of endearment; i.e., pet

name for a child. A little girl is often called *Chiquita*, or *Chica*, by her American parents and similarly a small boy would be called *Chiquito*. Literally the word means "little one."

1859 Reid, Samuel, *Scouting Expedition*, p. 108: Beneath you, sporting in the limpid element, you behold men and boys, and women with their chiquitos.

1903 O. Henry, *Heart of the West*, p. 38: But if you'll run in, chica, and throw a pot of coffee together . . . I'll be a good deal obliged.

chivarras See CHAPAREJOS.

chocolate See the *New English Dictionary*.

cholla (*Spanish*, chó: ja:; *English, the same*) A particularly spiny species (*Opuntia fulgida* and *bigelovii*) of the cactus family. The *cholla* grows to a height of six or eight feet and has stumpy branches which are easily detached from the main stem. This characteristic and numerous thorns enable the *cholla* to have the ugliest of reputations among cacti as a menace to passers-by. The *cholla* flower is usually yellow or red.

1907 North, A. W., *The Mother of California*, p. 18: . . . in seried ranks grew the cholla, most provoking of the cactus tribe . . . *Ibid.*, p. 36: They . . . entered upon vast plains covered with cholla, mesquit and other native growth.

1919 Chase, J. Smeaton, *California Desert Trails*, p. 31: Since the nightingale prefers to lean her breast against a thorn, it seems a pity she cannot try the effect of a cholla.

cholla gum An exudation or sticky substance that comes from the *cholla* cactus. It is found commonly on diseased or old cholla plants.

cienega or **cienaga** (*Spanish*, si:é: ne: ga:; *English*, sín I gi: or sín I gə) A spring of water that emerges from a mountain side or in a mountain valley, usually a watering place for range animals. The ground near the spring becomes saturated with water and therefore miry and grown over with verdure consisting of moss, weeds, etc., in fact becomes marshy; hence a marsh, swamp, or morass; a marshy valley. *Cienega* is commonly used.

1863 Fergusson, Major D., *Report to Congress*, p. 22: . . . a good road can be found coming into the Arivaca cienaga and avoiding the worst part of the route . . .

1886 McLane, H. H., *Irene Viesca*, p. 274: This mission was founded in the year 1703 in the *cienega* of the Rio Grande.

1907 Cozzens, S. W., *The Young Trail Hunters*, p. 200: Our route next day, passed through a fertile cienega, thence over an alkali plain.

1919 Chase, J. Smeaton, *California Desert Trails*, p. 151: . . . we resorted to the *cienaga* and ladled water over ourselves from a tepid pool.

1931 Austin, Mary, *Starry Adventure*, p. 4: Gard saw it in the cienaga below the house . . .

chuparosa (*Spanish*, chú: pa: ró: sa:; *English, the same*) A term applied to humming birds and literally meaning sipper or sucker of roses. "A good-sized bush (*Beloperone californica*), almost leafless, with purplish green, downy stems and handsome, dark red, tubular flowers. One of the earliest blooming desert plants, continuing all spring."

cientifico (*Spanish*, si:e:n tí: fi: ko:; *English, the same and* si:n tí: fi: ko: *also* sɪn tíf ɪ ko:) *Cientifico* literally signifies "one who is scientific." It is applied to the Mexicans and others who supported the Porfirio Diaz policy of government administration in Mexico. The *cientificos* were and are composed largely of the wealthy aristocracy as opposed to the middle and peon classes of citizens. The word is often used when subjects relating to Mexico are under discussion.

1929 Seldes, George, *You Can't Print That*, p. 319: The American embassy has always agreed with American business interests and the cientificos.

1929 Dos Passos John, *42nd Parallel*, p. 311: . . . the steamboats to Europe were packed with Cientificos making for Paris . . .

cigarrito English modification **segarrito** (*Spanish*, si: ga: rí: to; *English, the same*) This word is a Spanish-American contribution to the English vocabulary, but is being displaced by "cigarette." *Cigarrito* is at present used occasionally by Americans along the border.

1845 Stapp, William P., *Prisoners of Perote*, p. 124: . . . the old gentleman affected to have received a dispatch from Santa Ana . . . which was forthwith used to light his cigarrito.

1846 *New York Herald*, October 10, p. 322: He, Captain Cook, had been kindly treated while in Santa Fe and smoked many a segarrito from the fair lips of the ladies . . .

cimarron (*Spanish*, sí: ma: rró:n; *English*, sím ə ron) *Cimarron* is the augmentative of the word *cima*, which means the top, specifically the top of a mountain. A region in the Southwest bordering Arkansas and New Mexico; also a river the little Canadian. In Spanish the word *cimarron* signifies one who flees from civilization or organized society and becomes a fugitive or a wild person. Also a run-away slave may be known as a *cimarron*. See MAROON in Webster's *New International Dictionary*.

cincho English modifications **cincha, cinch;** (*Spanish*, sí:n cho:; *English*, sínch) "A saddle girth made of leather, canvas, or woven material such as horsehair. The two ends of the tough cordage which constitute the latigos (Spanish thongs) which connect the cinches with the saddle are run through an iron ring, called . . . the larigo ring . . . and then tied by a series of complicated turns and knots known only to the craft." In the colloquial speech of Southwesterners the word is used often, although English "girth" occurs as often as *cinch* in writings about the Spanish region. A *cinch* is usually made of horsehair. The hair is twisted into strands about the thickness of a clothes-line. About twenty of these strands approximately three feet in length are fastened together in the middle by another strand woven through them. At each end a ring about four inches in diameter is attached. The entire thing is known as the *cinch*. The word *cinch* has become widely known and used in the expression "It's a cinch." Although regarded as slang or a colloquialism this expression is used by cultivated people in all parts of the United States.

1874 Ingersoll, Ernest, *Knocking Round the Rockies*, p. 21: The crupper is gained, and the first hard pull made upon the *cincha* (as the girth is termed).

1912 Hough, Emerson, *Story of the Cowboy*, p. 65: The great broad cinches—especially the hind cinch so much detested by the pony . . . bind the big saddle fast to the pony until they are practically one fabric. *Ibid.*, p. 103: All his life he will hate a hind cinch . . .

1928 *The World* (New York) (Magazine Section), August 12: Regular Summer-Season Bout, in Which It Is a Cinch to Pick Vacation for the Winter.

1929 Lynd, Robert S. and Helen M., *Middletown*, p. 121: All you got to do is show non-support or cruelty and it's a cinch.

1931 *Lariat*, April, p. 7: It's a dead cinch that none of us kin ever hold our jobs . . .

cocaine South American borrowing.

cochineal See the *New English Dictionary*.

cockroach See the *New English Dictionary*.

cocoa See the *New English Dictionary*.

colear or **coleo** English modification **colliar** (*Spanish*, ko: le: ár; *English*, ko: li: ár) "To tail" an animal; the act of "tailing." This may consist of merely grasping a creature's tail and holding it or twisting it to obtain action, or throwing the animal by force applied to the tail. Often the tassel of the tail is wrapped about the horn of the saddle. If the *Coleador's* ("tailer's") horse is going at top speed behind a cow or steer, by dexterous turning, the animal is *coleared* (ko: li: árd) whether it be on its head, its side or merely turned about. The use of *colear* is restricted to those engaged in or familiar with the cattle business.
1844 Gregg, Josiah, *Commerce of the Prairies*, p. 242: Among the vaqueros, and even among persons of distinction, el coleo (tailing) is a much nobler exercise . . .
1847 Ruxton, George F., *Adventures in Mexico and the Rocky Mountains*, p. 94: . . . not a ranchero . . . could more dexterously colear a bull . . . *Ibid.*, p. 82: We arrived at the ranch of La Punta . . . in time to witness the colear de toros . . .
1932 White, Stewart Edward, *Ranchero* (in *Saturday Evening Post*, Feb. 27): I teach you the *colliar* . . .

coma (*Spanish*, kó: ma:; *English*, kó: mə) "An evergreen, stubborn, beautiful . . . with dirk-like thorns, and, in season, with blue berries . . ."
1929 Dobie, J. Frank, *A Vaquero of the Brush Country*, p. 202: A big mesquite or *coma* thorn in the joint of a horse's leg is as bad as a *viznaga* thorn in his foot.

comisario (*Spanish*, ko: mi: sá rio; *English*, ko mɪ sǽ rio) An officer of the law; inspector of police; a policeman. This word was used in Texas during the days of colonization. It has gradually gone out of use except in communities where the population and environment are dominantly Mexican. In such places *comisario* is used almost exclusively by Americans in the place of "policeman" or "officer."

compadre (*Spanish*, ko:m pá: ŏre:; *English, the same and* kom pǽd ri:) A close friend; companion; partner; godfather. *Compadre* is used in Spanish frequently to signify "godfather" synonymously with *padrino*. But the word also signifies in Spanish "companion"; that is, *compañero*. Godfathers are not so common among Americans as they are among Spanish-speaking peoples and for this reason, if no other, the use of this word in English is confined rather closely to the designation of friend, companion or partner. Such expressions as "Where is your *compadre?*" or "Bring your *compadre* and come along," are commonly heard.

1912 Bradley, G. D. (Carson, Kit), *Winning the Southwest*, p. 37: "Doctor, compadre, adios" are purported to be the last words of Kit Carson.

1925 Burns, W. N., *The Saga of Billy the Kid*, p. 119: Si, compadre.

1931 *Lariat*, April, p. 97: By this time them low down *compadres* of mine had mingled with the punch bowl . . .

compañero (*Spanish*, kó:m pa:n jé ro:; *English, the same and* kom pən jɛr o:) A companion; a friend; a partner. *Compañero*, although often used interchangeably by Americans with *compadre*, does not in general connote a relationship quite so intimate as the latter. Neither is the word used as commonly as is *compadre* among English-speaking people.

1923 Smith, Wallace, *The Little Tigress*, p. 209: I want to ride again with my companeros who sing with the hearts of children and die with the hearts of heroes.

1931 *Hew York Herald-Tribune*, July 5: The young Communist . . . compañero and understudy of Siquieros, has just written an exciting book . . .

concha (*Spanish*, kó:n cha:; *English, the same and* kón chə) Literally *concha* signifies a pearl. In the language of the *vaquero*, both Spanish and American, *concha* is the name for small, flat metal plates, circular in form and generally made of silver or brass, which are attached to various parts of the riding paraphernalia for decorative purposes. They might be found on the chaps, on the saddle skirting, on the vaquero's belt, or on the brow-band of his horse's bridle.

1922 Rollins, Philip Ashton, *The Story of the Cowboy*, p. 104: The belt commonly was studded with "conchas" which were flat metal plates, usually circular, generally of silver, in rare instance of gold, in much rarer instances set with jewels.

condor South American borrowing.

conquistador See Webster's *New International Dictionary*.

coon See BARRACON.

cordillera (*Spanish*, cor di:l jér a: *English*, ko:r díl ɛr ə) The range or chain of mountains in the western part of the Americas including the Rockies, Sierra Nevadas, etc. These mountains are spoken of as the "Cordillera Range" or simply the *Cordilleras*. The word was recorded early. It has been extended somewhat to include mountains in general and in this sense is synonymous with SIERRA.

corral (*Spanish*, ko: rrá:l; *English*, kə: rǽl *and* krɛl) Where the word has been learned from the printed page the pronunciation is *ko: rǽl*. As a noun the word signifies an enclosure, pen, or yard for the larger domestic animals. As a verb the word has at least two meanings: 1. That of the Spanish verb *corralar* to drive into a corral. 2. The one-time American slang usage meaning to lay hold of, to secure or obtain, to seize, to acquire. Its use is extensive and frequent in both senses by English-speaking people.
1845 Stapp, William P., *Prisoners of Perote*, p. 71: . . . we entered our former quarters (the coural of the ranch), and gladly sought repose for our wearied limbs . . .
1847 Ruxton, George F., *Adventures in Mexico and the Rocky Mountains*, p. 83: When all was ready the bars were withdrawn from the entrance of the corral and a bull driven out . . .
1891 Cody, William F., *Heroes of the Plains*, p. 437: The whole movement of corraling was done quietly and quickly . . .
1912 Hough, Emerson, *Story of the Cowboy*, p. 180: . . . the boy gathered up his horses into the rope corral made by two or three cow ponies and a couple of men as supports . . . *Ibid.*, p. 25: Each home ranch has a corral, and the corral of the Circle Arrow outfit is worthy of consideration. It is constructed of the most picturesquely crooked cedar logs, and there is not a nail in its whole composition. It is lashed together with raw-

hide at each joint or fastening, the hide being put on wet and drying afterward into a rigid and steel-like binding.

1928 *New York Herald Tribune*, April 14th: Smith Corrals Washington's fourteen delegates.

corrida (*Spanish*, ko: rrí: ða:; *English, the same*) From *correr*, to run. A shed along the walls of a corral; a cattle ranching outfit.

1929 Dobie, J. Frank, *A Vaquero of the Brush Country*, p. 1: Thus in one *corrida*, or outfit, may be found "Mexican vaqueros," "white vaqueros" and "nigger vaqueros."

corriente (*Spanish*, ko: rri:én te:; *English*, korí:ε n ti:) From Spanish *correr*, to run. Literally *corriente* means "current." As adopted by cattlemen and others in the Southwest it signifies inferiority or ordinariness and is used when referring to the quality of cattle or other commodities in such a phrase as "the herd is pretty (or *muy*) *corriente*."

cougar South American borrowing.

coumarin South American borrowing.

coyote English modifications **cayote, collote, kiote kiota** (*Spanish*, koi: jó: te:; *English*, kaɪ ó: ti: *or* kaɪ ó:t) From American Indian *coyotl*. The western prairie wolf (*canis latrans*). The animal is much smaller than the timber wolf and yellower in color. It is extremely shy. It preys on smaller animals and fowls but seldom attacks man unless rabid or enraged. The *coyote* is prone to bark with apparently nothing to bark at. Where *coyotes* abound their sharp staccato barks are frequently heard at night. The word *coyote* is used by extension to describe persons of various supposedly coyote-like characteristics. A skulking person given to petty thieving might be referred to as a "sneaking *coyote*." Likewise a person lacking in physical or moral courage might be called a *coyote*. The term is also applied to a half-breed by the Mexicans.

1923 Smith, Wallace, *The Little Tigress*, p. 31: Coyote-hearted foreigners! Hungry vultures dipping bloody beaks into the quivering body of Mexico.

1925 Scarborough, Dorothy, *The Wind*, p. 66: That's a coyote.

1931 *Lariat*, April, p. 59: He'd coyote on us right now . . .

coyote tobacco "A many-stemmed plant (*Nicotiana bigelovii* and *attenuata*) 1 to 2 feet high, with dark-green leaves and white, narrow-tubular flowers. Blooms midsummer to autumn." So named in derision and to distinguish it from "store" tobacco.

coyotillo (*Spanish* ko: jo: tí: jo:; *English, the same*) Diminutive of *coyote*. A shrub (*Karwinskia humboltiana*) with blackish poisonous berries and beautiful pinnate-veined leaves.

creole See the *New English Dictionary.*

cuarta English modification **quirt, quirto** (*Spanish*, kwá:r ta:; *English*, kwurt) A short riding whip used chiefly by cowboys, bronco busters, and horse tamers and trainers, or others who ride extensively, in the West and Southwest. The *quirt* is approximately a yard in length—butt, braid, and lash, or "popper" as it is often called. It is round and usually made of leather although it may be made of horsehair or more rarely of rawhide. The foundation of the *quirt* is the butt or handle, a piece of iron, about a quarter of a meter long (*un mango de cerra de una cuarta*). Around this piece of iron are braided the strands of leather each approximately the width and thickness of a shoe lace, or the strands of horsehair. Immediately below the handle the diameter of the *quirt* is increased from the three-quarters of an inch thickness to an inch or more. It then gradually tapers to less than half an inch in thickness where the lash is attached. The *quirt* is held on the hand of the rider by means of a leather strap loop. The cowboy uses it to insure proper action of his mount, to urge or to punish his cattle, or as a defense. The iron loaded *quirt*, when used as a weapon, is as effective as a policeman's night stick. For training broncos it is much more effective and satisfactory, when used judiciously, than are spurs. The word is almost universally used by riders in the West and Southwest. There it has been completely naturalized. No two authorities however seem to agree on the derivation of *quirt*, although all assume that it is derived from Spanish. It is doubtful whether the word is derived from Spanish *corto* as suggested. There is no relation between *corto* meaning short and *cuarta* meaning one-fourth, and the latter is the only designation given the article in Spanish. *Cuerdo*, another suggestion, is unlikely for the same reason. English *quirt* is probably derived from the Spanish *cuarta*. It is not entirely clear why the whip is called a *cuarta* in Spanish but it is not unlikely that this name was adopted because the accepted official length of the quirt stock seems to be *una cuarta de una vara*, a fourth of a vara. The form *quirto* is neither Spanish nor English but rather a literary hybrid. From the noun has come the verb to *quirt* and the Anglicized *quirting* used in such a phrase as "He gave the animal a sound quirting."

1899 Hubbard, Elbert, *Philistine*, p. 126: . . . with the butt end of a quirt he'd persuade you into his (Teddy's) own way of thinking.

1912 Hough, Emerson, *The Story of the Cowboy*, p. 62: The quirt was merely supplement to the spur which the cowpuncher wore on each foot.

1916 Benedict, H. Y. and Lomax, John A., *Book of Texas*, p. 180: Many stranded quirts and reatas, or lassos, were made of leather by skilled cowboys.

1928 Atherton, Gertrude, *The Splendid Idle Forties*, p. 8: He will not stand the quirto. *Ibid.*, p. 8: Their spurs were fastened to bare brown heels; the cruel quirto was in the hand of each . . .

cuartel English modification **quartel** (*Spanish*, kwa:r té:l:; *English*, kwar tl:) Barracks, soldiers' quarters, whether permanent or temporary. The term is seldom, if ever, used except when referring to such quarters occupied by Mexican soldiers.

1846 Kendall, George W., *Narrative of the Texan Santa Fe Expedition*, p. 300: . . . we were marched to a small room adjoining the soldiers' quartel.

1903 North, A. W., *Mother of California*, p. 128: . . . a Chinese conspiracy caused a rider to be thrown into the cuartel . . .

1917 McClellan, George B., *Mexican War Diary*, p. 91: We at first marched to the cuartel (barracks) where we remained some few hours.

1918 Bentley, J. C., [Unpublished Diary]: Next morning we got an early start, drove up to the quartel of government soldiers . . . and presented our passports.

1923 Smith, Wallace, *The Little Tigress*, p. 58: At the iron gate of the cuartel, Don Roberto begged to be excused.

cuesta See Webster's *New International Dictionary*.

cuidado (*Spanish*, kwi: ðá: ðo:, kwi: ðá: o:; *English*, kwi: ðá:o *also* kwi: dá:o) Look Out! Take care! Be careful! An exclamation of warning or danger. In Spanish it is used by workmen or construction "gangs" to warn fellow workmen or passersby of possible danger such as from blasting or falling timber, etc. It is also used in this sense by Americans in such expressions as the following "If you do not carry out his instructions you had better *cuidado*" or "Better *cuidado* or you will be hurt." The occurrence of *cuidado* is fairly well restricted to spoken English.

1855 Gringo, Harry, *Tales for the Marines*, p. 139: Qui-dow! marm! don't make lub to de baby. *Ibid.*, p. 276: O cuidado! Screamed the pastor. Beware it is certain death.

1903 Austin, Mary, *Land of Little Rain*, p. 265: There are still some places in the West where the quails cry "cuidado."

cuñado (*Spanish*, ku:n já: ðo: *or* ku:n já:o:; *English, the same*) Brother-in-law or often would-be brother-in-law. In the latter sense often facetious. Well known by Southwesterners with a knowledge of Spanish.

1932 Coolidge, D., *Fighting Men of the West*, p. 150: And then there were two uncles, both fighters and outlaws, and a host of *cuñados*.

cura (*Spanish*, ku: ra:; *English, practically the same*) A clergyman in general or a parish priest. In the general sense the word *cura* is synonymous with *padre*. Both are used frequently by Americans when referring to Catholic priests and their activities among the Mexican people. In spoken English *cura* promises to remain in the Southwest.

1836 Latrobe, Charles Joseph, *The Rambler in Mexico*, p. 63: ... four or five leagues higher up, shortly after the traveller has passed a large Hacienda belonging to a wealthy *cura* on the left bank ...

1844 Kendall, George Wilkins, *Narrative of the Texan Santa Fe Expedition*, p. 38: While at the cura's house he told me ... there was no further danger of being robbed ...

1889 Ripley, McHatton E., *From Flag to Flag*, p. 191: ... the *cura* in defiance of the law, carried her body to the village cemetery. *Ibid.*, p. 193: ... the amount ... collected was sent to the cura to pay for a mass for the repose of the soul of some relative.

dale vuelta English modification **dally welta, take dallies** (*Spanish*, dá: le: vu:e:l ta:; *English*, dǽ li: wɛl tə) From *dar la vuelta*, to give a turn or twist. An expression often used by cowboys when ordering someone to wrap a lasso rope around the horn of a saddle, a post, or the like. From a command it has been adapted to a noun phrase in such an expression as "he gave it a *dally welta*," or "he gave it a *vuelta*"; also "he took a *dally*."

1922 Rollins, Philip Ashton, *The Cowboy*, p. 139: . . . the users of that style needed more length in his rope than did the man who threw a free reata and thus, "dallied," "daled" "vuelted" or "dale vuelted" his rope

1929 Lomax, John A., *Cowboy Songs*, p. 382: . . . take your dolly weltas . . .

1930 James, Will, *Lone Cowboy*, p. 265: They had long rawhide ropes, made great big loops and instead of tying the other end, they take wraps, "dally welta," around the saddle horn.

de veras (*Spanish*, de: vé: ra:s; *English, the same and* də vέr əs) An exclamation meaning "For a certainty," "You don't say so," or "Is that possible?" Used chiefly in intimate and informal conversation by those who have a ready knowledge of both English and Spanish. Without the question mark it is used in the sense of "for certain" or "in earnest."

?156 Bolton, Herbert, *Fray Juan Crespin*, p. XIVIII: On the 11th the Santiago was towed out of the harbor once more and the voyage was begun *de veras*.

diablo (*Spanish*, di:á: blo:; *English*, di: ǽb lo: *and* di: ǽ bo: lo:) An ejaculation often used in conjunction with the word *que* as *que diablo* meaning "the devil," or "the deuce." *Diablo* is also common in place names as in "Diablo Canyon," "Mount Diablo," etc. Probably it is thus used with the descriptive connotation of the word in mind.

1931 *Time* (Magazine) August 24, *Que diablo!* it was too good a revolution to miss.

dichos (*Spanish*, dí: cho:s; *English, the same*) *Dicho* is the past participle of "decir" to say; dichos, therefore, literally means "What has been said," or "sayings."

1898 Lummis, Charles F., *The Awakening of a Nation*, p. 177: The *dicho* has a hundred forms; but in some shape it is current everywhere.

1930 Saunders & O'Sullivan, *Capistrano Nights:* . . . these stories, fables, dichos, form a unique contribution to the folklore of California . . .

dinero (*Spanish*, di: né: ro:; *English* di: nέr o: *or* dɪ nεr o:) Money. The word is well understood throughout the Southwest. A small town in Texas is named "Dinero."
1903 O. Henry, *Heart of the West*, p. 77: Here's a little bunch of the *dinero* that I drawed out of the bank . . .

dogie See ADOBE.

dueño (*Spanish*, dwe:n jo:; *English the same*) Owner; head of a family.
1919 Chase, J. Smeaton, *California Desert Trails*, p. 320: While I drank my milk and talked with the dueño . . . the phonograph was turned on for my pleasure.

dulce (*Spanish*, dú:l se:; *English, the same and* dú:l si:) Sweetheart; "girl"; "lady friend"; intimate acquaintance. It is common in the Southwest to hear the sweetheart of a young man referred to as his *dulce* or his *dulce corazon* (literally sweet heart).
1912 Hough, Emerson, *The Story of the Cowboy*, p. 212: It [a letter] may be from his "girl," as he calls it (his dulce, it would be in the South) . . .
1929 Stiff, James E., *The Spanish Element in Southwest Fiction*, p. 57: The old *ranchero* being a wily matchmaker, is ever offering inducements to his cowboys to join in matrimony some dulce of their choice.
1932 Coolidge, D., *Fighting Men of the West*, p. 275: . . . the next time I visit my *dulce* I could show her this pistol . . .

dulces (*Spanish*, dú:l ce:s; *English*, dú:lci: *or* dú:l ci:z) Sweets; candy of any kind.
1889 Ripley, McHatton E., *From Flag to Flag*, p. 244: . . . she was neighborly in her feelings, frequently sending us little bowls of delicious dulces of her own make . . .
1923 Smith, Wallace, *The Little Tigress*, p. 63: *Dulces!* Sweets! Sang the candy seller.

ejido (*Spanish*, e: hí: ðo:; *English, the same and* e hí do:) The land set aside for the common use of a village, generally pasture land for the small herds of goats, pigs and burros of the villages. *Ejido* may also signify the entire parcel of land of the township. Verbal use of the word by Americans is confined pretty much to the border territory and almost entirely to the Mexican side.

Ejido does, however, appear fairly commonly in recent books on Mexico and Mexican life.

1931 Beals, Carleton, *Mexican Maize*, p. 37: ... their ejidos (village commons) were again menaced.

1931 Frank, Waldo, *America Hispaña:* Meantime, the programme of the *ejido* ... was a failure.

empresario English modification **empressario** (*Spanish*, e:m pre: sá: rio; *English*, im pre sǽ rio) In the early days of colonization in Texas an *empresario* was one who was allotted by the Mexican government a tract of land on which he was by the terms of the agreement to plant a certain number of immigrant families, two hundred or more, under rules and regulations set down in the contract. The most common requirements of these contracts were that the immigrants should swear allegiance to the country and become good Catholics.

1834 Struble, George G., *A Visit to Texas*, p. 55: Thus the agent had not to purchase a title for the agent or empresario ...

1883 Sweet and Knox, *On a Mexican Mustang Through Texas*, p. 213: The title of the land cost him nothing; and they called him an empresario ...

1906 Garrison, G. P., *The American Nation, Western Expansion*, p. 25: Other *empressarios* joined in the movement, and the colonists were soon in practical possession of the country.

en pelo (*Spanish*, e:n pe: lo; *English, the same*) To ride *en pelo* signifies to ride bareback without saddle or other covering for the animals back, i.e., on the hair. It is occasionally heard among Americans acquainted with Spanish when referring to riding without a saddle. Its use is not extensive or important.

escopeta (*Spanish*, e:s ko: pé: ta; *English, practically the same*) A gun, rifle, escopet. This word finds occasional use in writings about Mexico and the border lands. It is used rarely in spoken English even by those well acquainted with both Spanish and English.

1912 Hough, Emerson, *The Story of the Cowboy*, p. 111: ... justice in this case perhaps tempered with a respect for the knife and escopeta of one's neighbour ...

factura (*Spanish*, fa:k tú: ra:; *English*, fæk tú: rə) An invoice of merchandise; a bill. The Spanish word is used in business parlance where the dealings and contacts with the Spanish-speaking element are many and the use of both languages is common by the business men. *Factura* is being used less frequently on the American side of the border but continues to be used by Americans in Mexico.

1844 Gregg, Josiah, *Commerce of the Prairies*, p. 66: . . . in the drawing up of the *factura* or invoice, the greatest care is requisite, as the slightest mistake might subject the goods to confiscation.

fandango See Webster's *New International Dictionary.*

fanega (*Spanish*, fa: né: ga:; *English, the same; or* fæ né: gǝ) A measure for dry matter, about 1.60 bushels. Rarely used except in communities of very intimate association and close business dealings between Mexicans and Americans. It is used also to signify the amount of land that may be sown by a *fanega* of seed.

1840 Turnbull, David, *Travels in the West*, p. 126: The . . . produce is stated as follows:—Of white or clayed sugar 3,901,835 arrobas of 25 lbs. each . . . of fanegas of Indian Corn 11,617,806.

1844 Gregg, Josiah, *Commerce of the Prairies*, p. 152: Husbandmen rate their fields by the amount of wheat necessary to sow them; and thus speak of a fanega of land . . .

1848 Emory, W. H., *A Military Reconnoissance*, p. 35: . . . the price (of wheat) is falling gradually to four dollars the fanega.

1863 Fergusson, Major D., *Report to Congress*, p. 9: Of wheat they raise annually 8,000 fanegas.

1901 Powell, L. P., *Historic Towns of Western States*, p. 454: The Indians paid an annual tribute of a vara of cotton cloth and a fanega of corn per family.

fiesta (*Spanish*, fi:é:s ta:; *English*, fi:és tǝ) A celebration; a holiday; a feast or religious holiday; festivity of any kind is generally termed a *fiesta*. Commonly used in the Southwest.

1925 James, Will, *The Drifting Cowboy*, p. 67: It started out with the fiesta.

1928 Stiff, James, *The Spanish Element in Southwestern Fiction*, p. 25: . . . the *fiestas* of the church attracted alike the pagan and the priest.

filibuster (*Spanish*, fi: li: bu: sté: ro:; *English*, fíl. ɪ bus ter) From Spanish *filibustero* which according to Alemany is the name of certain pirates who infested the seas of the Antilles during the seventeenth century. By extension it was applied to all buccaneers infesting the Spanish American coasts, then to all those who organize hostile expeditions to countries with which their own are at peace. The word later became closely associated with the Congress of the United States and is most commonly used at present to designate an attempt to obstruct or delay legislative action by means of extended talking about some phase of the subject at hand. In this sense as well as the former it has become fully naturalized in English.

fregar (*Spanish*, fre: gár. *English, the same*) The word means to "annoy," "injure," or "harm," following the Spanish meaning of *molestar*. It is used colloquially by Americans who have lived in intimate contact with the Spanish population and who more often than not use the word in Spanish in the same sense. It is used almost always in the infinitive form; for example "If we remain here they [bandits or the like] will come and *fregar* us," of "Ill *fregar* him."

frijol English modification **frijole, freeholays** (*Spanish*, frí: ho:l; *English*, fri: hó: li:) Beans. Although the word is used to designate any of the general variety of beans it specifies in particular Mexican pink beans or the more common *ojo de cabra* (goat's eye) beans. Like the Spanish *tamal* the singular form of the word has acquired an additional syllable in its English pronunciation. The combination *frijole-beans* meaning Mexican beans is occasionally heard in light conversation.

1844 Kendall, George W., *Narrative of the Texan Santa Fe Expedition*, Vol. II, p. 30: In fact, frijoles especially to the lower order of Mexican, are what potatoes are to the Irish.

1848 Emory, W. H., *Notes of a Military Reconnoissance*, p. 40: ... the whole (meal) terminated by chile the glory of New Mexico, and the frijole.

1930 Lyman, George D., *John Marsh, Pioneer*, p. 221: All the doctor gave them ... was ... some beeves and frijoles and a few clothes ...

1931 Austin, Mary, *Starry Adventure*, p. 34: All they understand is just meat and corn-meal and freeholays.

fuste (*Spanish*, fú:s te:; *English*, fú:s ti:) A saddle tree, a Mexican saddle, a pack saddle. In Spanish *fuste* signifies lumber or

board. It is used by Americans to distinguish the "Mexican saddle" from the western American saddle. The Mexican saddle
tree, or frame is constructed of wood and covered with a thin
skin preparation. The Mexican saddle has a minimum of leather
appurtenances and trimmings as compared with the western
American saddle with its tree completely covered with leather.
The *fuste* is distinguished by a large flat-faced horn or pommel
and a low cantel. It is notorious for its aptitude for injuring the
backs of horses on which it is used. The *fuste* is rarely used by
the American cowboy or rider and is becoming less popular with
the Mexican vaqueros who are adopting the American cowboy
saddle.

1844 Gregg, Josiah, *Commerce of the Prairies*, p. 212: . . . a
    cover of embossed leather embroidered with fancy silk and
    tinsel, with ornaments of silver, is thrown loose over the cush-
    ion and fuste or saddle-tree . . .

gachupin (*Spanish*, gá: chu: pí:n; *English, the same and* gǽ chu:
pí:n) From American Indian *cacth*, shoe plus *catsopin* to sting.
A Spaniard or native of Spain.

1847 Ruxton, George F., *Adventures in Mexico and the Rocky
    Mountains*, p. 87: I stayed in the house of the widow of a
    Gachupin . . .

1931 Austin, Mary, *Starry Adventure*, p. 100: . . . he was a
    gauchapin, whatever that meant.

galleta (*Spanish*, gaɪ jé: ta:; *English, the same*) "A coarse—
almost woody-stemmed, stiff grass [*Pleuraphis rigida*.] growing
in large dense clumps to a height of from 2 to 4 feet, and in the
driest of soils. The stems appear dry and dead except at the tips,
which are pale bluish green. It is an excellent forage-plant and
of the greatest value to desert travellers." *Galleta* literally means
"cracker." It is also spelled *gaieta*.

1872 *The Overland Monthly*, p. 146: The coarse, dry bunch-grass
    or *gaieta*, never abundant on this route, was unusually scarce
    that summer . . .

1919 Chase, J. Smeaton, *California Desert Trails*, p. 196: About
    ten o'clock I found a few scraps of blue-stem (galleta grass)
    and burro-weed . . . and we stopped to rest and lunch.

gambusino English modification, **gambosino** (*Spanish*, ga:m bu:
sí: no:; *English*, gæm bo: si: no:) A prospector; used also in
western mining parlance to designate an ore thief.

1844 Gregg, Josiah, *Commerce of the Prairies*, p. 174: The gambusinos being generally destitute . . . are often obliged to dispose of their gold daily . . .

1932 Coolidge, D., *Fighting Men of the West*, p. 147: . . . he made such an impression that he was invited to join the gambosinos . . .

garbanzo (*Spanish*, ga:r bá:n so:; *English*, gar bá:n zo: *or* gar bæn zo:) The chick-pea or garavance. The Spanish *garbanzo* has almost entirely replaced the English names for this pulse. Americans along the border and in Mexico engaged in the raising of this crop or in its merchandising seldom use chick-pea and garavance. The former is heard occasionally but the latter very rarely.

1840 Turnbull, David, *Travels in the West*, p. 126: The agricultural produce is stated as follows . . . of arrobas of wax, 63, 160 . . . rice, cotton, beans, garbanzos etc. . . .

1903 North, A. W., *The Mother of California*, p. 22: . . . around the present mission are immense orange . . . trees . . . and fields where garbanzas . . . thrive most wonderously.

garapatos (*Spanish*, gá: ra: pá: to:s; *English*, gára pá: toz *and* gara pǽ toz) A species of wood-bug. References to this insect indicate that it was very annoying to travellers and tourists on the frontier. Its name implies that it took hold of its victim by means of claws on the feet.

1836 Latrobe, Charles Joseph, *The Rambler in Mexico*, p. 35: Every leaf, every spray holds its myriads of *garapatos*, a species of wood bug.

gente de razon (*Spanish* 'he:n te: de: ra: 'so:n; *English the same*). Literally "people of reason." Applied to the more responsible or reliable among the common people and lower class of natives in Spanish regions.

1872 *The Overland Monthly*, p. 164: An incident is related, which is about as worthy of credence as the majority of ghost-stories narrated by the *gente de razon*.

golondrina "Rattlesnake weed (*Euphorbia polycarpa*) A flat-growing, mat-like plant with radiating reddish stems and small, roundish, bronze-green, white-edged leaves. Flowers very small, white or pinkish. Blooms in late spring."

grama (*Spanish*, grá: ma:; *English*, grǽ mə) Several species of grass (*Chondrosium foeneum* and *polystachyum;* also species of *Bouteloua*) common to the Southwest and Mexican border regions. *Grama* is highly regarded among stockmen and ranchers for its food value. *Grama* grass, as it is usually termed, is characterized by a slender stalk almost devoid of leafy structure but capped with a feather-like head. This latter is the fruit of the plant and when mature possesses food elements comparable to grain for horses, cattle and other live stock. It is harvested as a supplement to the alfalfa crop of many ranchers. See *zacate* in this study. Because of the commonness of the grass, no doubt, the word has become fully naturalized into the English vocabulary of Americans in the region under study.

1846 Gregg, Josiah, *Commerce of the Prairies*, p. 161: . . . the grama is only in perfection from August to October.

1848 Emory, W. H., *Notes on a Military Reconnoissance*, p. 71: Giving our animals a bite of the luxurious grama on the river banks, we . . . commenced the jornada.

1912? Cozzens, S. W., *The Young Trail Hunters*, p. 141: Notwithstanding its immense elevation, it was covered with a peculiar kind of grass called *grama*, which retains its nutritious qualities throughout the whole year.

greaser (*No Spanish pronunciation; English*, grí: zer *or* grí: ser) Not commonly regarded as of Spanish derivation. A Mexican, particularly one of low caste. The evidence that it is derived from the Spanish is not convincing. Reid in his *Scouting Expeditions* mentions that the *grazier* is a class of peons. He also spells the word *greaser* which is the more common spelling. Bret Harte specializes the word by assigning it to a "mixed race of Mexican and Indian." A common but questionable explanation of the word is that it comes from greasy; the outstanding characteristic of the Mexican cooks and laborers employed in the United States. *Greaser* applied to Mexicans by Americans in the border region carries with it depreciation, disrespect or even insult. It is more of this nature than the word *gringo* when applied by Mexicans to Americans. In careless and rude conversation and informal writing the word is too commonly used.

1859 Reid, Samuel, *Scouting Expedition*, p. 35: The Señoritas were all kneeling . . . while the greasers stood up on the right; there being no seats or pews. *Ibid.*, p. 89: The term greaser we suppose is a corruption of the word grazier, the class of peons of labourers of the country.

1912 Hough, Emerson, *The Story of the Cowboy*, p. 25: Most of the cowboys employed on the Circle Arrow outfit are Mexican or "Greasers," as all Mexicans are called by the American inhabitants.

gringo[4] (*Spanish*, grɪŋ go: *English, the same*) An American, a yankee. One of the specific hopes of this study was to clarify the derivation of this word. It is doubtful, however, if this can be done. Every dictionary, glossary word list, or idiom list in both English and Spanish that could be obtained was consulted. Of these the more conservative offer no specific source for the word. Several others suggest that *gringo* is a corruption of *Griego*. Others omit the derivation and merely offer a definition. And in the definitions there is no unanimity. One has it applied to Americans and English, and another to all foreigners, another to all those who speak a foreign language, and yet another indicated that *gringo* is applied to Italians only. For the purposes of this study it may be set down that in the territory of the Southwest the word signifies American either by birth or

[4] The subject of gringo was discussed in letters by P. de Klein, July 8; F. E. Foster and T. H. Jackson, July 11; W. C. Wells and myself, July 13, in the year 1916. At that time your editor was good enough to print the result of my investigations, which showed that gringo dates back to 1787. It is explained in P. Esteban de Terreros y Pando's "Diccionario Castellano," in volume 2, page 240, column 1 of that work, published in Madrid in that year: "Gringos—Llaman en Malaga a los estranjeros, que tienen cierta especie de acento que los priva de una locucion facil y natural Castellana; y en Madrid dan el mismo, y por la misma causa con particularidad a los Irlandeses." Roughly translated, this means: "Gringos—The name given in Malaga to those foreigners who have a certain accent which prevents them from speaking Spanish fluently and naturally; and in Madrid the same term is used for the same reason, especially with reference to the Irish."

The word may be found also in Melchior Emmanuel Nunez de Taboada's Dictionnaire Espagnol-Français, issued in Paris in 1838, where one may read, sub verbo: "Gringo, ga, adj. (figuré et familier) Grec, hébreu. On le dit d'une chose inintelligible." This serves to show that some "Spanish" was as so much Greek to the Hidalgos long before the Mexicans heard "Green grow the leaves on the hawthorn tree" or "Green grow the rushes, oh!"

FRANK H. VIZETELLY

New York, Sept. 23, 1929.
(In *New York Times*)

language. (Note. The commonly repeated story that *gringo* began with the Burns poem "Green grow the rashes, oh" set to
music is too naive to be accepted without more trustworthy evidence. It is, however, widely believed by the unlettered.)
1925 Smith, J. Russell, *North America*, p. 689 Mexico's enemy
    is not the hated gringo.
1926 Cather, Willa, *Death Comes for the Archbishop*, p. 139. Any
    European, except a Spaniard, was regarded as a gringo.
1928 Stiff, James E., *The Spanish Element in Southwest Fiction*,
    p. 4: At the time the gringo came . . . Indians still roamed the
    prairies . . .
1929 *Time*, Sept. 9, Coach Root's swart quarterback cried sig-
    nals in Spanish . . . held the gringos to a scoreless tie.
1929 De Castro, Adolph, *Portrait of Ambrose Bierce*, p. 337: Yes,
    it brings business; but it were best to live without the gringos.

grito (*Spanish* grí: to:; *English, the same*) A cry; a shout; a war
cry; as the latter it is an abbreviation of *grito de guerra*. This
word is used most commonly in narrative concerning an incident
involving Spanish-speaking people or in indirect quotation.
1844 Kendall, George Wilkins, *Narrative of the Texan Santa Fe
    Expedition*, Vol. II, p. 69: . . . the lesson they received
    prepared the minds of all to echo a grito (cry of revolution)
    whenever one was found bold enough to raise it.
1929 *New York Times*, Sept. 16: . . . members of the diplo-
    matic corps struck the liberty bell and gave the "Grito," or
    shout of liberty.

grulla English modifications **gruller, gruya** (*Spanish*, grú: ja:;
English, grú: jo:, grú jer) From *grulla*, a crane. A bluish-gray
colored object or animal. Usually applied to horses of this color.
Among the older ranch people of the Southwest the term is well
known and often used.
1903 O. Henry, *Heart of the West*, p. 147: The Mexicans, who
    have a hundred names for the colors of a horse, called him
    gruyo.
1925 James, Will, *The Drifting Cowboy*, p. 210: He was a big
    powerful *gruller* horse, tall and rawboned and all muscle.
1928 Dobie, J. Frank, *A Vaquero of the Brush Country*, p. 4: The
    horse my father gave me was a grulla (mouse colored) dun
    paint.

1931 *Lariat*, April, p. 4: . . . he had never roped much of anything except catclaw bushes and the . . . tail of his gruya mule . . .

guero See HUERO.

guia (*Spanish*, ǵi: a:; *English, the same*) A passport, or *salvo conducto*. A *guia* was often carried by a foreigner or other traveller in Mexico during the nineteenth century to insure him friendly reception by government officials. *Guia* is seldom used in spoken English today but is encountered in writings about the Southwest and Mexican border.
1844 Gregg, Josiah, *Commerce of the Prairies*, p. 67: Now, to procure this same guia, which is the cause of so much difficulty and anxiety in the end, is no small affair.

hacendado (*Spanish*, a: se:n dá: ᵭo:; *English, same*) The owner of an hacienda. *Hacendado* finds its chief usefulness in writings concerning those countries where haciendas are found.
1840 Turnbull, David, *Travels in the West*, p. 98: In the unexpected case of the confiscation of the rural property of a [sic] *Hacendado*, the civil judge of the district . . . is directed to proceed to the spot.

hacienda (*Spanish*, a: si:én da:; *English, the same*) A large ranch; a landed estate; a community built around such a ranch or estate; a plantation-like community. The word is derived from the Latin *facienda* from *facere*, "to do" or "to work." A distinctive feature of the *hacienda* as found in Spanish America is the *casa grande* in which lives the owner of the *hacienda* or his representative known as the *mayor domo* or in some instances the *caporal*. The *casa grande* of the *hacienda* and the other principal buildings are usually painted white or whitewashed and occupy the most prominent or favorable location of the *hacienda* site. Near the *casa grande*, are the various outbuildings including workshops, tool-sheds, granaries, stables and corrals. Another characteristic of the *hacienda* is the community of peons, or serfs, dependent upon it. The peons live in rude adobe houses, or *ramadas*, in close proximity to the *casa grande* yet outside the yard proper pertaining to the latter. These houses of the peons are provided by the owner of the *hacienda* and vary in quality according to his temperament or circumstances. Until the Madero revolution in

Mexico a great part of northern Mexico was made up of these *haciendas*. In the state of Chihuahua, Don Luis Terrazas owned about a score of them. It was customary for him to visit them all on occasions but to regard one or two as the official domicile. The word *hacienda*, although somewhat technical in aspect, serves a useful end in the English vocabulary of America.

1810 Pike, Zebulon M., *Expeditions*, p. 675: This hacienda was obliged to furnish accommodations to all travellers.

1834 Latrobe, Charles, *Travels in Mexico*, p. 88: After a two hours ride, we descended into a valley with occasional haciendas, scattered over its surface . . .

1885 Harte, Francis Bret, *Mystery of the Hacienda*, p. 220: . . . "her tall, erect figure . . . gave a new and patrician dignity to the melancholy of the hacienda . . ."

1927 Lawrence, David, *Walk to Huayapa*, p. 29: . . . along the foot hills, a few scattered trees, white dot and stroke of a *hacienda*, and a green, green square of sugar-cane . . .

1928 Stiff, James E., *The Spanish Element in Southwest Fiction*, p. 49: The movements of the hero are so rapid that there is little time for descriptions of rooms, haciendas, or gardens.

1929 Castro, Adolphe de, *Ambrose Bierce*, p. 334: The hacienda was not very far, and we made it in a few minutes at a gallop.

hammock See the *New English Dictionary*.

hasta la vista (*Spanish*, á: sta: la: ví: sta:; *English, the same*) Loosely translated it means, "I'll see your later." It is used frequently in the Southwest by those who know both Spanish and English at times of friendly leave-taking. It is also used by radio announcers. *Hasta luego* (lu:é:go:), a Spanish synonym of *la hasta vista*, is likewise used but not so frequently.

hatajo English modification, **atajo** (*Spanish*, a: tá: ho:; *English, the same and* ə tǽ ho:) From *hatajar* "to divide into flocks or small herds." A train of pack animals, burros, horses, or mules, usually the latter, used for the transportation of merchandise in the frontier regions of the United States and Spanish America. The typical *atajo* consists of from fifteen to forty animals equipped with *aparejos*. The *atajo* is cared for by one or more *atajaderos* or drivers. It is particularly useful in mountainous districts and in fact was long the only practical mode of transporting merchandise to and from mining, cattle, and other camps.

The word is used commonly in the Southwest. *Atajar*, the Spanish verb, signifies "to head off"; that is, "to stop," or "divide," and has no relationship to *atajo*, a clipped form of *hatajo*.

1844 Gregg, Josiah, *Commerce of the Prairies*, p. 79: we engaged an *atajo* of mules at El Paso, upon which to convey our goods across. *Ibid.*, p. 99: Arrieros with their *atajos* of pack mules always camp out . . . *Ibid.*, p. 181: Indeed it is apt to occasion much trouble to stop a heavily laden atajo . . .

havelina See JAVALINA

hectolitro English modifications **hectroliter, hec** (*Spanish*, e:k tó: li: tro:; *English*, hék tról ɪ tɛr *and more briefly*, hek) *Hectolitro* is the usual measuring unit in Mexico for the smaller grains. One *hectolitro* is equivalent to approximately two and one-half bushels. The abbreviated form, *hec*, is more commonly used by threshers, millers and farmers. There is also a transposition of the "r" in Spanish giving *hectrolito*.

hidalgo (*Spanish*, i: dá:l go:; *English, the same and* ɪ dǽl go:) A person of rank; a government officer; any person of prominent standing in a Spanish American community. According to popular etymology this word is derived from the phrase *hijo de algo*, meaning a son of someone of importance. *Hidalgo* is undoubtedly a duplicate borrowing, having been found in English contexts in Europe prior to its acquisition in America.

1912 Hough, Emerson, *The Story of the Cowboy*, p. 125: The hidalgo was pretty sure to locate his grant upon the best water he could find.

1921 Bolton, H. E., *The Spanish Borderlands:* In the midst of the crudities of a frontier, hidalgo and official . . . live joyously.

hombre (*Spanish*, ó:m bre:; *English*, ó:m bre, ó:m bri:, há:m br) A man; a person. *Hombre* is most commonly used in conjunction with an adjective such as "bad," "tough," "good," "mean," "great," and is heard in all parts of the United States although with varying pronunciations. In a New York daily newspaper appeared the picture of two endurance flyers [L. W. Wendell and R. B. Reinhart of Culver City, California] with the title "A couple of tough hombres." It is evident that *hombre* is often utilized for local color picturesqueness. This is particularly

true outside the region of the Southwest. There its use is more
natural as well as more common. The use of the word is increasing in all parts of the United States.

1925 Burns, W. N., *The Saga of Billy the Kid*, p. 115: The Kid's
a wise hombre.

1929 Dobie, J. Frank, *A Vaquero of the Brush Country*, p. 76:
He was a man of sound judgment and strict honor and he was
a great *hombre* among the Mexicans . . .

1929 Castro, Adolphe de, *Portrait of Ambrose Bierce*, p. 335:
Yes, but none of them [foreigners] was ever as his [Villa's] own
hombres.

1929 Dos Passos, John, *42nd Parallel*, p. 325: . . . everybody
was there . . . and this big hombre from New York . . . looked
like he didn't know whether he was coming or going.

1930 Ferber, Edna, *Cimarron*, p. 20: The fellow selling it was a
rat-faced hombre with one eye.

honda English modifications **hondoo, hondo** (*Spanish*, ó:n da:;
English hón do:; hon dú:) From *honda*, a sling for throwing
stones. The small loop in one end of a lariat or lasso rope of any
kind through which the other end of the rope is threaded, chiefly
for lassoing purposes. The *honda* on a good lariat is usually reinforced with leather or metal to eliminate the cutting and burning
caused by the swift friction of the rope surfaces when the noose
is tightening. This leather piece is sometimes called *honda*.

1922 Rollins, Philip Ashton, *The Cowboy*, p. 138: The loop was
formed by passing one end of the rope through the "hondo"
at the rope's other end.

1932 White, Stewart Edward, "Ranchero," *Saturday Evening
Post*, Feb. 27. He learned to braid the *reata*, to fashion the
honda, or ring, through which the loop was formed . . .

hoosegow See JUZGADO.

huajilla honey Honey the source of which is the huajillo flower.
(See huajillo.)

huajillo English modification **juagilla** (*Spanish*, wa: hí: jo:;
English, the same). A shrub (probably *Pittecolobium brevifolium*)
common in the Southwest. Its bloom is an important source of
honey highly valued for the flavor it imparts.

1916 Benedict, H. Y. and Lomax, J. A., *The Book of Texas*, p.

199: Texas should keep enough bees to utilize the myriad blossoms on her catclaws and juagillas.
1929 Dobie, J. Frank, *A Vaquero of the Brush Country*, p. 202: . . . balsam-breathed *huajilla*, over-spreading and making soft to the eye ten thousand hills . . .

huero English modification **guero** (*Spanish*, wé: ro:; *English*, gwɛr o: *and* wɛr o:) A person of fair or "sandy" complexion and light or red hair. Americans referring to Mexicans of this type seldom call them "blond" but rather *guero* or *huero*. On the other hand an American seldom refers to a fellow American as a *huero*. A Mexican, of course, referring to an American blond designates him as *un huero*.
1847 Ruxton, George F., *Adventures in Mexico and the Rocky Mountains*, p. 43: . . . from the caprice of human nature, the guero is always a favourite of the fair sex . . .
1929 Dobie, J. Frank, *A Vaquero of the Brush Country*, p. 50: In person he was a *huero*, or red-complexioned man . . .

huevosed (*English*, wé:vo:zd) From *huevo*, egg, plus "ed." The past participle of the improvised verb "to *huevo*" signifying to collect and take away by purchase or otherwise the eggs from a ranch, farm, or poultry yard. The use of the word is probably limited to the period of the Mexican War when American troops occupied parts of Mexico and *huevosed* the native poultry yards. It is probable also that "*huevosed* the ranche" was coined, by analogy, from "vamoosed the ranche."
1917 McClellan, George B., *The Mexican War Diary*, ed. 1917 by William Starr Meyers, p. 32: After dinner we started off to see Seth Williams but saw the mustangs at their feed and "huevosed" the ranche.

huisache (*Spanish*, wi: sá: che:, *English, the same and* wi: sǽch) Probably from American Indian *huitzo* meaning thorny and *achi* meaning a little. A shrub which grows extensively in Texas and other places in the Southwest.
1929 Dobie, J. Frank, *A Vaquero of the Brush Country*, p. 201: I worked for years in the *mogotes* of huisache and mesquite . . . and that brush is so bad that it could hardly be worse.

incommunicado (*Spanish*, í:n ko: mu: ni: ká: ðo:; *English, the same, and* ín kə mu: nı kǽ ðo:) Out of communication; incommunicable. Applied to a person under arrest who is held in custody without the privilege of communicating with others than officers or attorneys. The word is not unmistakably of Spanish origin but is distinctly of Spanish form except for the double "m." Its use is common in the Southwest in discussions of criminal and legal subjects.

1929 *San Antonio Express*, June 2: Jose Marin, 64-year-old Spaniard, today was held incommunicado in a cell in the county jail. *Ibid.*, June 3, 1929: Slayer of Attorneys held Incommunicado.

1931 *Nation*, June 24, p. 689: As the courts are closed, one . . . may be held for three days incommunicado before being arraigned in court.

insurrecto (*Spanish*, i:n su: rré:k to:; *English*, ɪn sə rék to:) Insurgent; revolutionist. The word commonly appears, or is heard, in the plural. Quite inoffensively one may suggest that the border territory has offered opportunity to use any word that signifies revolters. Others are *bandidos, colorados* and numerous *"istas."* During the activities of insurgent parties in Mexico one may frequently hear the word *insurrectos*.

Encyclopaedia Britannica, 14th Ed., Vol. XVI, p. 414: The Liberals laid down their arms, with exception of a single band of *insurrectos*.

ista (*Spanish*, i: sta:; *English* the same or i:s tə) A suffix indicating that one is the follower of a particular leader in a cause or a controversy; a believer in a particular philosophy; or a resident of a particular section of country. The period of unrest in Mexico following the revolution of 1912 during which time there appeared on the scene for long or short periods many individuals with their respective small or large bands of armed followers made it convenient to use the *ista* suffix. Followers of Villa were *Villistas*, of Carranza were *Carranzistas*, of Madero were *Maderistas*. By extension the suffix is occasionally attached to English surnames. Thus the followers of a Hoover might be referred to as "Hooveristas."

1931 *New York Times*, Jan. 18: . . . if ever the Sandinistas got into the building every American would die . . .

jacal (*Spanish*, ha: ká:l; *English*, hæ kǽ l, ha: ká:l, dzæ kǽl *and* dzǽ kəl) A rude habitation; a hut; a hovel; an adobe cottage.

Jacal is used frequently in writing and in speaking. It is, however, usually restricted to contexts relating to the life or habitations of Mexicans. The use of the word to signify an American habitation occurs but is not common. The Spanish usage is American; in Spain the same sort of habitation is termed a *choza* or *cabaña*.

1844 Gregg, Josiah, *Commerce of the Prairies*, p. 286: . . . they mostly live in rude jacales, somewhat resembling the wigwams of the Pawnees . . .

1859 Reid, Samuel, *Scouting Expedition*, p. 127: . . . on the other side of the road on a high eminence stood a little jacal for defence . . . *Ibid.*, p. 226: . . . the road wound itself around a chain of hills, dotted here and there with jacales and ranchos . . .

1889 Ripley, McHatton E., *From Flag to Flag*, p. 81: One of the men . . . was expert in finding Mexican jeccals (huts) . . .

1903 Lummis, C. F., *The Land of Poco Tiempo*, p. 17: It may be the veriest hut of a jacal amid the farther ranges . . .

1928 Stiff, James E., *The Literature of the Southwest*, p. 14: In the Mexican jacals . . . tales were told of El Dorado.

1930 Lyman, George D., *John Marsh, Pioneer*, p. 215: All were housed in adobe buildings, or jacals, clustered about a plaza . . .

n.d. Anonymous, *To California Over the Santa Fe Trail*, p. 138: . . . there the jacal, a poor mud hovel thatched with straw, is not quite extinct.

jaquima English modifications **hackamore, hackimore** (*Spanish*, há: ki: ma:; *English*, hǽk ə moːr *and* hæk ə mr) A rope halter, improvised in a loose fashion or permanently constructed. *Hackamores* made of horsehair rope, sometimes called *cabrestos*, or rope of other composition, are used extensively in the breaking, training, and handling of horses. The *cabresto* has a lead rope, as does in fact the *hackamore*. The word *jaquima* is in Spanish practically synonymous with *cabresto*, or "cabestro." *Hackamore* has been naturalized in English spelling, pronunciation and usage.

1912 Hough, Emerson, *The Story of the Cowboy*, p. 90: The reins of the hackamore are led back, and the saddle is put on and clinched up.

1925 James, Will, *The Drifting Cowboy*, p. 6: . . . nine times out of ten that loose bronc would steam past between him and the horse he was trying to hold, the hackamore rope would hook on the saddle of that bronc and it'd be jerked out of his hands. *Ibid.*, p. 44: . . . you're pawing at the hackamore without knowing what's hurting you.

javalina English modification **havalina** (*Spanish*, ha: va: lí: na:; *English, the same*) Peccary; a hog-like mammal formerly common to parts of Texas and Mexico but at present rarely found. The word is encountered in descriptive accounts or stories of the Southwest.
1912? Cozzens, S. W., *The Young Trail Hunters*, p. 46: Soon afterwards they discovered the tracks of the havilinas.

jefatura (*Spanish*, he: fa: tú: ra:; *English*, hɛ fə túr ə) The province or district under jurisdiction of a *jefe politico* (*q.v.*). Restricted in use to the border region and Mexico and writings about the latter.
1898 Lummis, Charles F., *The Awakening of a Nation*, p. 120: He drilled the half-naked Indians of his *jefatura* on Sundays . . .

jefe or **jefe politico** (*Spanish*, hé: fe:; *English*, héf fi:). A local magistrate; an officer of the law. The full title, *jefe politico*, is also heard in the Southwest. The shorter term, however, is much more common. The *jefe politico* may have jurisdiction in several townships or even an entire county.
1903 North, A. W., *The Mother of California*, p. 64: Luis Negrete became sub-jefe . . .
1925 Smith, Russell, *North America*, p. 678: The jefe . . . would often arrest a few harmless Indian farmers and fine them.
1930 Lyman, George D., *John Marsh, Pioneer*, p. 206: Noriega had obtained from Jose Castro—gefe politico ad interim—a grant to a large tract of land . . .
1931 Austin, Mary, *Starry Adventure* p. 283 he was still taking it out of you for that broken boast of his about being the *jefe* ,of the boy-gang . . .

jerky Of Peruvian origin, from American Indian *charqui.*

jigger See CHIGRE.

jinete (*Spanish*, hi: né: te:; *English*, hin ɛ́ ti:) A horse-rider. *Jinete* is often used in conjunction with the Spanish word *muy* as in "that man is *muy jinete*," signifying that so and so is an excellent rider, i.e., bronco buster. Likewise colloquially: "He is some *jinete*."

jornada English modification, **hornather** (*Spanish*, ho:r ná: ða:; *English, the same and* ho:r næ da) An expanse of desert country. There were two *jornadas* famous in the Southwest, the *Jornada del Muerto* (Desert of the Dead) and the Cimarron *jornada*. The former extended for about a hundred miles between El Paso and Santa Fe, beginning on the south at Doña Ana. The latter was a desert stretch of about sixty miles between the Arkansas and Cimarron rivers. *Jornadas* were dreaded and carefully prepared for by caravans and other travellers along the old Spanish trails during frontier days. They meant many hours without water, slow movement through heavy sand, perhaps attacks by Indians or relentless dumping of supplies to avoid disaster. The word is also applied to a day's journey, analagous to "a day's ride" or a "stone's throw" in English. Similarly it is used as a land measure to designate the approximate amount of land that can be plowed in one day; that is, one day's journey with a plow.

1848 Emory, W. H., *Notes on a Military Reconnoissance*, p. 71: . . . we filled every vessel capable of holding water, and commenced the jornada.

1853 House of Representatives, *Ex. Doc.* No. 91, p. 31: Lieut. Edwards had, on the Tucson *jornada*, an abundance of water, where not a drop was found early in July. *Ibid.*, p. 161: The range . . . drops down to the northward, where it forms the hills which lie on the east side of the Jornada del Muerto . . .

1930 Duffus, R. L., *The Santa Fe Trail*, p. 87: . . . his expedition had twelve bad hours on this plain the terrible *jornada*.

juagilla See HUAJILLO.

junta (*Spanish*, hu:n ta:; *English, the same, also* hən tə *or* dzэn tə) A gathering; a reunion; a meeting; a political party or group; a social party. *Junta* is known to readers of American newspapers as signifying a political party or group in Mexico or South American countries.

1851 *New York Herald*, Dec. 25: General Almonte had sent in a memorial to congress recommending the formation of a junta of the principal officers of the army and navy . . .

1903 North, A. W., *The Mother of California*, p. 71: . . . a *junta* managed the fund—for a time.

1928 Stiff, James E., *The Spanish Element in Southwestern Fiction*, p. 19: Most of his [Bret Harte] information was obtained through disjointed memoranda, the proceedings of . . . early departmental juntas . . .

1931 Adams, J. T., *The Epic of America*, p. 134: Hamilton and the Junto were mad with rage, and determined to ruin Adams.

juzgado English modification **jusgado, hoosegow** (*Spanish*, hu:s gá: δo: *English*, húz: ga:u *or* hu:z gá:u) The past participle of *juzgar* "to judge." A court of justice; a jail; a prison. *Juzgado* is commonly heard in colloquial English throughout the southwestern country and to some extent in other parts.

1931 *Lariat*, April, p. 122: And I had to stay in the nearest *jusgado* for three days . . .

1931 *The Vanity Fair Book*, p. 42: . . . the whinings in the hoosegow are extremes to which wet-minded folk often go . . .

Key West A Florida place name said to be derived from the Spanish *Cayo Hueso;* *hueso* (wé: s o:) meaning bone and *cayo* (kái jo:) signifying in Spanish "a low reef or small island." Old guide books; such for instance as the *American Coast Pilot* published by Edmund M. Blunt in 1817 support this theory. In the table of latitudes and longitudes Blunt lists *Key Cruz, del Padre, Key Carenero, Cayo Confites, Cayo* or *Key Verde, Keys Jardines, Key Lobos, Cayo Largo* or *Long Key*. No such supporting evidence was encountered for the *hueso* element of the name.

labor (*Spanish*, la: bór; *English*, lə bór) *Labor* as once used in the Southwest signified either a section of land of about 177 acres. With the passing of the Spanish régime and the disposal of the land parcelled out in *labors* the need for this word has gone. It is rarely heard today among English-speaking people of the Southwest except as a legal term. It is still used by Mexicans as the common word for field. The spelling of the plural is anglicized. In Spanish it would of course be *labores* as spelled by Gregg.

1834 Struble, George G., *A Visit to Texas*, p. 262: A foreign settler shall receive two *labors* unless the land is susceptible of irrigation and then one *labor*.

1836 Parker, *A Trip to the West and Texas*, p. 189: This land is laid off in what is called *labors* of one hundred seventy acres each.

1836 *Texas Constitution, General Provisions Section*, 10. Every head of a family shall be entitled to one league and labor of land . . .

1844 Gregg, Josiah, *Commerce of the Prairies*, p. 150: The labores and milpas (cultivated fields) are often (fenced) . . .

1883 Sweet and Knox, *On a Mexican Mustang Through Texas*, p. 213: . . . they "persuaded" the latter (Anglo-American) with a league and a labor of land . . .

labrador (*Spanish*, la: bra: ðó:r; *English*, lǽ brə do:r) A laborer. According to the *Century Dictionary of Names*, "Labrador," a geographical division of North America, got its name from the fact that slaves and other laborers (*labradores*) were found there by the early explorers. The word is not often used except as a proper name either in spoken or written English even by those who speak both Spanish and English.

1844 Gregg, Josiah, *Commerce of the Prairies*, p. 134 . . . the Indians . . . killed several *labradores* who were at work. *Ibid.*, p. 192: . . . wonderful stories are told of them and dreadful combats between them and the labradores . . .

ladino (*Spanish*, la: ðí: no; *English*, *the same*) Crafty; sagacious; also dissimulative or deceptive. Applied to vicious animals, horses in particular.

1929 Dobie, J. Frank, *A Vaquero of the Brush Country*, p. 14: They were all outlaws, *ladinos*, as wild as bucks, cunning, and ready to fight.

ladron (*Spanish*, la: ðró:n; *English*, lə dró:n) A *ladron* of the Southwest is a robber of either high or low degree. A *ladrone* in early England was more of a rogue than a thief. The *New English Dictionary* gives Old French as the source of the word rather than Spanish. It is likely, however, that the use in the Southwest is of Spanish origin. The word appears in writings and is used occasionally in English conversation.

1840 Turnbull, David, *Travels in the West*, p. 36: Lest I should meet with a ladron on the road, I carried no more money with me . . . than would be quite sufficient.

1847 Ruxton, George F., *Adventures in Mexico and the Rocky Mountains*, p. 34: Thinking a ladron was in sight, I seized my gun . . . *Ibid.*, p. 30: . . . is there anything new?—always having reference to the doings of the ladrones.

1932 Coolidge, Dane, *Fighting Men of the West*, p. 225: . . . recruited from captured bands . . . were *ladrones* and former outlaws.

laguna English modification **lagoon** (*Spanish,* la: gú: na: *English, the same and* lə gú:n) A lake or pond; an area of brackish water especially one near the sea. The word *lagoon* was used in English writings as early as the first part of the seventeenth century. Its earlier meaning, however, seems to be confined to "an area of salt or brackish water." In America the word is used more frequently to describe a small lake or a large pond of water and is sometimes spelled *laguna.*
1836 Latrobe, Charles Joseph, *The Rambler in Mexico,* p. 30: A little above this point, the river, Tammasee, draining the Lago Chairel, and many other lagoons covering a vast tract of country westward . . .
1840 Turnbull, David, *Travels in the West,* p. 178: On many parts of the surface the pitch approaches often to a liquid state . . . but never certainly to justify the name of lagoon.
1912 Hough, Emerson, *The Story of the Cowboy,* p. 15: Sometimes this artificial water supply of the ranch is supplemented by a few natural lagoons of fresh water.
1926 Cather, Willa, *Death Comes for the Archbishop,* p. 90: Jacinto got firewood and good water from the Lagunas . . .

largo (*Spanish,* lá:r go: *English, the same and* lár ə go:) The part of a saddle girth which connects or binds the cinch to the saddle; i.e., a long piece of leather approximately two inches wide and three to five feet long. This is secured and fastened at one end to the cinch ring (or larigo ring) on the saddle. The other end is passed repeatedly through the ring on the end of the cinch and back through the saddle ring until the proper adjustment in length is attained. A knot is then tied securely to hold the cinch at the desired adjustment. *Largo* is also used to designate the "hind cinch" of a two-cinch saddle. This may be due to the fact that often such a cinch is no more than a strap of leather similar to the *largo* itself. Such expressions as "he broke his *largo,*" "the *largo* is hanging," "take up the *largo,*" are commonly heard on cattle ranches and other places where the western type of saddle is used. The word *latigo* means the same thing in English.

lariat See REATA.

lasso-cell. A microscopic cell given the name *lasso-cell* because of a characteristic of throwing out a stringy substance as a part of its organic activity.

latigo (*Spanish*, lá: ti: go:; *English*, lǽ ti: go:) A strap or thong used to fasten the cinch of a saddle to the iron ring on the saddle tree. It is usually three feet or more in length and is wrapped back and forth between link and cinch and adjusted according to the size of the animal on which the saddle is being used. *Latigo* is used synonymously with *largo* (*q.v.*).

1922 Rollins, Philip Ashton, *The Story of the Cowboy*, p. 124: Such riders "rode heavy," had frequent cause to taughten latigos, and caused many a saddle sore upon their ponies' backs.

1930 James, Will, *Lone Cowboy*, p. 21: . . . for every piece of the latigo he took away he brought back a chip . . .

1931 *Lariat*, April, p. 9: Big Wagner is jerkin' the latigo tight . . .

lazo English modifications, **lasso, laso** (*Spanish*, lá: so:, lá: θo:; *English*, lǽ so:) 1. As a noun *lazo* signifies a rope or a lariat. It is a generalized term for all cordage used for roping, that is, noosing purposes. It might be noted that the definition in the *New English Dictionary* for *lazo* would be more accurate as regards the present-day usage if applied to *lariat*, *lariat* being a specific term while *lazo* is generic. 2. As a verb the word is a synonym for "to rope" or "to noose." As noun or verb *lazo* is used with about equal frequency as English "rope."

1834 Struble, George G., *A Visit to Texas*, 66: A man came hurrying down on horseback, provided with a lasso; a rope with a noose at the end as before described. *Ibid.*, p. 60: Lazoing a horse on the Prairie. (Caption for picture facing p. 60). *Loc. cit.*: A horse which has been lazoed is blindfolded, mounted by a rider armed with the heavy and barbarous spurs of the country.

1846 Kendall, George Wilkins, *Narrative of the Texan Santa Fe Expedition*, p. 89: The latter had nothing but a lasso or lariat with him—a long rope made either of hemp or horsehair, but generally the latter . . .

1876 Besant and Rice, *Golden Butterfly*, p. 3: The horsehair lariette, which serves the western Nimrod for lassoing by day and for keeping off snakes at night.

1912 Hough, Emerson, *The Story of the Cowboy*, p. 62: The common name gives the verb form, and the cowpuncher never speaks of "lassoing" an animal, but of "roping" it.

1917 Atherton, Gertrude, *The Splendid Idle Forties*, p. 29: Lassoing another mustang, he pushed on, having a general idea of the direction he should take.

1929 de Castro, Adolphe, *Portrait of Ambrose Bierce*, p. 163: One of the Indians immediately got his lasso ready, which was a long rope made of hide plaited like whip cord, with an iron ring at the end . . .

lepero (*Spanish*, le: pé: ro:; *English*, le pɛ ro:) A person of the lower classes; a peon; a plebe; a begger. *Lepero* is not used extensively in the United States but is found often in writings descriptive of travels in Mexico and in the Spanish territory prior to the Mexican War.

1844 Gregg, Josiah, *Commerce of the Prairies*,: . . . crowds of *leperos* hung as usual to see what they could pilfer. *Ibid.*, p. 254: In New Mexico, however, this procession is not . . . accompanied by armed soldiers and followed by crowds of leperos of all sexes and ages (as in the South).

1847 Ruxton, George F., *Adventures in Mexico and the Rocky Mountains*, p. 67: Leperos whine and pray for alms, and lavanders for your clothes to wash . . .

ley fuga (*Spanish*, le: fú: ga:; *English, the same*) A law or regulation, probably extra legal, which allows a guard to fire at a prisoner who attempts to escape or flee when under arrest. This law was popular under the Porfirio Diaz régime in Mexico. Its abuse for political or personal advantage was one of the most thoroughly denounced policies of the Diaz government. It has not entirely disappeared, and its corollary, the *ley suicidio*, also exists. A prisoner found dead with a pistol in his hand, or near him, is pronounced "a suicide."

1928 Gruening, Ernest, *Mexico and Its Heritage*, p. 61: Of course, under the *ley fuga*, only the prisoner was to blame. Dead men refute no charges.

1932 Coolidge, Dane, *Fighting Men of the West*, p. 227: . . . all ten had suffered the *ley fuga*, being killed while attempting to escape.

llama South American borrowing.

llano (*Spanish*, já: no, ljá no; *English*, já: no: *and* lá: no: *or in parts of Texas* lǽ no:) Flat country without trees; a plain. In general it is not uncommon for one reared along the border to speak of the *llanos* rather than of the plains; of a "small *llano*" or the "*llano* country."

1903 North, A. W., *The Mother of California*, p. 104: The large sections of the Peninsula which are not sierra regions are usually either wide deserts or hot barren llanos, or plains. *Ibid.*, p. 99: Up from the silent desert and boundless llanos, comes the mystic call . . .

1912? Cozzens, S. W., *The Young Trail Hunters*, p. 28: . . . if we don't ketch 'em afore they git into the Llano, that's the end of 'em . . .

Llano Estacado (*Spanish*, já: no: e: sta: ká: ðo:; *English*, *the same and* lǽ no: es tə kǽ ðo: *or* do:) A vast plateau in Texas and New Mexico. The meaning of the term is usually given as "staked plain." It could, however, as well be called the "palisaded plateau." "*Of the Llano Estacado.*—Upon the eastern or left bank of the river (Pecos) commences the "Llano Estacado," or Staked Plain, which derives its name from a tradition that, in early times, the Spaniards had staked a road upon it from San Antonio, in Texas, to Santa Fe, in New Mexico. This famous desert, without wood or water, extends from the vicinity of the 30th to about the 35th parallel of latitude, is about one hundred and seventy-five miles across at its point of greatest width, and divides the Rio Grande and its tributaries from the affluents of the Mississippi and the streams of eastern Texas. The formation of the Llano Estacado is one of the most marked physical features of the American continent. Its surface, rising over a broad area to an altitude, in almost every part, of over 4,000 feet, at the lowest estimate, and but little broken or traversed by river valleys, constitutes one of the most perfect examples of an elevated plateau, or *mesa*, that is found. The Llano is not broken by a single peak; and there is nothing to break the monotonous desert character of its surface, except an occasional river gorge or canon invisible from a distance, and often apparent only when the traveller stands on its brink."—"Report of Explorations for a Route for the Pacific Railroad," by E. G. Beckwith. H. of R., *Ex. Doc.*, No. 91.

1883 Sweet and Knox, *On A Mexican Mustang Through Texas*,

page 620: And vanished . . . On the Llano Estacado.
1925 Burns, W. N., *The Saga of Billy the Kid*, p. 1: . . . and
Jingle-Bob pastured over nearly half of New Mexico, from the
escarpments of the Llano Estacado westward to the Rio
Grande . . .

lluvia de oro See PALO VERDE.

loafer See LOBO.

lobo; English modifications, **loper, loafer** (*Spanish*, ló:bo: *English, the same*). A wolf. "In Texas the larger wolf is called *lobo wolf* (*canis occidentalis*) to distinguish it from the prairie wolf or *coyote* (*canis latrans*)." Lobo is also used as a synonym for wolf, sometimes for the purpose of lending an atmosphere of greater fierceness when referring to this animal.
1903 O. Henry, *Heart of the West*, p. 11: Lobos have killed three of the calves.
1909 Rye, Edgar, *Quirt and Spur*, p. 9: Far out into the vast expanse of country . . . where the gray lobo wolf and mountain lion stalked their prey . . . Major George H. Thomas established an army port.
1912 Hough, Emerson, *The Story of the Cowboy*, p. 225: . . . an incessant war was waged by the whole ranch force, this more especially applying to the great gray wolf known as the timber wolf, buffalo wolf, "loper," "loafer," or "lobo" wolf . . .
1922 Rollins, Philip Ashton, *The Story of the Cowboy*, p. 213: The lobos were often very hard to capture . . .
1925 Scarborough, Dorothy, *The Wind*, p. 66: We do have wolves, though, loboes or loafers, we call 'em . . .

loco (*Spanish*, ló: ko:; *English, the same*) Crazy; stupid; miner's craze. Originally applied to cattle. When applied to humans *loco* is synonymous with craziness for any reason. *Loco* in cattle and horses is usually caused by eating the *loco weed*, or "stagger grass," as it is sometimes called. This weed may be one of several varieties; *astrogalus molissumus* or *hornii*, or *Oxytropis lamberti*. It is not entirely clear whether the weed gave the name to the affliction, or the affliction gave the name to the weed. The latter is probable from the fact that several plants have the name of *loco weed*. The United States Department of Agriculture has published a bulletin on the subject of *loco weed*. "Horses, oxen, and sheep which have for some time eaten *Astragalus mollissimus*

Torr., in the prairies of Texas, New Mexico, Dakota, Colorado, Montana, etc., exhibit a state of mental excitation and also become the victims of illusions, which cause the animal, for instance, to jump with an enormous expenditure of energy over a small object seen on the ground. If an arm is suddenly lifted before their eyes the intoxicated animals fall down as if paralyzed with fright. They turn round in circles or do other similar things. In horses other sense-illusions are also produced. The animals behave in such a manner that we must conclude that a special state of mental disorder is present similar to the state of man under the influence of alcohol or other substances. This state lasts for months. During this time the animals refuse to take any other kind of food and greedily seek to procure their old fodder, like the morphinist his morphia. This phase of excitation is succeeded by physical decay to which the animals succumb. This is the cause of great losses in cattle-breeding."—*Phantastica Narcotic and Stimulating Drugs*, by Louis Lewin.

1916? *Sunset Pacific Monthly*, Vol. XXXVI, p. 29: Thereafter she shifted for herself until she made her way west to Colorado and the miner's loco claimed her.

1926 Branch, Douglas, *The Cowboy and His Interpreters*, p. 40: He's the kind of horse with a far-away look. Some folks call 'em locoed.

1929 *United States Daily*, July 1: The purple loco affects horses particularly. The white causes heavy losses of all three classes of animals.

1931 *Lariat*, April, p. 102: Slim, yo're plum loco.

loma (*Spanish*, ló: ma; *English, the same*) A hill; a mound. It is used occasionally in California and the Southwest.

1863 Fergusson, Major D., *Report to Congress*, p. 30: . . . and the new road is to follow the bottom at the edge of the lomas . . .

1930 *New York Times*, June 6: The landscape, usually characterized by bare sand dunes and buttes and lomas of tan and chocolate, was changed into a splash of marvelous color.

1931 Austin, Mary, *Starry Adventure*, p. 41: . . . suddenly, in the dark, fires began to break, through the town and up along the lomas.

machete (*Spanish*, ma: ché: te:; *English*, mə ché ti: *and* mə chet i:) A knife; a cane-knife or any large knife used as a weapon or cutting tool. The cane-knife signification is current chiefly in Cuba and the other sugar-cane regions. Along the Mexico-United States border *machete* is used for the knife as commonly carried by Mexicans chiefly as a means of defense. The *machete* may be nothing more than a case knife well sharpened or it may be of highly refined steel with carved handle. It is usually carried concealed in the belt, the jacket pocket, or other convenient place. During times of quarrels and drunken brawls among the rougher element of Mexicans, *machetes* play freely, either in threats or in actual cutting affrays. As a result knife wounds are common. A "friendly" gash across the cheek, around the neck, or down the side of the head or a slash down the back and the combatants are separated. Those who carry this weapon are in general skillful in its manipulation. It is not uncommon for an argument to be clinched through the quick and dexterous cutting of a hat or shirt of the adversary, perhaps as an indication of what might be done should the argument become more serious. *Machete* is used in the speech of Americans rather commonly along the border. Perhaps there is more atmosphere in the connotation of *machete* than in the word knife or carving knife.

1847 Ruxton, George F., *Adventures in Mexico and the Rocky Mountains*, p. 98: But Juan Maria had fearful odds to contend against and was unarmed save by a small machete.

1889 Ripley, McHatton E., *From Flag to Flag*, p. 235: . . . none of the indigenous fruits and vegetables require more cultivation than the machete affords . . .

1929 Dobie, J. Frank, *A Vaquero of the Brush Country*, p. 267: One of the Mexicans who understood English, rushed at the captain with a *machete* . . .

madroña See MANZANITA; see also Webster's *New International Dictionary*.

maestro (*Spanish*, ma: é:s tro:; *English*, máis tro:) The chief artisan or head workman in a factory where articles are made by hand, such as a shoe factory, or in other industries. The *maestro* is appealed to for advice or for answers to questions arising in the work of other employees. *Maestro* is a term of respect. It indicates skill and ability in a field of one kind or another.

maguey (*Spanish*, ma: gé:; *English*, *the same*) A species of the *Agave Americans*. The term *maguey* is not used with discrimination by Americans, nor by Mexicans, but is applied to the *Agave* of whatever species. The word is used alone, or in conjunction with "plant," as in the "*maguey* plant."

1912? Cozzens, S. W., *The Young Trail Hunters*, p. 216: This beverage is made from the roots of the maguey, a plant common to this region.

mahogany See the *New English Dictionary*.

malpais (*Spanish*, ma:l pa:í:s; *English, the same and* mæl país) Bad country. Usually land covered with lava rock.

1919 Chase, J. Smeaton, *California Desert Trails*, p. 193: The spur ran out at last in a tongue of yellowish rock of the *malpais* kind . . .

1929 Lomax, John A., *Cowboy Songs*, p. 381: A sort of an old outlaw that ran down in the malpais.

manada (*Spanish*, ma: ná: ða:; *English, the same and* mə n ǽ ðə) A herd or flock. A small drove of horses or mules. "In Spain it usually means a flock of sheep."

1929 Dobie, J. Frank, *A Vaquero of the Brush Country*, p. 8: Literally "like a streak of greased lightening" she broke into the manada of mares and colts . . .

mañana (*Spanish*, ma:n já: na:; *English*, mən já: nə *and* mæn jǽ nə) Tomorrow, later; indefinitely later, perhaps never. *Mañana* is universally associated with a policy of postponement and leisureliness commonly assigned to those who speak the Spanish language in any country. Such phrases as "the land of mañana," "they live in the mañana," are commonly and readily understood by Americans everywhere. In the conversation of Americans along the Mexican border the word is, of course, used freely.

1889 Ripley, McHatton E., *From Flag to Flag*, p. 164: Their mañana never came, never was intended to come . . .

1903 Adams, Andy, *Log of a Cowboy*, p. 138: Flood had had years of experience in the land of mañana, where all maxims regarding the value of time are religiously discarded.

1917 McClellan, George B., *The Mexican War Diary*, p. 34: We encamped in a hollow before the town—had a small eggnog and dreamed of a hard piece of work we had to commence on the morrow mañana.

1929 Dobie, J. Frank, *A Vaquero of the Brush Country*, p. ix: He was deep in the joys of constructing, purely in an imaginative and mañana manner, a ten-storied marble hotel . . .

1930 Lyman, George D., *John Marsh, Pioneer*, p. 251: He was well-read, spoke French fluently, but was addicted to indolence and mañana.

n.d. College Song of University of New Mexico: Yes, mañana is the day, When our poco we shall say . . .

mangana (*Spanish*, ma:ŋ gá: na:; *English*, mæŋ gǽn ə) A loop or noose thrown about the fore-feet of an animal in order to tumble the creature to its side with ease. The word is not used except in the parlance of cowboys or others whose work is with and conversation or writing about the cattle or ranching business.

1929 Dobie, J. Frank, *A Vaquero of the Brush Country*, p. 8: I picked up my rope . . . and as she came down the side fence, threw a *mangana* on her fore-feet and at the same time tossed a half hitch over a post . . .

manta (*Spanish* má:n ta:; *English* 'mæn tə) A course, unbleached white cotton cloth used extensively by the Mexicans in Mexico and formerly in the Southwest territory.

manzanita (*Spanish*, ma:n sa: ní:ta; *English*, mæn sə ní: tə *and* mæns ní: tə) Diminutive of *manzana*, apple. A shrub (*Arctostaphylos*, various species; probably *Ahania malvaviscus* also) common to the mountains of the border region and California. The smaller variety resembles a lilac bush in shape but has a rugged red bark and fewer leaves than the lilac. The large, tree variety resembles a cherry tree and also has a mottled red and yellow bark. In popular parlance the smaller species are called *manzanita* bushes and the larger species *manzanita* trees. The fruits are known as *manzanita* berries and are edible. In California a species of *Arctostaphylos* is known by its Spanish name, "madroña."

1872 Evans, A. S., "Manuel" in *The Overland Monthly*, p. 333: . . . she had reached a clump of manzanita-bushes, growing on the edge of a ravine . . .

1903 Austin, Mary, *Land of Little Rain*, p. 86: South the land rises in very blue hills, blue because thickly wooded with ceanothus and manzanita.

1913 Stevenson, R. L., *Silverado Squatters*, p. 19: He taught me the madroña, the manzanita, the buck-eye, the maple.
1931 *Lariat*, April, p. 8: I spot some old renegade steers bunched up in the big manzanita thickets . . .

marihuana English modifications **marajuana, marijuana** (*Spanish*, ma: ri: wá: na:; *English, the same*) Indian hemp. *Hasheesh* (*cannabis indica* and *sativa*). A narcotic plant, the dried leaves of which are used for smoking or for the making of a beverage. The plant grows wild in Mexico and is also cultivated commercially. It is sometimes referred to as the "dope plant." Taken in excess it is said to cause insanity. "When *cannabis indica* is taken in large doses, or when it is smoked, it usually produces a characteristic state of pleasure and exhilaration . . . Very soon after taking a large amount of hashish, the individual passes into a drowsy state, during which he has vivid dreams, and forgets everything—cares, worries, troubles, events which occur about him. He has beautiful visions and is usually joyful and happy." A. S. Blumgarten, *Materia Medica*, p. 285.
1923 Smith, Wallace, *The Little Tigress*, p. 102: The Cockroach is unable to stagger around any more because he has no more *marijuana* to smoke.
1925 Scarborough, Dorothy, *The Wind*, p. 90: Marajuana. That's a Mexican weed that has intoxicatin' properties.
1931 *Salt Lake Tribune*, (Salt Lake, Utah) Aug. 23: Give one of these professional murderers a few whiffs of a marihuana mixed with tobacco and he loses all sense of fear.

matachina dance (*Spanish*, ma: ta: chí: n; *English, the same and* mæ tə chí: nə) A dance or fiesta of dances in which the performers dress themselves as grotesque figures wearing masks and other paraphernalia. The masks usually cover the entire head and body and often are in the likeness of the devil or hideous imaginary creatures.
1929 Applegate, Frank G., *Indian Stories from the Pueblos*, p. 7: There are many different kinds of the matachina dance.

mate South American borrowing.

mayordomo English modification **majordomo** (*Spanish*, mai jor dó: mo:; *English, practically the same*) The head officer of an hacienda; the manager. A wealthy *hacendado* owning several haciendas has under him as many *mayordomos* or *caporales* as there are haciendas. For example; Don Luis Terrazas, former governor of the state of Chihuahua, had many haciendas or ranchos and over each of the larger ones presided either a *mayordomo* or a *caporal* under a *mayordomo*. This word was used in Europe for "head butler" or chief servant in charge of the economic administration of a household or an estate. In America the use of the word has been in connection with the haciendas of the Spaniards and Mexicans and may therefore be listed in this study as an American borrowing. In the mind of the American who uses the word it is not synonymous with butler nor chief servant. The word *mayordomo* connotes distinction and authority just as it did in its earlier significance in Spain.

1844 Gregg, Josiah, *Commerce of the Prairies*, p. 124: I was confident I should meet either with a *mayordomo* or some of the *vaqueros* to whom I could pay the value of the beef . . .

1889 Ripley, McHatton E., *From Flag to Flag*, p. 95: The mayordomo was loud and vociferous in his language . . .

1898 Nicoll, Mrs., *A Ranchwoman in New Mexico*, p. 48: Go, and request the mayordomo to look into this affair.

1912? Cozzens, S. W., *The Young Trail Hunters*, p. 27: I ascertained, however, that Magoffin himself was not with the train, which was in charge of his majordomo, or head man, Don Ignacio.

1930 Lyman, George D., *John Marsh, Pioneer*, p. 208: Next morning, before the others were up, the mayordomo went out to gather wood to cook the breakfast. *Ibid.*, p. 380: . . . he established as mayordomo, John Beener and his pretty Spanish wife.

mecate (*Spanish*, me: ká: te:; *English, the same and* mə ká ti:) From American Indian *mecatl*. A horse hair headstall with lead rope; a horsehair rope. Hair is obtained by clipping the tails of horses, often on the range without permission of the owners. The longest hair possible is obtained. By the aid of a twisting apparatus it is made into strands or *cuerdas* about the size of heavy wrapping cord. These in turn are twisted into a hard rope or *mecate*. The *mecate* is much used as a "tie rope" or "lead rope" on a *cabresto* (*cabestro*). The usefulness of the *mecate* for lassoing purposes is restricted by the fact that it becomes swollen and somewhat unmanageable when wet. See also LARIAT, SOGA, and PITA. *Mecate* is synonymous with rope or *soga* in parts of Texas.

1916 Benedict and Lomax, *Book of Texas*, p. 180: Equally elaborate and beautiful were the mecates made from the tails of mares.

1919 Chase, J. Smeaton, *California Desert Trails*, p. 182: Before I left I bought of him a *mecate* or rope of plaited horsehair, of his own making.

mesa (*Spanish*, mé: sa; *English, the same, also* mɛs ə) A tableland (the word means table in Spanish); any relatively high flat country is termed a *mesa*. *Mesa* has been adopted universally in the United States although the English "table-land" still remains in constant use. *Mesa* is also used as an adjective in such combinations as "up in the mesa country" and the "mesa pasture." Eight states have communities named "Mesa."

1844 Gregg, Josiah, *Commerce of the Prairies*, p. 47: We resumed our march and soon emerged into an open plain or *mesa* which was one of the most monotonous I have ever seen . . .

1882 *Report to House of Representatives, Precious Metals in The United States*, p. 636: The top, sometimes several miles wide, mesa-like and comparatively level.

1912 Hough, Emerson, *The Story of the Cowboy*, p. 19: Snow never falls at this latitude over the lower valleys and mesas.

1916 Lummis, C. F., *The City in the Sky*, p. 59: If there is any sight in the world which will cling to one, undimmed by later impressions it is the first view of Acoma and its valley from the mesa as one comes in from the West.

1926 Cather, Willa, *Death Comes For the Archbishop*, p. 90: Behind their camp, not far away, lay a group of great mesas.

1929 *New York Times*, Sept. 7, p. 1: Report of Party on Mesa Fails on Later Investigation.

meson (*Spanish*, me: só:n; *English, the same*) An inn; a hostelry; rarely used by Americans except in descriptions of Mexico.

1836 Latrobe, Charles Joseph, *The Rambler in Mexico*, p. 61: After some trouble we discovered a poor meson, where we were allowed to dry and refresh ourselves.

mesquital (*Spanish*, me: ski: tá:l; *English*, məs ki: tǽl) A landscape or region covered with mesquite.

1929 Dobie, J. Frank, *The Vaquero of the Brush Country*, p. X: The cattle industry of America began in the *mesquitals* along the Rio Bravo.

mesquite English modifications **mesquit, mesquits, musqueto, musquito, musquit** (*Spanish*, me: skí: te:; *English*, mə skí:t *and* mes kí:t) A shrub or tree the larger *prosopis glandulosa* the smaller *pubescens* that grows in arid regions. Said to be a species of the true *Acacia*. It is found extensively throughout the Southwest and the border territory, especially on the flat or llano country adjacent to hills or mountains. Here it grows very dense in places. The *mesquite* has a small pinnate leaf of a fresh green color. Thorns are found on the shrub in abundance and the wood itself is exceedingly hard. Its chief use is as fuel. But it is gathered for this purpose at the expense of much labor. Occasionally the *mesquite* grows as high as twenty feet. *Pubescens* is sometimes called the "curly mesquite" "screwbean" or tornillo.

1830–1834 Pattie, S., *Early Personal Narratives*, p. 340: A few miserable, stinted shrubberies of a diminutive growth called musqueto wood is only found at intervals.

1834 Struble, George G., *A Visit to Texas*, p. 25: The musquito grass which overspreads the ground is green all the year. Among the timber is also found the mesquito tree, which is very useful for fences and fuel.

1856 Webber, C. W., *Tale of the South Border*, p. 42: He can brag the knot off a musquit limb, and that's tough a little. *Ibid.*, p. 39: The mesquit grass covering this basin was a fresher green than the up-land grass; while the mesquit-timber, a scrubby growth, differed much from the grand live oak, and was destitute of moss.

1917 McClellan, George B., *The Mexican War Diary*, ed. in 1917 by William Starr Meyers, p. 11: The banks are covered with mesquite trees, caves, etc. The ranches are rather sparse . . .

mesquite bean The fruit of the mesquite which grows in a long pod similar to that of the string bean. The bean is sometimes used for food.

mesquite grass See quotations under MESQUITE.

metate English modifications **matete, matet** (*Spanish*, me: tá: te:; *English*, mə tǽ ti:) A rectangular stone, measuring approximately eighteen inches by thirty, on which is ground corn and other grains and food by the natives of Mexico. Porous, volcanic rock which makes an admirable grinding surface is generally used for *metates*. With a few years of use, however, the rock wears down until it is nothing but a shell. The word *metate* is as nearly naturalized as such specialized name words become. The spelling of the word often shows metathesis when it occurs in English writings.

1836 Parker, *A Trip to the West and Texas*, p. 275: You can hear the plump, plump of the metate from the alcoves . . .

1844 Gregg, Josiah, *Commerce of the Prairies*, p. 152: The corn is boiled in water with a little lime; and when it has been sufficiently softened, so as to strip it of its skin, it is ground in the metate, and formed into a thin cake.

1854 Bartlett, John R., *Personal Narrative of Explorations . . .* vol. II, p. 245: Several broken metates, or corn-grinders, lie about the pile.

1889 Ripley, McHatton E., *From Flag to Flag*, p. 112: A few drowsy women with stone metates were laboriously grinding corn for tortillas . . .

1903 North, A. W., *The Mother of California*, p. 123: . . . metates are still in general use for the grinding of corn and wheat for tortillas.

1910 Lummis, C. F., *Lo, Who Is Not Poor?* p. 49: Each brought to an appointed house her metate and sack of corn.

mezcal English modifications **muscal, meschal, mescol, mescal** (*Spanish*, me: ská:l; *English*, mə skǽl) A species of the Agave; a strong alcoholic beverage distilled from the sap of the agave or *pita* root. *Mescal* is one of the varieties of native Mexican intoxicants. Others are *tequila*, (*q.v.*) *pulque*, and *sotol*. As pointed out in the treatment of *tequila* in this study, these terms are not used discriminantingly by Americans although *tequila* and *pulque* are the most commonly used of the four words.

1824–1830 Pattie, S., *Early Personal Narratives*, p. 363: It is of this juice (maguey) they make a kind of whiskey called *vino meschal*.

1903 North, A. W., *The Mother of California*, p. 57: . . . they made and consumed overmuch mescal and wine.

1903 O. Henry, *Heart of the West*, p. 28: . . . her father . . . herded a hundred goats and lived in a continuous drunken dream from drinking *mescal*.

1912? Cozzens, S. W., *The Young Trail Hunters*, p. 216: . . . we came upon a party of Mexicans and Papago Indians, engaged in manufacturing mescal, the native whiskey of the country.

1927 Bolton, H. E., *Fray Juan Crespi*, p. 10: Even the mescal, their daily bread, is not to be found in the great part of the mountains . . .

1932 White, Stewart Edward, "Ranchero," in *Saturday Evening Post*, Jan. 16, p. 6: . . . not every greaser that cashes in from mescal shot Joe Byers.

milpa (*Spanish*, mí:l pa: *English*, míl pə) A small plot of land cultivated by the humbler classes of Indians and Mexicans in the Spanish territories of the United States or Mexico. These plots of land are usually planted to corn or chile and occasionally tomato. The term is becoming more generally known as a result of the increasing number of books written about the Indians of Mexico and simple Mexican life.

1919 Chase, J. Smeaton, *California Desert Trails*, p. 326: After a dozen miles or so we came to a clearing where Mexicans had cultivated their little patches of maize, *milpitas*, as they call them.

mimosa (*Spanish*, mi: mó: sa:; *English*, final ə) A sensitive leguminous plant found in Texas and elsewhere one species of which is notable for the way its long slender leaves contract when touched. *Mimosa* signifies delicate or sensitive in Spanish.

1836 Latrobe, Charles Joseph, *The Rambler in Mexico*, p. 84: The whole of the stony surface of the mountains on both sides of the valley is covered with a profusion of maguey, mimosa, cactus, gigantic nopal or other prickly pear.

1872 Evans, A. S., "Manuel," in *The Overland Monthly*, p. 453: His laugh made her shrink a little—like the *mimosa sensitiva*, when touched by ever so dainty a finger . . .

mochila (*Spanish*, mo: chí: la:; *English, the same and* mo: chíl ə) Originally a military term for knapsack or haversack. During the days of the Pony Express it was applied to the mail pouches built into the skirting of the saddles. Each official Pony Express saddle usually had four such *mochilas*. The word is rarely heard today but is encountered in writings descriptive of the Pony Express.

1932 Chapman, Arthur, *The Pony Express*, p. 234: King's horse stumbled and the rider and *mochila* were thrown off.

mocho (*Spanish*, mó cho:; *English, the same*) From *desmochar* to decapitate or cut off. An animal or a person, usually the former, which is short of some limb or other member of the body. An animal with a bob-tail is, for instance, often characterized as a *mocho*. A burro, or mule, or even a horse that has met with an accident and has lost a portion of an ear, or of its tail, is often given the name of *mocho*. The word provides a convenient descriptive word and synonym for the English "bob-tailed" or "bobbed."

1824–1830 Pattie, S., *Early Personal Narratives*, p. 117: When we had done laughing, Mocho asked us how we baptised among our people.

1853 House of Representatives, *Ex. Doc.* no. 91, p. 123. In the proximity of the Lagoons the trail was on hard clay, and thence to Alamo Mocho it was mostly sand.

mogote (*Spanish*, mo: gó: te:; *English*, mo: gó: ti:) A hillock; applied also to thick patches of shrubbery.

1929 Dobie, J. Frank, *A Vaquero of the Brush Country*, p. 201: I worked for ten years in the *mogotes* of huisache and mesquite . . . *Ibid.*, p. 233: The brush here was rather spotted, very thick in some places with open intervals between the *mogotes*.

moharrie See MUJER.

mole (*Spanish*, mó: le:; *English*, mó: li:) From American Indian *mulli*. A sauce used in Mexican cookery in connection with the serving of meats. Its chief ingredient is chile and sometimes *ajonjoli* (*benne*). *Mole* is not infrequently heard among speakers of English who have been in Mexico or come in contact with Mexican foods. The unpalatability of *mole* to most Americans unaccustomed to *chile* gives it a certain notoriety.

morral (*Spanish*, mo: rrá:l; *English*, mor ǽl) A nose-bag; a feed bag. *Morral* is widely current in the cattle country of the Southwest, particularly in Texas.

mosey "To be off; to leave; to sneak away. A low expression. Sternberg gives 'malter' and 'moulter,' as provincial in Northamptonshire, with the same meaning as to *mosey*. The word more properly originated from the Spanish vamose, very common at the Southwest and in California, which has the same meaning."—Bartlett, John, *Familiar Quotations*.

mosquito See the *New English Dictionary*.

mozo (*Spanish*, mó: so:; *English, the same*). A young man; a servant, assistant or valet; a person in low or humble circumstances. Young men who assist in various occupations and trades such as the cattle industry, pack trains, *et cetera*, are commonly termed mozos.

1836 Latrobe, Charles Joseph, *The Rambler in Mexico*, p. 49: The remainder were sent in advance under his domestics or mozos . . .

1847 Ruxton, George F., *Adventures in Mexico and the Rocky Mountains*, p. 48: I at length hired a mozo to proceed with me as far as Durango . . .

1912 Lawrence, David H., *Corasmin and the Parrots*, p. 23: And . . . the Indian *mozo* looks up at me with his eyes veiled by their own blackness . . .

1923 Smith, Wallace, *The Little Tigress*, p. 5: An aged and stooping mozo came to answer his knocking.

muchacho (*Spanish*, mu: chá: cho:; *English*, mu chǽ cho:) A boy, or youth. *Muchacho* is used for variety or local color occasionally by Americans who have an intimate knowledge of Spanish. The term is generally understood by Americans in the Southwest.

1925 Burns, W. Noble, *The Saga of Billy the Kid*, p. 280: No, muchacho, protested Celsa.

mugre (*Spanish*, mú: gre:; *English*, mú: gri:) Dirty; greasy; general uncleanness. The use of the word has been extended to apply to anyone in disreputable circumstances and occasionally to the lower classes of Indians or Mexicans. Not widely used except by those having an intimate knowledge of Spanish.

mujer English modification **moharrie** (*Spanish*, mu: hé:r; *English, the same and* mu: hé:r i:) Woman; sometimes a girl or young lady. The term is seldom used except for local color or variety; although during a certain period when cowboy life was prominent in the West and Southwest the term was common in his vocabulary. The spelling was often *moharrie* and the pronunciation distinctly Anglicized.

mulada (*Spanish*, mu: lá: ða:; *English, the same, and* mu: lǽ ðə) A drove or herd of mules analogous to *caballada* for a drove of horses. A mixed herd is always termed a *caballada* (*q.v.*) and some-times a herd of mules is thus called. Words like *mulada* are used by Americans because of the convenience over the English method of expressing the idea in a phrase rather than a word. "Wood's Report on the Pacific Wagon-Road, p. 7: As this accident prevented us keeping up with the *mulada* ahead, the conductor went to the assistance of the men driving the herd."—Bartlett, John, *Familiar Quotations.*

mustang (*Spanish, none: English,* məs tæŋ) It is generally conceded that this word is derived from a corruption and combination of the two Spanish words of related meanings, i.e., *mesteno,* signifying something pertaining to the *mesta* or cattle industry and *mostrenco* that which belongs to no one. Although *mustang* is often regarded as signifying the native wild pony of the West, in the Southwest it has also come to be practically synonymous with "horse," "bronc," or "steed." *Mustang* is commonly used in speech and occurs frequently in writings about the West.
1925 Scarborough, Dorothy, *The Wind,* p. 24: . . . the wind comes . . . over the prairie like wild mustangs on a stampede.
1926 Branch, Douglas, *The Cowboy and His Interpreters,* p. 32: The Spanish mustang caught in Texas in the early days of the cattle trade might be a thoroughbred.
1930 Ferber, Edna, *Cimarron,* p. 29: Then something made me turn. The girl had mounted my mustang.

mustangers "The business of entrapping mustangs has given rise to a class of men called mustangers, composed of runaway vagabonds and outlaws of all nations, the legitimate border-ruffians of Texas.—Olmsted's *Texas,* p. 443."—Bartlett, John. *Familiar Quotations.*

navaja (*Spanish* na: vá: ha:; *English, the same*). A pocket-knife.

noche triste (*Spanish,* nó: che: trí: ste:; *English,* nó: chi: trí: sti:) The night of July 1, 1520, when the Spaniards under Cortes were sorely beset by the people of Montezuma on the causeway of Mexico City. It is referred to as the *noche triste* in American histories and other accounts of this particular event.
1865 Brownell, Charles D., *The Indian Races of North and South America,* p. 105: During the "noche triste" . . . eight hundred and seventy Spaniards are recorded to have perished.

1884 Conkling, A. R., *Guide to Mexico*, p. 190: The horse cars run through the Riviera de San Cosme, passing . . . the School of Agriculture, and the noche-triste tree, before reaching their destination.

nopal (*Spanish*, no: pál; *English, the same and* no: pǽl) The flat-leaved prickly pear (*Opuntia chlorotica*). Although the term "prickly pear" is more frequently used by English speaking people along the border, *nopal* seems to be regarded as a bit more learned.
1836 Latrobe, Charles Joseph, *The Rambler in Mexico*, p. 84: The whole of the stony surface . . . is covered with a profusion of maguey, mimosa, cactus, gigantic nopal or other prickly pear . . .

noria (*Spanish*, nó: ri:a; *English*, nór: j:ə) A well; a spring; a water hole. A machine or apparatus for the lifting of water from a well or cistern. In Spanish the word is used synonymously with the word *pozo*. Its use is not extensive in the Southwest.

norte (*Spanish*, nór te: *English* nór ti:) The term *norte*, literally "north," is used to signify the cold, severe winter winds blowing from the north, characteristic of the Gulf of Mexico and adjacent regions. Although *norte* was used commonly by the early colonizers of Texas, the English "norther" was also used. *Norte* is encountered in writings descriptive of the Texan and Mexican territory where such winds prevail.
1836 Latrobe, Charles Joseph, *The Rambler in Mexico*, p. 21: . . . the ill-fated Halcyon . . . had been compelled to speed on the breath of a second violent Norte out of the sea . . .
1840 Turnbull, David, *Travels in the West*, p. 4: The first time there had been some derangement of the machinery; the second it was blowing a norte . . .

novia (*Spanish*, nó: vi:a:; *English*, no: vi:ə Sweetheart; girl friend. The Spanish usage of the word is properly confined to a young lady about to be married, or to one just married. The English usage in the Southwest is more free and *novia* is used interchangeably with "lady friend," "girl," "sweetheart," "dulce," or *moharrie*. Its use is common in Spanish and in spoken informal English.
1929 Dos Passos, John, *42nd Parallel*, p. 322: . . . he [Salvador]

felt romantic and wanted to serenade his novia and they went out.

ocelot See Webster's *New International Dictionary.*

ocote (*Spanish*, o: kó: te:; *English, the same and* o: kó: ti:). A resinous species of pine found in parts of Mexico. The word, being a specialized name, is not encountered frequently.
1927 Lawrence, David H., *Walk to Hyauapa*, p. 29: The mountains are clothed smokily with pine, ocote, and, like a woman in a gauze rebozo.

ocotillo (*Spanish*, o: ko: tí: jo:; *English, the same*) Diminutive of *ocote*. "A tree or shrub of the tamarisk family with long bright scarlet flowers (*Fouquieria splendens*)." This plant is not a cactus although often mistaken as such. It grows in tall stalks about an inch in diameter and is covered completely with long sharp thorns. The *ocotillo* stalks are used extensively by the poorer citizens for making fences about yards and gardens in the Southwest.
1919 Chase, J. Smeaton, *California Desert Trails*, p. 50: The ocotillo, *Fouquieria splendens* (commonly but wrongly taken for a cactus) is to me the most striking and characteristic of the desert plants.
1922 Bogan, P. M., *The Ceremonial Dances of the Yaqui Indians:* . . . the majority are made from upright Sahuaro ribs or Ocatillos . . . but some of the sport small gardens, ramadas and fences.

olla (*Spanish*, ó:l ja: *and* ó: ja:; *English*, ó:jɔ) A vase-like vessel made of baked clay or of hewn stone. *Ollas* are of many sizes. They are used by Americans chiefly as drinking-water containers and coolers. In rural districts in the Southwest it is common to see a large *olla* set in the forks of a tree in the yard or hanging elsewhere in the shade serving as a water cooler. It is frequently wrapped with burlap or other cloth which is kept moist. Smaller *ollas* are used as pitchers, for cooking, and for other purposes.
1847 Ruxton, George F., *Adventures in Mexico and the Rocky Mountains*, p. 70: . . . numerous ollas simmering in the ashes of a fire containing frijoles and chile . . .
1854 Bartlett, John S., *Personal Narrative of Explorations . . .*

Vol. II, p. 360: . . . in all that have been excavated have been found jars (cantaros), pitchers, ollas, etc. of pottery . . .

1919 Chase, J. Smeaton, *California Desert Trails*, p. 30: How many years the *olla* had stood there is a matter for free guessing . . .

1926 Cather, Willa, *Death Comes for the Archbishop*, p. 196: Each woman owed the Padre so many ollas of water a week from the cisterns . . .

olla podrida (*Spanish*, ó: ja po: ðrí: ðә; *English, the same*) A conglomeration of meat and vegetables. Used figuratively to denote a conglomeration of anything, a "hodge podge." Commonly understood in the Southwest and quite commonly used.

1841 McCalla, W. L., *Adventures in Texas*, p. 4: He [the author] hopes that the reader will give him due credit, for the jugulation of matter which would have filled a large volume, besides the olla podrida of an index.

orejano (*Spanish*, o: re: há: no:; *English, the same and* or ә hǽn o:) From *oreja*, ear. A longear; that is, an animal usually cow, calf or steer, that has not been branded or earmarked. Its use at present is less frequent than formerly.

1925 James, Will, *The Drifting Cowboy*, p. 87: I'd find myself all tangled up with a big two-year old "orejana."

pack burro A burro, equipped with a pack saddle or aparejo, used for carrying merchandise. A companion term to the English "packhorse."

1909 Austin, Mary, *Lost Borders*, p. 63: His pack-burro in hobbles strayed off to hunt for a wetter mouthful than the sage afforded.

padre (*Spanish*, pá: ðre:; *English, the same and* pá: dri; also pǽ dri) A priest; a catholic priest; a clergyman. *Padre* was taken into English in Europe and fully naturalized there. Its adoption in America has been just as complete.

1844 Gregg, Josiah, *Commerce of the Prairies*, p. 128: . . . the unsuspecting padre was asleep in the convent.

1845 Stapp, William, *Prisoners of Perote*, p. 76: His reverence, the padre was allowed but little time to enlighten them . . .

1886 McLane, Hiram H., *Irene Viesca*, p. 221: I shall seek repentance and perhaps constitute your padre and make confession.

1902 Atherton, Gertrude, *The Splendid Idle Forties*, p. 26: The padres in their brown hooded robes . . . welcomed the traveller. *Ibid.*, p. 30: . . . not a white man but the padre and his assistant was in it . . .

1906 Stoddard, C. W., "Old Mission Idyls," in *Sunset Magazine*, Vol. XVII, p. 86: Even then the padres . . . selected the most pleasing site for the laying of those consecreated foundations that were so long to outlive them.

1918 White, Steward Edward, *The Forty Niners*, p. 3: The original padres were almost without exception zealously devoted to poverty . . .

1926 Cather, Willa, *Death Comes for the Archbishop*, p. 66: The Bishop was going to Mora to assist the Padre there in disposing of a crowd of refugees . . .

padrino (*Spanish*, pa: ðrí: no:; *English, the same and* pə drí: no:) Literally "godfather" but used in the Southwest to designate the rider who attends a broncobuster while the latter is riding a mean horse in order to assist the buster if necessary; i.e., a hazer.

pagare (*Spanish*, pa: ga: ré:; *English*, pa: gə ré: *and* pæ gə ré:) A note or "due bill"; a promise to pay. The Spanish note form usually begins with the word *pagaré*, i.e., "I will pay," or "I promise to pay." In communities on the Mexican side of the border, where legal documents are worded in Spanish, Americans often refer to notes as *pagares*. The primary accent on the last syllable in Spanish, indicating future tense, is less prominent in English.

paisano (*Spanish*, pa:i: sá: no:; *English, the same and* pai: sǽ no:) From *pais* meaning country. A fellow countryman; a peasant. *Paisano* is often used colloquially. The common species of road runner is called a *paisano* in some sections of the Southwest.

1844 Gregg, Josiah, *Commerce of the Prairies*, p. 195: There is to be found in Chihuahua and other southern districts a very beautiful bird called paisano (literally "countryman").

1885 *Harper's Magazine*, Feb. 4: The paisano deserves . . . kindness from man.

1893 Lummis, C. F., *The Penitent Brothers*, p. 88: Every one was out, but they were no longer the friendly paisanos we had known. *Ibid.*, p. 103: The crucified was . . . lifted to his feet, and carried . . . a stout paisano under each shoulder . . .

palo fierro (*Spanish*, pá: lo: fi:é rro:; *English, practically the same*) A tree-like desert plant (*Olneya tesota*) with dull blue flowers. The fruit of the plant is a bean. *Palo fierro* is found in parts of California and Arizona. The literal translation is "iron wood."

palomino (*Spanish*, pa: lo: mí: no:; *English, the same and* pæ lo: mí: no) Diminutive of *paloma*, dove. A term commonly used in the Southwest and California to describe a horse of a silver yellow color. Such a horse often is given no other name but is known as the *palomino*. *Palominos* are favorites with Western riders and are supposed to be intelligent and enduring.
1932 White, Stewart Edward, "Ranchero," in *Saturday Evening Post*, Apr. 23, p. 19: The *palomino* snorted and leaped. At full speed it raced . . .

palo verde See Webster's *New International Dictionary*.

pampa South American borrowing.

pan dulce (*Spanish*, pa:n dú:l se:; *English, the same and* pæn dú:l si:) Sweet bread; sweet meats. The phrase is only occasionally used by English-speaking people when referring to the particular Mexican confections to be found in border towns.
1922 Bogan, P. M., *The Ceremonial Dances of the Yaqui Indians*, p. 27: Booths for the sale of soda water, pan dulce, pies and coffee appear as if by magic.

panzon (*Spanish*, pa:n só:n; *English, the same and* pæn so:n) Spanish *panza* meaning stomach or belly. *Panzon* is the augmentative of *panza*. *Panzon* is used in describing a person or an animal with a large stomach. Americans acquainted with Spanish occasionally use *panzon* colloquially as a convenient and seemingly unobjectionable substitute for "big-bellied" or "pot-bellied." It is used in such phrases as *muy panzon*, "he is *muy panzon*," "what a *panzon*," etc.

partida (*Spanish*, pa:r tí: ða:; *English* final ə) From *partir*, to divide. A party, a band, squad; an outlaw band.
1929 Dobie, J. Frank, *A Vaquero of the Brush Country*, p. 66: . . . Mustang Gray . . . rounded up a *partida* of Cortina bandits . . .

pasear See PASEO.

paseo (*Spanish,* pa: sé: o :; *English, the same*) A walking trip; a pleasure ride; a public promenade; a trip of almost any kind. *Paseo* seems to add something to the English vocabulary by way of connotation not found in such words as "journey" or "trip." It is quite commonly used by Americans in the Southwest. As indicated by the citatitions the infinitive, *pasear,* is often the form used.

1840 Turnbull, David, *Travels in the West,* p. 57: Next to . . . the paseo, is the public work which his admirers have praised . . . most . . .

1886 Harte, Francis Bret, *The Mourners of Todos Santos,* p. 165: I don't know but I'd take a little *pasear* into the town if I had my horse ready.

1909 Austin, Mary, *Lost Borders,* p. 86: And so, when the camp went on another pasear . . . she stayed. *Ibid.,* p. 99: . . . I learned . . . of his three morning paseos into the hills.

1914 Fitch, A. H., *Junipero Serra,* p. 23: The paseos, or public promenades, were the pride and delight of the people.

1929 Dobie, J. Frank, *A Vaquero of the Brush Country,* p. 129: . . . I made . . . a considerable *pasear* into the Devil's River country to the south and west.

patio (*Spanish,* pá: ti:o:; *English, the same and* pǽ ti:o:) A courtyard; an open garden surrounded by walls; a garden. *Patio* has been fully naturalized in most parts of the United States. The increasing popularity of Spanish architecture in California and other parts of the Southwest may be responsible to some extent for this. *Patio* is usually preferred to the English "courtyard" or "court."

1840 Turnbull, David, *Travels in the West,* p. 61: . . . they . . . are encouraged to amuse themselves . . . in the spacious patio, or inner court, of the building.

1847 Ruxton, George F., *Adventures in Mexico and the Rocky Mountains:* . . . the houses present to the street a blank wall of stone without windows, and one large portal, which leads to the patio-corral, or yard, around which are the rooms . . .

1894 Harte, Francis Bret, *The Mystery of the Hacienda,* "Works" (Argonaut Edition), Vol. 19, p. 213: . . . behind those blistering walls was a reposeful patio surrounded by low-pitched verandas.

1926 Cather, Willa, *Death Comes for the Archbishop,* p. 143: The fellow got to his feet in great confusion, escaping through a door into the patio.

patron (*Spanish*, pa: tró:n; *English, the same and* pə tró:n) Master; chief; head supervisor. The nearest equivalent to the Spanish *patron*, as used in the Southwest, is the English word "boss." *Patron* is commonly used.

1859 Warren, Thomas Robinson, *Dust and Foam*, p. 154: . . . the fifth, the patron or captain, was arrayed in a broad-brimmed hat, in possession of which he considered himself dressed . . .

1931 Austin, Mary, *Starry Adventure*, p. 161: It would be well, while the *Patron* is away, that Alfredo should not come . . .

pedregal English modification **pedrigal** (*Spanish*, pe: dre: gá:l; *English, the same and* pedri gǽl) Spanish *piedra*. A rocky section of country; a lava flow.

1929 *Encyclopaedia Britannica*, 14th Edition, Vol. 6, p. 350: He decided to build a road over the *pedrigal* toward the West.

pelado (*Spanish*, pe: lá: ðo: *and* pe: lá: o:; *English, the same*) From *pelar*—to remove the hair or skin; by extension to strip one of his possessions. A disparaging term applied to persons of the poorer class. Often used in the plural in such a colloquial expression as "a bunch of *pelados*" (pe lá:oz). By extension it is used to describe anything low class as for example "his language was *pelado*." *Pelado* is used with good effect where the significance of the word is generally understood.

1883 Sweet and Knox, *On a Mexican Mustang Through Texas*, p. 556: In nine cases out of ten the men who get up a revolution . . . are foreigners . . . *pelados* (scum), riff-raff, soldiers, God, and liberty . . .

1923 Smith, Wallace, *The Little Tigress*, p. 90: Only the *pelados* —die with their hats on.

1929 Dobie, J. Frank, *A Vaquero of the Brush Country*, p. 173: . . . a few Mexican girls of the *pelado* class danced with him.

1931 *New York Herald Tribune*, July 5, xi, p. 7: At the other extreme . . . is the picaresque type—the life of a young pelado.

peon (*Spanish*, pe: ó:n:; *English*, pi: ó: n *and* pí: ən) From Latin *pedo* meaning foot. A servant; a peasant; a day laborer. *To peon out* is to hire out on a servile basis.

1856 Webber, C. W., *The Tale of the South Border*, p. 43: She has near five hundred peons about her.

1859 Reid, Samuel, *Scouting Expedition*, p. 15: What added to the singularity of the bustling scene . . . was the gangs of peones who were employed in loading teams.

1886 McLane, Hiram H., *Irene Viesca*, Vol. IV, p. 240. The peons increased to such an extent that the patrons made this objection to the abolition of the system.

1894 Harte, Francis Bret, *The Mystery of the Hacienda*, p. 216: But we'll find servants enough in the neighborhood—Mexican peons and Indians

1903 Lummis, C. F., *The Land of Poco Tiempo*, p. 20: They were his peons—slaves without the expense of purchase. And peonage in disguise is still effective in New Mexico. . . . *Ibid.*, p. 218: . . . three peons picked up at Los Pinos, bore their transplantation with singular equanimity.

1912 Hough, Emerson, *The Story of the Cowboy*, p. 3: Life here was very calm, alike for the hacendado and the barefoot peons. *Ibid.*, p. 218. The honest cowboys . . . were referred to as being "peoned out" to their employers . . .

peonage (*English*, pi: ó:n ɪdge or pí: ə nɪdze) From *peon* plus English suffix "age." The state of being a *peon;* a system of serfdom. The term *peonage* is used almost exclusively in referring to the social conditions and class distinction in the Mexican Republic. The word is completely naturalized in the English language.

1903 Lummis, C. F., *The Land of Poco Tiempo*, p. 20: They were his peons—slaves without the expense of purchase. And peonage in disguise is still effective in New Mexico.

1925 Smith, J. Russell, *North America*, p. 678. The debtor cannot stop working for the lender until his debt is paid. Here the system of peonage appears.

petate (*Spanish*, pe: tá: te:; *English*, pə tǽ ti:) A mat usually made of palm-leaf strips or straw loosely woven. Used by humbler Mexicans as a floor covering and, in the absence of chairs for mats to sit on. Bags are made of the *petate* matting and are used in the shipping of rice, coffee, etc. These bags are known as *petates*. Along the border one speaks of a "*petate* of rice" or a "*petate* of coffee."

1847 Ruxton, George F., *Adventures in Mexico and the Rocky Mountains*, p. 118: . . . we had completed out little fort, and

spreading a petate, or mat, the animals were soon at their
suppers of corn . . .

peyote English modifications **piote, pyote** (*Spanish*, pe: jó:
te:; *English*, pi: ó: ti:) A plant of the cactus family (*Mamillaria
fissurata*), sometimes called "dry whiskey," as it is said to produce intoxication when chewed.
1930 Ferber, Edna, *Cimarron*, Her quick eye had leaped to the
   table where lay the little round peyote disk or mescal button
   which is the hashish of the Indian.

picacho (*Spanish*, pi: ká: cho:; *English*, pə: kǽ cho:) A mountain
peak; a projection of rock; a promontory on the landsçape.
Picacho is limited in use but is occasionally heard in the Southwest as the name of some prominent mountainous feature of
landscape.
1903 King, Charles, *An Apache Princess*, p. 207: If Stout made
   even fair time he should have reached the picacho at dusk.
   Ibid., p. 208: Not a sign, except Stout's signal blazes at the
   picacho.

pickaninny (*Spanish* Pequeño niño)"Generally applied to a negro
or mulatto infant in the southern States. Negroes apply the same
term to white children." Bartlett John, *Familiar Quotations*.

pilon English modification **pelon** (*Spanish*, pi: ló:n:; *English,
the same*) A favor; a gratuity. Literally the word signifies a small
cone-shaped cake of sugar. It may be conjectured that a small
dulce of this sort constituted the *pilon* originally. Among the
poorer class of Mexicans it is common to expect from the clerk
at a store, particularly a grocery store or the like, some small gift
or additional portion free of charge after a purchase has been
made. This is the *pilon*. Should the clerk fail to volunteer the
pilon it is not unusual for him to be reminded of it by some such
phrase as *"¿Y el pilon"*? Among Americans dealing with the
Mexican people *pilon* is practically synonymous with the phrase
"one for good measure." An American closing a bargain might
add that he would "throw in" one portion, be it corn, cow, or
horse, for *pilon*.
1883 Sweet and Knox, *On a Mexican Mustang Through Texas*,
   p. 348: Pelon was nothing more nor less than any little trifle
   thrown in, a kind of voluntary commission to the customer.

1887 Gooch, F., *Face to Face with the Mexicans*, p. 90: . . . come what would, he was determined to have his pilon in the market.

piloncillo Diminutive of *pilon*. Brown or cane sugar loaf of conical shape. The standard *piloncillo* cone or loaf as it appears on the market is approximately five inches in length and two inches in diameter at the larger end. *Piloncillo* serves commonly as a candy for Mexicans and American children along the border. By them it is always called *piloncillo* and never cane sugar or candy.

1844 Kendall, George Wilkins, *Narrative of the Texas Santa Fe Expedition*, Vol. II, p. 84: I accepted his offer so far as to purchase some clothing, chocolate, piloncillos, and other little luxuries for the road . . .

piñata (*Spanish*, pi:n já: ta:; *English, the same*) From Spanish *piña*, *piñe* cone or *pine* nut. (1) A bag containing nuts and other confections usually suspended from the ceiling or other overhead object, in connection with a Christmas celebration. (2) A party at which a *piñata* is a feature. The *piñata* feature constitutes the climax of the celebration. Near the end of the party someone is blindfolded, given a rod or staff, and requested to strike down the *piñata*. When the *piñata* bag or jar breaks the contents scatter on the floor and a general scramble is made by all participants to acquire a share of the confections. High school and college Spanish clubs sometimes make the use of *piñata* a feature at Christmas parties.

1930 Purnell and Weathereaux, *The Talking Bird*, p. 22: After the corn eating there had been piñatas for the children.

pinole (*Spanish*, pi: nó: le:; *English*, pi: nó: li:) From American Indian *pinolli*. A gruel-like beverage made from parched corn ground and mixed with sweetening. *Pinole* may likewise be made from the vanilla bean and other such spices. The word has become generally known in the United States.

1844 Gregg, Josiah, *Commerce of the Prairies*, p. 54: . . . a bag of bread and maybe another of pinole which they barter away to the savages for horses and mules. *Ibid.*, p. 159: This pod [they] grind into flour to make their favorite *pinole*.

1848 Emory, W. H., *Notes of a Military Reconnoissance*, p. 85: Several acquaintances . . . offered water melons and pinole.

Pinole is the heart of Indian corn, baked, ground up, and mixed in sugar.

1919 Chase, J. Smeaton, *California Desert Trails*, p. 78: Mixed with flour it becomes the famous *pinole* of the Mexicans, the staff of life of the common people.

piñon See Webster's *New International Dictionary*.

pinto (*Spanish*, pí:n to:; *English*, pɪ:n to: *and* pɪn to:). From *pintar*, to paint. Piebald, dappled, spotted. *Pinto* is encountered commonly in written English and is used in the Southwest in preference to piebald. It is common as a proper name for spotted horses.

1885 Harte, Francis Bret, *Maruja*, It was you, who took before you on your pinto horse.

1902 Connor, Ralph, *Sky Pilot*, p. 9: She sprung upon her pinto and set off down the trail.

1922 Rollins, Philip Ashton, *The Story of the Cowboy*, p. 140: What makes a pinto the hardest bucker of all?

1925 Burns, W. N., *The Saga of Billy the Kid*, p. 236: "Dad" Peppin's pinto pony was lame in its off hind foot . . .

1929 La Farge, O., *Laughing Boy*, p. 134: One day he met two braves . . . one on a roan and one on a pinto.

1930 Ferber, Edna, *Cimarron*, p. 86: Indian ponies, pintos, pack horses . . . and occasionally a flashing eyed creature who spurned the red clay with the disdainful hoof . . .

pita (*Spanish*, pí: ta:; *English*, pi: tə) Probably from Peruvian. The fiber of the *maguey* plant or the *agave*. *Lazo* rope is made of this fiber. The *pita* fiber when twisted into a rope makes a very strong and hard cord known as a *pita* or a *maguey*. It is the most commonly used lassoing cord of the vaqueros and cowboys in the Southwest. The fact that it is cheaper than the leather *reata* and serves for all general purposes as well as does the latter accounts for its commonness among cowboys. There are several kinds of *pita* classified by connoisseurs of lassoing rope according to the fiber from which they are made and the characteristic "twist" by which they are put together.

1844 Gregg, Josiah, *Commerce of the Prairies*, p. 88: There is one species whose fibres, known in the country as *pita* are nearly as fine as dressed hemp, and are generally used for sewing shoes, saddlery, and similar purposes.

1889 Ripley, McHatton E., *From Flag to Flag*, p. 235: The cordage, ropes, and bridles of pita caruja are strong and durable.

placer (*Spanish*, pla: sé:r; *English*, plǽ ser) appears also as place mine From Spanish *placer* meaning a bank of sand. (1) The mining process whereby gold or other metals are extracted from sand, gravel or dirt deposits. (2) The location or mine site itself. Adopted by the mining industry in the Southwest and California during the nineteenth century. The fact that one of the best-known mines of New Mexico in the early nineteenth century was known as *El Placer* may account in part for the general currency of *placer* in mining circles.

1844 Gregg, Josiah, *Commerce of the Prairies*, p. 175: . . . at a point called Sangre de Cristo a very rich placer has been discovered.

1858 Lowell, James Russell, *Study Wind*, p. 296: It is a vast placer full of nuggets.

1883 Ingersol, Ernest, *Knocking Round the Rockies*, p. 85: Therefore placer-gold is sometimes known as "floated" gold.

1909 *The Evening Post*, New York, Feb. 22: A placer-mine was the ideal poor man's mine from which with simple contrivance of a sluice box he washed out the precious nuggets of gold from the gravelly soil of mountain gulches . . .

1927 Read, G. W., *A Pioneer of 1850* The old placers are still exceedingly productive and new ones are almost daily discovered.

placeta (*Spanish*, pla: sé: ta:; *English, the same and* pla: sí: tə) A small plaza or court. *Placeta* is a diminutive of Spanish *plaza* and practically synonymous with it in both Spanish and English.

1925 Burns, W. N., *The Saga of Billy the Kid*, p. 53: A rude balladry in Spanish and English has grown up about him, and in every placeta in New Mexico, Mexican girls sing to their guitars songs of Billy the Kid.

1931 *Lariat*, Apr., p. 27: Anyway, he pulled me out . . . down at a placita by the Brushy Ford.

plata (*Spanish*, plá: ta:; *English*, plǽ tə) Silver; along the border where Mexican and American silver coins are in circulation the term *plata* is commonly applied to the Mexican coins. One speaks of fifty cents *plata* meaning fifty cents Mexican silver.

1932 Private correspondence: Everything is figured in plata for next year and there is a reduction in all prices.

playa See Webster's *New International Dictionary.*

plaza (*Spanish*, plá: sa:; *English*, plǽ zə) A public square; a park. It is customary in Spanish-American towns to set apart in a central location a square for public purposes such as meetings, concerts, entertainments, fiestas and other celebrations, as well as for less formal recreation. Many towns and cities in the Southwest have retained, intact, the old *plaza publica* of Spanish days. The word *plaza* is fully naturalized in the region where such *plazas* are still maintained and is generally known throughout the United States.

1836 Latrobe, Charles Joseph, *The Rambler in Mexico*, p. 79: . . . our party entered . . . across the Plaza, with ringing spurs and jingling arms . . .

1844 Gregg, Josiah, *Commerce of the Prairies*, p. 111: Each . . . on driving through the streets and the plaza publica, everyone strives to outdo his comrades . . .

1859 Reid, Samuel, *Scouting Expedition*, p. 103: Ancient Cathedrals and churches stood gray with age before the grass-grown plazas.

1891 Cody, William Frederick, *Heroes of the Planes*, p. 287: . . . the Mexicans retreated to what had been a monastery . . . which stood opposite the plaza.

1897 Lummis, C. F., *Lo, Who is not Poor?* p. 53: . . . the terraces and doors facing only the safe plaza . . . were eloquent witnesses to the dangers of old . . .

1926 Cather, Willa, *Death Comes for the Archbishop*, p. 82: Every Sunday her carriage . . . waited in the plaza after mass . . .

1927 Lawrence, David H., *Walk to Huayapa*, p. 39: In front of the church is a rocky *plaza*, leaking with grass . . .

1929 *San Antonio Express*, June 2: . . . on the northwest west corner of North Bridge Street and the *plaza* . . .

pobrecito (*Spanish*, pó: bre: sí: to:; *English, the same*) An expression of sympathy and pity meaning literally poor little thing.

1923 Smith, Wallace, *The Little Tigress*, p. 59: He is captain of the guard. But he has fallen asleep. Pobrecito!

poco (*Spanish*, pó: ko:; *English, the same*) A small amount. *Poco* is often used in connection with such words as *tiempo, malo* or *frio*. It is commonly used by Americans in the border territory. n.d., College Song of the University of Nex Mexico: Yes, mañana is the Day When our poco we shall say.

poncho (*Spanish*, pó:n cho:; *English, the same, and* pa:n cho:) A blanket-like covering used by Mexicans and cowboys as a protection against the weather and for sleeping purposes when out camping. The official *poncho* usually has a hole cut in the center through which the head of the wearer is inserted so that the *poncho* rests directly on the shoulders. See also SERAPE.
1844 Kendall, George Wilkins, *A Narrative of the Texan Santa Fe Expedition*, p. 315: Over his uniform he now wore a poncho of the finest blue broadcloth, wrought with various devices in gold and silver, and through the hole in the center peered the head . . .

posada (*Spanish*, po: sá: ða:; *English* final ə) From *posar*, to stay. A guest house; an inn; a hostelry. *Posada* is synonymous with the Spanish word *meson*. Its occurrence is limited in American English to descriptions or narratives about Mexican territory in the Southwest although it was used in England according to the *New English Dictionary*.
1889 Ripley, McHatton E., *From Flag to Flag*, p. 114: The posada did not close its doors till a very late hour . . .
1891 Harte, Francis Bret, *Tam Tassajara*, Vol. II, p. 102: There were some Mexicans lounging about the *posada*.
1917 McClellan, George B. *The Mexican War Diary*, ed. by William Starr Meyers, 1917, p. 91: Soon after we had established ourselves at the posada we were astonished by a great commotion in the streets.

potato See the *New English Dictionary*.

potro (*Spanish*, pó: tro:; *English, the same*) A colt; a young horse; used interchangeably with *colt* by ranchers and cattlemen in the Southwest.
1929 Dobie, J. Frank, *A Vaquero of the Brush Country*, p. 8: . . . a rancher told me that if I would break seven wild *potros* (young horses) he would let me have my pick of the seven.

pozo (*Spanish*, pó: so: *English*, pó: so: *and* pó: zo) A water hole; a well; a cistern; a spring. *Pozo* is restricted in written use to descriptive or other writings dealing with the Spanish American territory in the Southwest and elsewhere. In spoken English in the Southwest its use is not uncommon among those who know Spanish well.

1863 Fergusson, Major D., *Report to Congress*, . . . I left . . . the boat in a gulley near the beach and the "Pozo" partially filled with sand . . . *Ibid*. There are seven arrastras at work at the pozo reducing silver.

presidente (*Spanish*, pre: si: ð̵é:n te:; *English*, prez: ɪ dɛn ti:) A local government official; a civil officer holding powers corresponding to those held by both the police chief and a judge of a district court. The smaller towns in Mexico and formerly in all Spanish territory now a part of United States were governed by a *presidente* under whom operated a few *comisarios* or policemen. Americans invariably use the term *presidente* when referring to the officer in question.

1863 Fergusson, Major D., *Report to Congress*, p. 2: The "presidente" of the municipality . . . has set about repairing and changing the road in the vicinity. *Ibid*., p. 16: . . . the presidente has given orders to construct a new road to the left of the present one.

1923 Smith, Wallace, *The Little Tigress*, p. 166: But the white-whiskered presidente changed that.

1929 Private Correspondence, July 3: Although the presidente says he will marry any couple found out together after ten o'clock we have been out until after twelve every night.

presidio (*Spanish*, pre: sí: ð̵i:o:; *English*, *the same and* prɔ sí dɪ o:) A military stronghold; a fort. *Presidios* were established early by the Spanish explorers and colonizers throughout the Southwest and California. A few of the old sites of *presidios* have developed into present day cities; one at least still carries the name.

1844 Kendall, George W., *Narrative of the Texan Santa Fe Expedition*, Vol. II, p. 66: On arriving at the presidio we were halted and counted.

1847 Ruxton, George F., *Adventures in Mexico and the Rocky Mountains*, p. 168: El Paso is situated at the head of the valley and at the other extremity is the presidio . . .

1891 Blackmar, Frank W., *Spanish Institutions of the Southwest*. Around the presidio were located the traders, the families of the soldiers, and numerous settlers . . .

1914 Fitch, A. H., *Junipero Serra*, p. 153: The business of selecting a suitable site for the presidio and mission soon occupied the attention of the Spanish.
1929 Stoddard, C. W., "Old Mission Idyls," in *Sunset Magazine*, Vol. XVII, p. 89: The presidio had two gates, open by day but closed at night.

pronto (*Spanish*, pró:n to:; *English, the same and* prón to:) Quickly; suddenly; hurry. *Pronto* is used in conversation, by those acquainted with Spanish, to indicate the same meaning as any of the following English phrases: "Quickly," "hurry up," "get a move on you," "be quick about it," "get along," "very soon." It is often used in combination with the Spanish word *andale* from the Spanish phrase *andale pronto* meaning "move along fast." In written English it is used chiefly for picturesqueness or local color. *Pronto* is commonly understood throughout the United States and is common as army slang.
1903 O. Henry, *Heart of the West*, p. 147: Get him and saddle him as quick as you can. "Prontito, *senor*."
1912 Hough, Emerson, *The Covered Wagon*, p. 47: But she heard the rush of hoofs and the high call of Basion's voice back of her: "Ho, pronto, pronto!"
1917 Chapman, Arthur, *Out Where The West Begins*, p. 5: This game of get-rich-pronto seems a foolish sort of thing.
1925 James, Will, *The Drifting Cowboy*, p. 11: Me being only about a thousand pounds lighter than that shadow I'm knocked out of the way pronto.
1925 Scarborough, Dorothy, *The Wind*, p. 37: You'll have to get ready and be off *pronto* . . . *Ibid* p. 96: Now you pick them up *pronto!*
1931 Austin, Mary, *Starry Adventure*, p. 308: . . . see that he gets off the place. *Pronto!*

pronunciamiento (*Spanish*, pro: nú:n si:a mié:n to:; *English, the same*) A proclamation; a pronouncement; a report. Also a revolutionary uprising. The revolters themselves are sometimes termed *pronunciados* (pro: nu:n si: á:os).

pulque (*Spanish*, pú:l ke:; *English, the same*) An alcoholic beverage distilled from the sap of the maguey. Of the four Mexican beverages, *sotol, mescal, tequila,* and *pulque,* the latter is the most generally used and the best known to Americans.

1929 Dos Passos, John, 42nd *Parallel*, p. 317: They drank pulque and they had a bottle of whisky with them . . .
1930 Purnell and Weathereaux, *The Talking Bird*, p. 48: King Zotzel was greedy first for another king's kingdom, and later for the pulque.

pulqueria (*Spanish*, pu:l qe: rí:a:; *English*, final ə) A shop where pulque is sold; a saloon.
1847 Ruxton, George F., *Adventures in Mexico and the Rocky Mountains*, p. 43: After leaving the pulqueria we visited . . . the dens . . . *Ibid.*, p. 68: . . . I was detected as a stranger by a knot of idle rascals standing at the door of a pulque-shop . . .
1923 Smith, Wallace, *The Little Tigress*, p. 163: Do you think you are in some low *pulqueria?*

puma South American borrowing.

puro oro (*Spanish*, pú: ro: ó: ro:; *English, the same*) Literally, pure gold. A synonym for the colloquialism "cold cash" or "spot cash."
1929 Dobie, J. Frank, *A Vaquero of the Brush Country*, p. 269: I plugged down $500 *puro oro* on the jack for an ace.

quadroon See the *New English Dictionary*.

que dice (*Spanish*, ke: dí: se:; *English, the same and* ke: dí: si) "What do you say?" in its slang sense: "What do you think about it?" This expression is used in informal conversation or informal writing by those Americans in close contact with Spanish.
que hubo le (*Spanish*, ke: ú: bo: le:; *English*, ke: u: bo: le *and* ki:u: bo: le) Hello; the term is common as an informal salutation among younger Americans. It is often shortened to *kiu: bo:* or *kiu: bo: li:*.

que le hace (*Spanish*, ké: le: á: se:; *English*, ké: li: ǽsi:) "What do I care?" "What difference does it make?" "No matter." An expression used informally and often accompanied by a significant shrug of the shoulders. It use is restricted to those Americans who have had intimate contact with Spanish. Among such it is used naturally, effectively and often.

querida (*Spanish*, ke: rí: ða:; *English, the same and* kɛr í: də) From *querer* to wish or to love. Sweetheart; dear one; well beloved. In the Southwest one may speak informally of "going to see his *querida.*" *Queredisima*, the intensified form is also used.

1925 Burns, W. N., *The Saga of Billy the Kid*, p. 185: In every placeta in the Pecos some little senorita was proud to be known as his querida.

1930 Harris, Frank, *Reminiscences of a Cowboy*, p. 71: Some of them were very pretty, and soon I was seeing Rosariga— Charles' querida—a very pretty girl.

1931 Raynolds, Robert, *Brothers in the West*, p. 243: . . . she pressed her palm against his forehead . . . and said with a low fierceness, a passion that must have sunk into his heart, . . . queridisimo! queridisimo!

que tal (*Spanish*, ke: táːl; *English, the same*) "How goes the world?" "How do you like it?" "What success?" etc. This neat phrase has found a useful place in the popular vocabulary of Americans along the border. It is the most succinct phrase to use when inquiring into the condition of any situation or learning one's reaction to anything used or tried out or experimented with. It is restricted to individuals having a working knowledge of Spanish.

1930 Ferber, Edna, *Cimarron*, p. 122: He looked at the Spaniard. Miro eyes him innocently "Que tal?"

quien sabe English modifications, **quien savvy, no savvy** (*Spanish*, kiːén sáːbeː; *English*, kiːen sǽ biː, kɪ n sǽ biː, kɪ en sǽ viː, kɪn sǽviː) Who knows? I don't know. (Often implying "It is none of my affair"). Few Spanish words or phrases are more used in modern Wild West fiction or other writings with a Spanish-American setting. In spoken conversation the use of *"quien sabe?"* is often accompanied by a non-committal shrug of the shoulders.

1859 Reid, Samuel C. J., *Scouting Expedition*, p. 53: . . . the government was charitably bound to suppose . . . they had recklessly laid violent hands upon their own lives! "Quien sabe?"

1888 Johnstone, E. M. *By Semi-Tropic Seas:* . . . they [hieroglyphics] may have been . . . meaningless figures in the sand and on the rocks. Quien sabe?

1912? Cozzens, S. W., *The Young Trail Hunters*, p. 84: . . . he will simply shrug his shoulders and say, "Quien sabe?"

1912 Hough, Emerson, *The Story of the Cowboy*, p. 3: The cattle might have come from another land, at another time. Quien sabe?

1916 Benedict, H. V. and Lomax, John, *Book of Texas*, p. 181: Even more curious were such brands as the quien sabe? *Ibid.*, p. 199: But the decline in production of honey may have robbed Uvalde of her world's championship. Quien sabe?

quien vive English modification **King Beebe** (facetious) (*Spanish*, ki:e:n ví: ve:; *English*, ki:e:n ví: vi: *and* kɪn vi: vi:) Halt! Who goes there? In other words "Declare yourself, whom would you have live?" This phrase is the universal challenging call by Mexican soldiers, doing guard duty, to unknown persons who may come into their territory of duty. By English-speaking people it is used chiefly in indirect quotation or narration. *Quien vive*, therefore, is not extensively used in English.

1859 Reid, Samuel C., Jr., *Scouting Expeditions*, p. 233: The scouting party was immediately challenged with quien vive?

1889 Ripley, McHatton, E., *From Flag to Flag*, p. 115: I have the password; why when one of them lightening-bug fellows [alluding to lanterns they carried] ses to me, King Beebe (quien vive) I jes ses back to him—Lem me go! (Amigo!) and they let me go right on.

1923 Smith, Wallace, *The Little Tigress*, p. 165: Quien vive? There is a pointed rifle with a nervous, impatient finger at the trigger.

quinine South American borrowing.

quirt See CUARTA.

ramada (*Spanish*, ra: má: ða:; *English, the same and* rə mǽ ðə) From *rama*, branch or limb. An improvised shelter or shed made of tree branches with the leaves left on. The *ramada* is a common thing in the Southwest both for temporary and permanent use.

1919 Chase, J. Smeaton, *California Desert Trails*, p. 316: . . . the family was already breakfasting . . . under the *ramada*, or brush-roofed shed, which is the general living-room during the hot months.

1931 Austin, Mary, *Starry Adventure*, p. 355: . . . Eurdora had sent all over the State for grapevines of the old Colonial stock for the ramada.

ramal English modification, **romal** (*Spanish*, ra: má:l; *English*, rə mǽl *and* ro: mǽl) From *rama*, branch. A thong usually braided and divided into lashes, attached to the saddle or reins and used as a "quirt."

rancher See ranchero.

rancheral (*Spanish*, ra:n che:rá:l; *English*, ræn cher ǽl) Pertaining to a ranch.
1847 Ruxton, George F., *Adventures in Mexico and the Rocky Mountains*, p. 94: . . . he who bore away the palm of rancheral superiority was the third son . . .

rancheria (*Spanish*, ra:n che: rí:a; *English*, ræn chur ía) Recorded usage indicates that the word was sometimes applied to a temporary *junta* of *rancheros* with their tents, families, and equipment. It was also synonymous with "rancho." Its use in English today is not common except in historical writings. The Spanish meaning is "a collection of ranchos" or rude dwellings.
1844 Gregg, Josiah, *Commerce of the Prairies*, p. 301: . . . I happened to pass near their rancherias (temporary villages) with a small caravan which mustered about thirty-five men.
1912? Cozzens, S. W., *The Young Trail Hunters*, p. 183: . . . he managed to remove the skin from both animals; and . . . bore them in triumph to the rancheria, . . .
1914 Fitch, A. H., *Junipero Serra*, p. 222: There were many rancherias on the banks of the Colorado.

ranchero (*Spanish*, ra:n ché: ro:; *English*, ræn chér o:) One who lives on or operates a ranch or rancho; a rancher; a cattleman; a dairyman. Its use is not so common now as it was during the latter part of the nineteenth century. Rancher is used more commonly today. A *ranchero* is always a Mexican; a "rancher" may be either Mexican or American.
1836 Latrobe, Charles Joseph, *The Rambler in Mexico* . . . p. 27: you have here . . . every degree from the substantial *Ranchero*, bespurred, embroidered vest, and gaudy *serape;* or the trusty *arriero*, with his long string of mules, his previous cargo of specie, and his train of assistant mozos . . .
1847 Ruxton, George F., *Adventures in Mexico and the Rocky Mountains*, p. 30: . . . there is hardly a ranchero who is not in league with the robbers . . .

1856 Webber, C. W., *Tale of the South Border*, p. 10: Wonderful indeed were the narrations which he had to give concerning its Mexican rancheros, traders, and robbers.

1889 Ripley, McHatton E., *Rough and Ready Annual*, p. 246: Altogether it was a motley procession—rancheros, officers, soldiers, women, children, mustangs, burros, burrestos, parrots, dogs, monkeys, and heaven knows what else, I don't!

1912 Hough, Emerson, *Story of the Cowboy*, p. 124: All the gold of the cattle range lay before the first ranchero, all the untouched resources of an empire.

1912 Stevenson, R. L., *The Silverado Squatters*, p. 19: I think we passed but one ranchero's house in the whole distance . . .

1926 Cather, Willa, *Death Comes for the Archbishop*, p. 81: . . . he and the *rancheros* had run their church to suit themselves, making a very gay affair of it.

1929 *New York Herald Tribune*, Aug. 20: There is a very funny story of a ranchero . . .

ranching (*English*, ræn chiːn) The participle of "to ranch." It is likely that the verb forms come directly from English "ranch" and not from Spanish *rancho*. *Ranching* is a relatively late development of the word. No example of its usage was found for the period when *rancho* and not "ranch" is the form recorded. No example of *ranchoing* was encountered in writings or in spoken language. The word is also used as an adjective in such phrases as "a ranching outfit."

1912 Hough, Emerson, *The Story of the Cowboy*, p. 79: This ended what was probably one of the very first of the attempts at horse ranching east of the Rockies on the cow range.

1929 *Provo Herald* (Provo, Utah), Aug. 16, . . . Russ Mangleby, halfback, is ranching near his home town . . . "red" Clark . . . is ranching in Nevada . . . Pearl Pollard . . . is ranching at Winnifred, Montana . . .

rancho English modifications **ranch, ranche** (*Spanish*, raːn choː; *English*, ræntʃ and ræn choː) A stock-raising establishment for cattle, sheep or horses; a farm; an orchard; a country place where livestock of any kind are raised as, for instance, a rabbit ranch, a chicken ranch or a turkey ranch. Also a resort or retreat in the West or Southwest where guests, that is, tourists or those on vacation, may live an out-of-door life similar to that of cowboys. Such a place is usually known as a "dude ranch" or a "guest ranch." *Ranch* has been completely taken over by English and serves usefully indeed, whether alone or in combinations such as "rancher," "ranchman," "ranchwoman," "ranch house," "ranch owner," etc.

1841 McCalla, W. L. *Adventures in Texas*, p. 38: I . . . encamped with the party on the Sevilla Creek on which Patton's rancho was soon after attacked by Indians . . .

1844 Kendall, George Wilkins, *Narrative of the Texan Santa Fe Expedition*, p. 269: The shepherd had sent to their rancho, or farm, during the night and supplied themselves with flour.

1856 Webber, C. W., *Tale of the South Border*, p. 39: Facing me, were three stockade-houses, or lesser "ranchos."

1894 Harte, Francis Bret, *The Mystery of the Hacienda*, p. 238: . . . haven't I seen all sorts of queer figures creeping along by the brink after nightfall between San Gregorio and the next rancho?

1914 Thomas, Augustus, *Arizona*, p. 56: That's one of the vaqueros on the ranch here.

1929 *San Antonio Express* (Advertising Section), June 2: Bargain of Bargains, Goat, Sheep and Cattle Ranch; Chicken Ranch Supreme, Finest in South Texas, 15 acres . . . Goat and Cattle Ranch $6 . . . located about 125 miles southwest of San Antonio . . . Chicken ranch, at station, 20 acres . . . chickens, cows . . .

real (*Spanish*, re: ál *and plural* re: á:le:s:; *English*, ri: ǽl *and plural* ri: ǽl i:z *or* ri: ǽl s). A monetary denomination; a coin; a bit; usually for the amount of twelve and a half centavos. The word is not used so commonly as the English "bit" but one does hear occasionally such expressions as "I give him a couple of reales." It is possible, however, that the common use of *dos reales, seis reales, ocho reales* by the Spanish-speaking element along the border has increased the use of the English "two bits," "four bits," and "six bits" in the same region.

1840 Dana, R. H., *Two Years Before the Mast*, . . . without a real in his pockets and absolutely suffering for something to eat . . .

1844 Gregg, Josiah, *Commerce of the Prairies*, p. 112: . . . both plain and twilled stripes . . . are rated at two or three *reales* per *vera. Ibid.*, p. 173: When short of means they often support themselves upon only a real each per day.

1903 O. Henry, *Heart of the West*, p. 28: The man sawed them [coconuts] in two and made dippers which he sold for two *reales* each.

1930 Duffus, R. L., *The Santa Fe Trail*, p. 28: . . . their profits, owing partly to an ingenious system of accounting, by which a "dollar" might mean eight, six, four or only two reales, were large.

1930 Lyman, George D., *John Marsh, Pioneer*, p. 246: He ended the conversation by remarking that his guests had already cost him over one hundred dollars, and that God knew whether he would ever get a real in return.

reata English modifications **lariat, lariette** (*Spanish*, re:á: ta:; *English*, ri: ǽtə, lær i:ét) From *reatar* to retie or re-bind, hence the word *reata* in Spain means a cord with which to tie horses together so that they will travel in a line. It also means a line of horses thus tied. In America *reata* signifies a cord or rope made of woven or braided leather or rawhide strands; a hard-twisted rope of any kind used for lassoing purposes. *Reata*, the Spanish form of the word, is used about as often by English-speaking cowboys and others along the border as *lariat*. Grammatically, of course, it is more correct to say "This is my *reata*" than to say "This is my *lariat*." The latter when translated is literally "This is my *the* rope"; *lariat* being nothing more than an adaptation of *la reata*, "the rope." It is true that *lariat* has been extended to include any rope used for lassoing, much more generally than has *reata* and both terms are used loosely for *mecate* the proper name for a rope made of horsehair, and for *pita* the lasso rope made of hemp (*cañamo*). The early use of *lariat* by Americans who visited or lived in the frontier country indicates that it was taken by them to signify a rope for picketing animals while they fed either at noontime, or at other resting periods. This restricted usage was not long current. Properly it applies, in the border regions at least, to the particular rope made of braided leather or rawhide. Other names are assigned to other kinds of rope. See also MECATE, PITA, and SOGA for additional information about ropes.

1838 Irving, Washington, *A Tour of the Prairies*, He was again led forth by . . . a long halter or lariat.

1841 McCalla, W. L., *Adventures in Texas*, p. 27: . . . during the day I had purchased a lariat from a Mexican.

1844 Kendall, George Wilkins, *Narrative of the Texan Santa Fe Expedition*, p. 93: It is deemed that they [rattlesnakes] will never cross a hair lariat.

1856 Webber, C. W., *Tale of the South Border*, p. 78: The bridle, lariat, quirt, and buffalo-robe had belonged to some Comanche warrior . . .

1876 Besant and Rice, *Golden Butterfly*, p. 3: The horsehair lariette which serves for lassoing by day and for keeping off snakes at night.

1891 Cody, William F., *Heroes of the Plains*, p. 642: On the second day I lariated, or roped a big buffalo . . .

1903 King, Charles, *An Apache Princess*, p. 11: . . . but never mustering energy enough to stamp a hoof or strain a thread of his horsehair reata.

1926 Branch, Douglas, *The Cowboy and His Interpreters*, p. 18: Fifty dollars for a gold-mounted sombrero, another fifty for a blanket, and twenty-five for a quirt and a lariat.

reboso English modifications **rebosa, robezo, rebozo** (*Spanish and English,* re: bó: so:) A shawl-like covering for the head and shoulders worn by Mexican and Spanish women in Mexico and along the border. It is made of cloth, cotton or silk and usually black or of other dark color.

1836 Latrobe, Charles Joseph, *The Rambler in Mexico* . . . the population was partly engaged in the manufacture of the cotton cloth which serves as *reboso* . . .

1845 Stapp, William P., *Prisoners of Perote*, p. 110: A woman with her head and face enveloped in a battered reboso, stood under the sombre doorway as we entered . . .

1856 Webber, C. W., *Tale of the South Border*, p. 190: . . . the men in white cotton shirts, loose trousers, and . . . the women in striped "robesos" . . .

1909 Austin, Mary, *Lost Borders*, p. 167: Marguerita leaned her fat arms on the table, wrapped in her blue rebosa.

remuda (*Spanish,* re: mú: ða:; *English,* rə mú: ðə; *also* rə mú: ðər) The horses, mules and other riding, pack, or harness animals of a ranching, camping, freighting, or traveling outfit or expedition when considered as a group, as for example, when they are out for the night feeding together. In such companies or expeditions a member (wrangler) or members of the party are usually assigned the responsibility of taking out the *remuda* to suitable grazing grounds and bringing it in when the outfit is ready to move. One or more of the *remuda* is usually equipped with a bell to facilitate locating the *remuda* when it is wanted. *Remuda* is practically synonymous with *caballada* but is used more generally; *caballada* being rather restricted to cattlemen parlance. *Remuda* is a useful acquisition and widely used in the Southwest but it is difficult to determine how permanently it is established in the vocabulary of the English language. Although the general meaning of *remuda* signifies a change, i.e., of clothes or any such thing, its meaning in America has been specialized as indicated in the foregoing explanation.

1925 James, Will, *The Drifting Cowboy*, p. 10: . . . I sure had to do some tall scrambling when the remuda broke out of the corral.

1925 Burns, W. N., *The Saga of Billy the Kid*, p. 1: He came with . . . a caravan of wagons, a remuda of cow ponies . . .

1926 Branch, Douglas, *The Cowboy and His Interpreters*, p. 43: . . . the cowboy . . . held the *remuda* overnight in a rope corral.

1931 *New York Times* (Rotogravure Section), July 5: Turning out the Remuda or string of Cowboy Saddle Horses.

remudera (*Spanish*, re: mu: ðé: ra:; *English, the same and* re: mu: dɛr ə:) From *remuda* (*q.v.*). A bell mare.

1929 Dobie, J. Frank, *A Vaquero of the Brush Country*, p. 251: Our method was to pen them at night . . . and then during the day while not riding them to herd them with the bell mare— the *remudera*, as the Mexicans call her.

remudero WRANGLER (*q.v.*).

ricos (*Spanish*, rí: ko:s; *English*, rí: koz) The rich. It occurs most commonly in the phrase *los ricos* referring to any wealthy class or group of people. It is not widely used.

1844 Gregg, Josiah, *Commerce of the Prairies*, p. 134: The rancheros and others of the lowest class, however, were only the instruments of certain discontented ricos. *Ibid.*, p. 189: This business has constituted a profitable trade to some of the ricos of the country.

1931 Austin, Mary, *Starry Adventure*, p. 204: She'd think you

would think she didn't know how *ricos* should be fed. *Ibid.*,
p. 286: And the *ricos* are the ones that are losing the old way
the quickest

rincon (*Spanish*, ri:ŋ kó:n; *English*, rɪŋ kó:n) In Spanish the
word means a corner and by extension a secluded or retired spot.
In English *rincon* signifies a nook, a secluded place, or a bend in
the river. It is used commonly by ranchers and others in the
Southwest.
1888 Johnstone, E. M., *In Semi-Tropic Seas:* The territory . . .
included all the arable lands from the "Rincon" west to the
sea.
1919 Chase, J. Smeaton, *California Desert Trails*, p. 243: In a
rincon or elbow at the foot of the rise lay the hamlet . . .

rodeo (*Spanish*, ro: ðé: o:; *English, the same and* ró: di: o: *and*
ro: dí: o:) From *rodear*, to surround, to gather together. *Rodeo*
in Spanish means a gathering in of cattle for inspection or inventory; a round-up. In English, except along the border it is becoming known as a large show or performance, usually held out
of doors, of cowboy stunts involving bronco riding, steer riding,
bulldogging of steers, calf-roping, steer-roping for speed, horse
racing and clown or other miscellaneous stunts for the display
of riding or roping skill. A show of this kind is a *ró: di: o:* and not
a *ro: ðe: o:*. The word in this sense has a different pronunciation,
a different accent and a different meaning from the original
Spanish. In fact, for those who still use *rodeo* for its original
meaning there exist two words: *ro: ðe: o:* a round-up and *ró: di:o:*
a show. It is in the latter sense that the word has gained widest
currency in the United States. One of the first instances of word
writing in the sky by airplane was on the occasion of advertising
a *rodeo* in Madison Square Garden in New York. A meteorite
and a shoe have been named *rodeo*. A western magazine has a
department known as "The Month's Rodeo" with a subtitle "A
roundup of strays worth corraling." Although it is quite probable that every American youth and adult is acquainted with
the word *rodeo* in one sense or the other, both meanings may pass
into obsolescence if the two activities which they label pass out
of practice.
1903 Atherton, Gertrude, *The Splendid Idle Forties*, p. 4: . . .
thousands of cattle would pass to other hands at the next
rodeo . . .

1912 Hough, Emerson, *The Story of the Cowboy*, p. 112: . . . the rodeo was shiftless and imperfect, and many cattle got through year after year unbranded.

1925 James, Will, *The Drifting Cowboy*, p. 6: At them rodeos there's two men handling each horse . . .

1929 *Encyclopaedia Britannica*, 14th Edition, Vol. I, p. 196: . . . pictures sky-writing by airplane; the word Rodeo appears at an altitude of 12,000 feet; the letter R is one mile long and the five letters are five miles in length.

1929 *New York Times*, Oct. 25: Rodeo on at Garden for Hospital Fund.

1930 Lyman, George D., *John Marsh, Pioneer*, p. 280: Here by his rodeo grounds, he built a slaughterhouse . . .

rurales (*Spanish*, ru: rá: l e:s; *English*, ru: ráel iz) Mounted police [*Guardia rural*] of Mexico usually serving in rural and outlying districts. The *rurales* system was originated by President Porfirio Diaz of Mexico to wage a war of annihilation against bandidos and other undesirables who preyed upon the Mexican populace and American property holders in Mexico and along the border. No little cunning and knowledge of human nature was shown in selecting the *rurales*. Many who were on the borderline of banditry were definitely lined up on the side of the government by holding out to them the temptation of a horse, a gun and the free life of a *rural*. So effective did this police system become in Mexico that the cry "the *rurales* are coming" seldom failed to strike terror into the hearts of outlaws. "Their service uniform was of a dark-grey whipcord, with black braid down the legs of the tight trousers; but for parades they had a *charro* costume of soft brown leather, and at all times they were gorgeously arrayed. On their high-crowned sombreros the eagle-and-snake ensignia of Mexico was laid in solid, gleaming silver, and their horses were the pick of the land. The men received high pay and took pride in their appearance; but their faces were hard as iron. Over this body of man-killers [Emilio] Kosterlitsky ruled like a king."—*Fighting Men of the West*, by Dane Coolidge.

1907 North, A. W., *The Mother of California*, p. 85: . . . heavily indebted to him for the establishment of the mounted . . . rurales.

1919 Chase, J. Smeaton, *California Desert Trails*, p. 292: A couple of burly brigands with huge pistols projecting from their hip-pockets . . . proved to be *rurales* . . .

1925 Smith, J. Russell, *North America*, p. 677: Thirty-two men were arrested . . . taken out into the bushes beside the track and shot by the Rurales (police).

1929 *World's Work*, November 23: The other day, rurales caught and executed a cattle rusher and murderer.

1932 *New York Times*, April 14: Other great men discussed are . . . the Russian, who commanded the rurales in northern Mexico.

sabe English modifications **savy, savvy, savez** (*Spanish*, sá: be:; *English*, sǽ bi:, sǽ vi:) From Spanish *saber* "to know." Know; understand; be acquainted with; sense; knowledge. *Savy* was used extensively by unlettered persons during the frontier times in the Southwest and still maintains an extensive colloquial use. It also occurs often in western-story writing.

1909 Rye, Edgar, *Quirt and Spur*, p. 41: . . . the old man has caught on to the mutual admiration between Wilhelm and Sallie Washington, and don't propose to give a free exhibition of the Pocahauntas and Captain Smith act. Sabe?

Clemens, Samuel Langhorne, *Goose-Rancher:* "He has no savy."

1925 Scarborough, Dorothy, *The Wind*, p. 47: Oh, I *savez*.

1930 James, Will, *Lone Cowboy*, p. 70: I didn't savvy what he meant but I understood. (Savvying means more than understanding.)

1931 *Lariat*, April, p. 53: . . . you ain't got much sabe . . .

saguaro See Webster's *New International Dictionary*.

sala (*Spanish*, sá: la:; *English, the same and* sǽ lɔ). A large room; a hall; a room. *Sala* is used occasionally in description either written or verbal of Spanish dwellings or houses.

1902 Atherton, Gertrude, *The Splendid Idle Forties*, p. 12: The floor was bare, the furniture of horsehair ̇. . . it was a typical Californian sala of that day.

1926 Cather, Willa, *Death Comes for the Archbishop*, p. 55: Lujon and his two daughters began constructing an altar at one end of the sala.

salvo conducto (*Spanish*, sá:l vo: ko:n dú:k to:; *English, the same*) Literally, "safe conduct." An official letter of introduction giving information about and requesting protection and courtesies for a traveller, usually on the Mexican frontiers.

sarsaparilla See the *New English Dictionary*.

sassafras See the *New English Dictionary*.

seguro (*Spanish*, se: gú: ro:; *English, the same and* sɪ gú: ro) Sure; certainly. *Seguro* is used colloquially to emphasize sureness and certainty in a particular situation. In conversation one might ask "Are you coming with us?" and be answered with "*Seguro*" or "*Seguro que si.*" This use is restricted to those places where contact with the Spanish or Mexican element has been, or is, intimate.

1931 Austin, Mary, *Starry Adventure*, p. 160: You hadn't yet lost the deep delight of the last look around . . . seguro . . . seguro. *Ibid.*, p. 419: . . . the *frijoles*, are they to be eaten? *Seguro* . . .

sendero (*Spanish*, se:n dé: ro; *English*, sen déro:) A trail, path or clearing.

1929 Dobie, J. Frank, *A Vaquero of the Brush Country*, p. X: I have sought to open a *sendero*, as we say on the border—a clearing that will allow people to hold some of the secrets that the brush has hidden.

señor (*Spanish*, se:n jó:r; *English, the same and* sí:n jor) A man; a husband or head of a household. The word is used chiefly in direct or indirect address. It is often substituted for a proper name.

1856 Webber, C. W., *Tale of the South Border*, p. 72: Señor Kentucky I have been a great traveller.

1925 Burns, W. Noble, *The Saga of Billy the Kid*, p. 24: So, Señor McSween was a young lawyer looking for a good town in which to settle . . .

1926 Cather, Willa, *Death Comes for the Archbishop*, p. 70: The Bishop drew his pistol. No profanity señor.

señorita (*Spanish*, se:n jor í: ta:; *English, the same and* si:n jor í: tə) Diminutive of *señora*. A young unmarried woman. The word is used throughout the Southwest in both written and spoken language when referring to a young unmarried Spanish lady or a woman of Spanish birth or associations. Occasionally it is used when referring to an Anglo-American woman.

1889 Ripley, McHatton E., *From Flag to Flag:* . . . the señoritas proposed to unpack the hampers and array themselves in full evening dress.

1912? Cozzens, S. W., *The Young Trail Hunters*, p. 152: Instead of the plump, rosy-cheeked, smiling señorita who entertained us so charmingly at Fort Davis . . .

1912 Hough, Emerson, *The Story of the Cowboy*, p. 127: Some wandering teamster . . . met and wooed and married the señorita, and so after a fashion got control of the water front . . .

1928 Stiff, James E., *Spanish Literature of the Southwest*, p. 32: Harte's *señoritas* in Maruja are not clearly pictured.

si (*Spanish*, si:; *English, the same*) Yes. Used commonly in colloquial parlance in the Southwest.

siembra (*Spanish*, si:é:m bra:; *English, the same*) A planting (of trees or seed). This term is used in Cuba especially in connection with the planting of coffee trees.

1840 Turnbull, David, *Travels in the West*, p. 304: The siembra "a la estaca" is differently executed.

siesta (*Spanish*, si:é:s ta:; *English*, si: és tɔ) A noonday or afternoon rest or nap; a short sleep; a rest. *Siesta* was borrowed in Europe before it was borrowed in America. It is included in this vocabulary because it is probable that the word was borrowed independently. *Siesta* is used frequently in conversation in the Southwest.

1810 Pike, Z. M., *Expeditions*, p. 660: I forgot their siesta, or repose after dinner.

1821 Bingley, William, *Travels in North America*, p. 244: . . . they drink a few glasses of wine, sing a few songs, and then retire to take their siesta or afternoon nap.

1836 Latrobe, Charles Joseph, *The Rambler in Mexico*, p. 33: . . . leaving my two companions to their siestas . . . I might be seen stealing off up to the Bluff . . .

1840 Turnbull, David, *Travels in the West*, p. 24: . . . the peninsula custom prevails of dining at three in the afternoon, and afterwards, indulging in the siesta.

1929 *New York Times*, July 7: A short after lunch siesta will be followed by an automobile ride over his [Mr. John D. Rockefeller's] estate and at 7:30 the birthday dinner will be served.

1929 Stoddard, C. W., "Old Mission Idyls," in *Sunset Magazine*, Vol. XVII, p. 91: These "forty winks" the seductive yet refreshing siesta were the prevailing custom of the country . . .

sitio (*Spanish*, sí: ti:o; *English, the same*) "A Spanish superficial measure, used in the States and Territories of Spanish origin. The *sitio* is a league of land of 5,000 varas, and is equal to 4,428 English acres." Bartlett, John. Familiar Quotations.)

soga (*Spanish*, só:ga; *English, the same*) In Spanish the word *soga* is used in a general sense to designate a rope of any kind. In English it has the same general usage to some extent but is applied more particularly to a particular loosely-twisted hemp rope. This rope is not used for lassoing purposes and is usually called "*soga* rope" to distinguish it from *reata* "pita," or *mecate*.

soldadera (*Spanish*, so:l da: ðe: ra; *English, practically the same*) A woman who accompanies her soldier husband, or man, in the field or on a campaign. She cares for his personal wants—cooking, sewing, laundry, etc., nurses him when necessary, and at times joins him in actual fighting maneuvers. The term, already restricted in use to a discussion of the Mexican army is being further restricted in use by the modernization of that organization.

1923 Smith, Wallace, *The Little Tigress*, p. 15: The soldadera in Mexican armies, with few exceptions, is the wife, married or not of the man at whose side she sleeps.

solo (*Spanish*, só: lo:; *English, the same*) Alone; single. *Solo* is applied in particular to Mexican workmen who come to the United States . . . without their families.

1928 McLean, R. N., *That Mexican*, p. 124: . . . there exists a large number of "solos" in the country.

sombrero (*Spanish*, so:m bré: ro:; *English*, som bré: ro: *and* som brí: ro:) A hat with relatively broad brim and high, peaked crown; also a hat of large proportions. *Sombreros* are made of straw and of felt. They vary from the simple inexpensive kind worn by peons in Mexico and laborers along the border to the elaborately trimmed *sombreros* coveted by many and worn by those who are able to buy them. The word is found frequently in situations where local color or picturesqueness is sought.

1836 Latrobe, Charles Joseph, *The Rambler in Mexico*, p. 33: My accoutrement consisted of . . . a bag for seeds, and a broad-eaved palmetto sombrero.

1851 *The New York Herald*, Feb. 19: The Californians, with broadbrim sombreros, had probably plenty of gold dust.

1903 Atherton, Gertrude, *The Splendid Idle Forties*, p. 17: "At your service, señor," he said, lifting his sombrero.

1914 Thomas, Augustus, *Arizona*, p. 289: Off came the great sombrero and it swept to the ground gracefully.

1922 Rollins, Philip Ashton, *The Cowboy*, p. 105: . . . while these two legitimate titles were interchangeable throughout the West, the Northwest leaned toward "hat" the Southwest toward "sombrero."

1929 Advertisement of *Fiesta*, a Broadway play: The Experimental Theatre Inc. flings with considerable dexterity its sombrero into the Broadway arena.

1930 Ferber, Edna, *Cimarron*, p. 91: His eyes, steel gray beneath the brim of the white sombrero . . .

1930 *New York Times*, Feb. 9: . . . giving his sombrero a jerk down over his left eye . . .

sotol (*Spanish*, so: tó:l; *English, the same*) A number of desert plants, among them *Dasylirion texanum* and *wheelerii* and *Beaucarnea œdipus*, are known locally as *sotol*. The alcoholic beverage distilled from the sap of these plants is called *sotol*. See also TEQUILA.

1908 McDougal, D. T., *Botanical Features of the North American Deserts*, p. 9: This is the typical sotol region.

stampede See Webster's *New International Dictionary*.

suerte (*Spanish*, swe:r te:; *English*, swer ti) Chance; lot; a quantity of land in a newly-founded town, for which the settlers drew lots. These were situated within the limits of the *ejidos* (*q.v.*), and were intended for gardens, orchards, etc. The *suerte* was generally irrigable, and contained 152,352 square varas, or 27 acres. *Suerte* is now applied to any small lot of land. It is occasionally used by Americans familiar with Spanish in the sense of chance or turn in such a phrase as "I will try my *suerte*."

tamal English modifications **tamale, tamaule** (*Spanish,* ta: má:l; *English,* tə má: li:) A common Mexican food made of corn ground (usually in a *metate*) flavored with pepper or chile, mixed with meat or with a piece of meat inserted, rolled into a pasty loaf the size of a biscuit and about the same shape, wrapped in wet corn husks and baked in coals or an oven. The *tamale* is without doubt the most popular with Americans of all Mexican foods. Evidence of this is to be found in the numerous street vendors of *tamales* encountered in American cities and towns. *Tamales* may be obtained in all parts of the United States. Some definitions and descriptions of *tamales* leave the definite impression that they are a sort of hash composed of any number of ingredients. As a matter of fact *tamales* are of a rather standard composition. Corn is the chief and sometimes only constituent except for flavoring; meat is an important ingredient but when not obtainable *tamales* are made without it. *Tamales* are served hot or cold. It should be noted that the Spanish word is *tamal* but that the English borrowing is *tamale;* that is, it has the final *e*, which is sounded as *i:*. In Spanish one would say *deme un tamal.* In English one says "give me a *tamale.*" *Tamale*, therefore, is the English word and *tamal* the Spanish. This may be accounted for by the fact that the word occurs much more frequently in the plural in both Spanish and English than it does in the singular. In making the plural *tamales* into a singular, the American has merely left off the *s*. In Spanish the rule for plurals and singulars requires that the *es* be omitted. American boys use "Hot *tamale*" as an exclamation or ejaculation both alone and in the nonsensical combination "Hot tamale, Billy Goat."

1836 Parker, *A Trip to the West and Texas*, p. 275: You can hear the plump, plump . . . from the alcoves of the vines where comfortable old dames . . . are pounding out corn for tamales.

tapadero English modifications **tapidero, tapaderas** (*Spanish,* ta: pa: ðé: ro:; *English,* tæp ə dér o: *and* tæp i: dér o) From Spanish *tapar*, to cover. A stirrup guard. There being no word in English except in army parlance that describes the stirrup covering so accurately and neatly as *tapadero* this word is used exclusively by Americans who have occasion to refer to the apparatus in question. The *tapadero* is made of heavy cowhide, sometimes reinforced by a wooden frame. It covers the foot when in place in the stirrup and protects it from minor injuries such as bruising, scruffing, and the biting of vicious animals. It also prevents the foot of the rider from slipping completely through the stirrup during occasions of rough riding or bronco-breaking.

1844 Gregg, Josiah, *Commerce of the Prairies*, p. 213: Formerly the stirrups constituted a complete slipper, mortised in a solid block of wood, which superseded the use of tapaderas. *Ibid.*: The stirrups . . . over which are fastened the tapaderas or coverings of leather to protect the toes . . .

1929 Dobie, J. Frank, *A Vaquero of the Brush Country*, p. 204: To work effectively in this brush a vaquero had to have tapáderos (toe fenders) on his stirrups, boots on his heels . . .

tapaojos English modification **tapojos** (*Spanish*, tá: pa: ó: ho:s; *English*, tǽ pɔ ó: ho:z) From *tapar*, to cover; 3rd p. sing. *tapa+ojos*, eyes. A blind; an eye cover for animals. It consists of a strip of leather about three inches wide and long enough to extend across the brow of a horse or mule and be fastened to the headstall of the bridle or hackamore on each side of the animal's head. The *tapaojos* is used extensively by Mexican vaqueros on broncos, mules, and horses of mean disposition. When the rider mounts he pulls the *tapaojos* over the animal's eyes to insure himself against being bitten or kicked. After seating himself securely in the saddle he leans over and raises the *tapaojos*. This device is used on a bronco that is being mounted for the first time, as an animal when blindfolded hesitates to cavort about as it would otherwise be likely to do. *Tapaojos* are also used very commonly in connection with *atajos* of pack mules. While the mule or burro is being packed. to avoid exciting it, the *tapaojos* is drawn over the eyes. The rather general use of the Spanish word in preference to the English "blindfold" may be attributed to the fact that the device itself is used much more extensively by Mexican riders than by American.

1847 Ruxton, George F., *Adventures in Mexico and the Rocky Mountains*, p. 112: I instantly stopped . . . dismounted, and, catching the wildest mule, immediately tied her legs together with a riata, and covered the eyes of all with their tapojos . . .

tapioca South American borrowing.

tasajo (*Spanish*, ta: sá: ho:; *English, the same and* tə sǽ ho:) Dried meat, jerked beef, or other meat. The terms jerked beef or jerked meat are more commonly used by Americans. *Tasajo*, however, is not uncommon and is encountered in writings which have a Mexican or Spanish background or element.

1926 Branch, Douglas, *The Cowboy and his Interpreters*, p. 4: Occasionally he visited his stock . . . to mark the oxen to be killed for his *tasajo*.

1929 Dobie, J. Frank, *A Vaquero of the Brush Country*, p. 28: A staple article of diet with many of them was *carne*, or *tasajo* . . . which is still prepared and used on many Texas ranches . . .

tecolote (*Spanish*, te: ko: ló: te:; *English*, te: kó: lo: ti:) From American Indian, *tecolotl*. Small owls of various species in Texas and other parts of the Southwest and northern Mexico are known as *tecolote* owls or merely *tecolotes*.

1928 Austin, Mary, *Children Sing in the Far West*. Black beetle and tecolote owl Between two winks their ancient forms will take.

tegua (*Spanish*, té: gwa:; *English*, té: wə, *occasionally* té: wi:) From American Indian. A handmade moccasin worn by many Mexicans and also by American children in Mexico. *Teguas* are heeless, pointed-toed, ankle high, and laced in front. They are never made of buckskin although they are often swede together with buckskin string. *Teguas* are never decorated with beads, etc., as the Indian moccasins frequently are. They are plain and homely looking footwear, but are popular with American boys because of their lightness in weight and great comfort in wearing.

1889 Lummis, C. F., *Lo, Who is not Poor?* p. 49: . . . the men . . . kept time with the tap of the hammer as they shaped rawhide soles for their teguas.

1922 Bogan, P. M., *The Ceremonial Dances of the Yaqui Indians*, p. 60: He is barefoot or shod with teguas.

1932 Coolidge, Dane, *Fighting Men of the West*, p. 158: . . . he found the *tegua* tracks of an Indian or Mexican who had picked it up.

tejano Variant spelling, *texano* (*Spanish*, te: há: no:; *English*, *the same and* tə hǽ no:) A Texan; one who was born or lives in Texas. *Tejano* is regarded as a term of distinction. Its popular implications are courageousness and manliness in general.

1925 Simpson, Charles, *El Rodeo*, p. 42: . . . the little cowpony Tejano, pricks up his ears.

1929 Dobie, J. Frank, *A Vaquero of the Brush Country*, p. 63:

... many [bad Americans] were overbearing and cruelly unjust to the *Tejanos* (Texanized Mexicans).
1932 Coolidge Dane, *Fighting Men of the West*, p. 120: Almost in a day, thirty thousand Texas steers were shipped into the country ... and with them a bunch of fighting Texanos.

temblor (*Spanish*, te:m bló:r; *English, the same*) A thunder storm; a violet storm of any kind accompanied by thunder or thunder and rain. Related to Spanish *temblar* "to tremble."
n.d. Anonymous, *To California over the Santa Fe Trail*, p. 132: ... the dreaded temblor upset the 120-foot tower of the Mission San Juan Capistrano ...

temporal See page 218.

tequila (*Spanish*. te: kí: la:; *English, the same*) From American Indian. An alcoholic beverage distilled from the agave plant. The four beverages common in Mexico—*pulque, mescal, tequila,* and *sotol* are not very distinguishable in composition and effect and are not discriminated by Americans nor carefully by the Mexicans themselves. Of the three, however, *tequila* and *pulque* are more commonly used by Americans as the name for Mexican beverages. All these drinks except *sotol* (*q.v.*) are made from the sap of various species of the agave and are strong intoxicants.
1929 De Castro, Adolphe, *Portrait of Ambrose Bierce*, p. 337: An American who drinks too much tequila soon loses himself.
1929 Dos Passos, John, *42nd Parallel*, p. 321: They had a tequila each before dinner at a little bar where nothing was sold but tequila out of varnished kegs.
1932 DeVoto, Bernard, "Accolade," in *Saturday Evening Post*, Jan. 16, p. 6: The cops found him ... at the fair grounds. He smelled of *tequila. Ibid.*, p. 7: He died drunk—*tequila.*

tiempo (*Spanish*, ti:é:m po:; *English, the same*) Time; i.e., time to stop work. *Tiempo* is commonly used by foremen and workmen in building and construction work along the border to indicate that the hour for stopping work has come. This may be at noon or at the close of the day. The rhythm of the word makes it more easily sung forth as the clock strikes the hour than the monosyllable "time." Furthermore, along the border a large proportion of the laborers are Mexican.

tierra caliente (*Spanish*, ti:é: rra: ka: li:én te:; *English*, tie: rra kæ li: en ti:) The hot country of Mexico and Central America. Used rather generally in American contexts such as history, geography, etc., where the country in question is being described. It occurs also in narrations and descriptions which refer to Mexico and Central America.

1856 Webber, C. W., *A Tale of the Southwest Border*, p. 82: I have sucked the nectar from the yellow flowers in my way from 'Tierra Calliente' . . . up to 'Tierra Frier' . . .

tierra fria (*Spanish*, tierra *plus* fri:a; *English, the same*) Cold country; frigid zone.

tierra templada (*Spanish*, ti:e: rra: te:m plá: ða:; *English*, tem plæ da *and* tierra templa: ðə) The temperate zone in Mexico used similarly to *tierra caliente*.

tinaja (*Spanish*, ti: ná: ha:; *English*, tɪ ná: hə). Literally vase or jar. Natural water tanks, usually hollowed-out basins in the course of a small canyon stream. These *tinajas* retain water long after it has disappeared from the arroyo or canyon, and are therefore great boons to desert animals and men.

1919 Chase, J. Smeaton, *California Desert Trails*, p. 347: Somewhere near the mouth of the cañon is a tinaja known as Granite Tanks . . .

tlaco English modifications, **thlack, claco** (*Spanish*, tlá: ko:; *English*, klæ ko:) From the Mexican *tlacoualoni*. A copper coin, about the size of a United States copper cent of the old style, valued at one-quarter of a real, also called *cuartillo*. The *claco* was used in the nineteenth century in Mexico and consequently along the border, but has practically gone out of currency.

1844 Gregg, Josiah, *Commerce of the Prairies*, p. 220: In the large cities . . . the limosneros . . . may be seen . . . inviting the blessings of heaven upon every man, woman or child, who may have been so fortunate as to propitiate the benison by casting a few clacos into his outstretched hand.

1898 Lummis, Charles F., *The Awakening of a Nation*, p. 60: And when you have bestowed the copper *tlaco* . . . he says . . . "God give more to you!"

tobacco See the *New English Dictionary*.

tomato See the *New English Dictionary.*

tonto (*Spanish*, tó:n to:; *English, the same*) A fool. *Tonto* is used synonymously with English "fool" by those in the Spanish-English territory and is not uncommon as a proper name for animals. For example a horse may as a result of certain characteristics of temperament, which develop during his being tamed and trained, be given the appellation of *tonto*, and carry it with him as a permanent name.

1903 King, Charles, *An Apache Princess*, p. 12: . . . the handclap was repeated, low but imperative, and Tonto, the biggest of the two hounds, uplifted one ear and growled a challenge.

tornado English modifications **tornada, tornadeo** (*Spanish*, to:r ná: ðo; *English* tor né: do:) From *tornar* "to twist," "to turn." *Tornado* is the regular past participle form. *Tornado* seems to have been first used in connection with violent wind storms in and about the region of the Gulf of Guinea. It has been extended to mean a hurricane anywhere. In Spain the word *huracán* is used rather than *tornado*. The word *tornado* may be regarded as completely naturalized in the English vocabulary. See dictionaries.

1856 Webber, C. W., *A Tale of the South Border*, p. 97: . . . he ought to express gratitude . . . towards the "Blessed Virgin" for her mercy . . . in not leaving him exposed . . . to the tornadeos of Mexican ire.

tornillo (*Spanish*, to:r ní: jo: *English, the same*) A whirl of dust caused by the wind. Also applied to the mesquite plant (*q.v.*).

1931 Austin, Mary, *Starry Adventure*, p. 89: And at the same time hot and dry like the *tornillo;* you saw it rise and twist, going skyward . . .

1932 Coolidge, Dane, *Fighting Men of the West*, p. 154: . . . the Rangers crossed the river and rode through the heavy willows and tornillos . . .

toro (to:ro *in Spanish and English*) A bull; a steer. *Toro* is commonly used as a synonym for bull in informal conversation. It is also a place name in the state of New York.

torreon (*Spanish*, to: rre: ó:n; *English, the same and* tor i: ó:n) Augmentative of *torre*, tower. An outlook hill or mountain usu-

ally in a position to command a view of the surrounding plains
or valleys. Commonly used in the Southwest.

1931 Austin, Mary, *Starry Adventure*, p. 56: . . . Gard . . . had
climbed up and up, quite to the top of the tree, pretending it
was a *torreon* from which he was looking for Apaches.

tortilla English modifications **tartilloes, tortillia** (*Spanish*, tor
tí: ja: *English*, tor tí:ə *and* tor tíl ə) A flat, round, very thin, un-
leavened griddle cake. *Tortillas* are usually made of ground corn,
that is, corn flour, or they may be made of wheat flour. When
made of corn, the corn is first soaked in water, or lime water,
until softened. The hulls are removed and the kernels ground on
the metate into a pasty mass. Portions of this dough are then
patted and flipped back and forth between the palms of the
hands until the desired size has been attained for the cake, usually six or eight inches in diameter and one-fourth of an inch
thick. The cake is placed on the coals of an open fire, or preferably on a piece of metal over the fire, and browned on each side.
Tortillas made of wheat flour are invariably much larger than
corn *tortillas*. *Tortillas* are most delicious when served hot, but
they are used extensively for cold lunches at midday. They often
serve, among the poorer classes, as scoop-like dishes from which
beans and other foods are eaten.

1836 Latrobe, Charles Joseph, *The Rambler in Mexico*, p. 78:
We ascertained that he had had . . . a dozen and a half tortillas, smeared with chile . . .

1859 Reid, Samuel, *Scouting Expedition*, p. 18: . . . the neat little rancho on the opposite side of the river furnished us with
a supply of fruit, milk and tortillas . . .

1889 Ripley, McHatton E., *From Flag to Flag*, p. 104: . . . it was
not unusual to see women making chocolate and tortillas for
their teamster lords.

1917 McClellan, George, *The Mexican War Diary*, ed. 1917 by
Wm. Starr Meyers, p. 12: They [the Mexicans] . . . eat their
horrible beef and tortillas and dance all night at their fandangos.

toston (*Spanish*, to: stó:n; *English, the same*) A Mexican fifty-
cent piece. Because of the use along the border of both American
coins and Mexican coins any terms that distinguish them are
useful. For this reason, if for no other, *toston* is commonly used by
Americans in business to designate the Mexican half-dollar.

Likewise *peso* is used for the Mexican dollar, while "dollar" or Spanish *dolár* is used for the American dollar piece.

tripas (*Spanish*, trí: pa:s; *English*, trí: pɜz) Entrails, tripes, guts. *Tripas* of beef prepared as a food are eaten by a certain class of Mexican people. Americans use the word often in preference to the English entrails, tripe, or guts. It seems that *tripas* signifies to the American the prepared tripe more than do the English terms. The word is also used by Americans who would not say "entrails" and prefer not to use the unmentionable "guts." *Tripas* is convenient as a respectable medium.

1929 De Castro, Adolphe, *Portrait of Ambrose Bierce*, p. 330: He promised to speed a bullet into my *tripas* for the fine things I wrote about his enemies.

triste (*Spanish*, trí:s te:; *English*, trí:s ti:) Sad; gloomy. *Triste* is commonly heard in informal conversation, sometimes alone and often in conjunction with Spanish *muy*. A person may be described as "very *triste*" or as *muy triste*. A person accosted by "How are you today? might reply, "Pretty *triste*" if he were in a sad state of mind. It is doubtful whether *triste* will become obsolete in America so long as there is contact of Spanish-speaking and English-speaking peoples.

1932 Whetten, N. L. *Letter*, June 18: The situation for next year looks rather triste as yet.

tulares A region or place covered with tules.

tule English modification (*Spanish* tú: le:; *English* tú: li:) In Texas the name *tules* is applied to several species of yuca, and to certain kinds of reeds not identified. The name of Tooele (pronounced *tu:* ɪ *lə*) County, Utah is thought by some to come from *tule*.

1836 Parker, *A Trip to the West and Texas*, p. 266: Below the town . . . the land dips away to the river pastures and tulares.

1850? Bryant, Edwin, *Rocky Mountain Adventures*, p. 224: In crossing the valley on the southern side, we passed through several miles of *tule*, a species of rush, or reed, which here grows to the height of eight feet . . .

uña de gato (*Spanish*, ú:n ja: de: gá: to:; *English*, *the same and* ú:n ja de: gǽ to:) Cat's claw. Shrubs (*Mimosa biuncifera* and

Acacia greggii) with sharp spines found in western Texas and other parts of the Southwest. The leaves are similar to the mesquite leaves.

valgame Dios (*Spanish*, vá:l ga: me: ðiːóːs; *English the same and* væl gə mi:) An ejaculation meaning literally "Lord appraise me" but equivalent in meaning to the English "God bless my soul" or the more vigorous "Well I'll be damned." *Valgame Dios* is widely current in the Southwest among those acquainted with Spanish. It may be used to express surprise, disgust, disappointment, contempt or pleasure, or in fact almost any emotion. The tone of voice determines the meaning.
1873 Wallace, Lew, *The Fair God*, p. 291: . . . what an exchange. *Valgame Dios*!
1903 O. Henry, *Heart of the West*, p. 44: Valgame Dios! It is a very foolish world . . .
1931 Austin, Mary, *Starry Adventure*, p. 159: Pablo began talking as soon as he came within reach, and you said . . . *Valgame Dios* or whatever was required.

vamos English modifications **vamose, vamoos, vamoose, bamos, bamanos** (*Spanish*, vá: moːs:; *English, the same and* və: múːs; *also* vǽ moːs). From *ir* to go. *Vamos* is first person plural of the Spanish. "Let's go," "let us go," "shall we go," "be gone," "get out," "beat it," "to go." This word is not found in formal writing or speech, but is encountered commonly both in informal writings and conversation. The first occurrence of the word seems to have been in the phrase *"vamoose the ranch."*
1844 Kendall, George Wilkins, *Narrative of the Texan Santa Fe Expedition*, p. 390: The Mexican now pointed to his horse, and uttered the well known bamanos (Come, let us be moving—a word we heard forty times a day.)
1847 Ripley, McHatton E., *Rough and Ready Annuls, Soldier's Letter to his Mother*, p. 245: On the morning after I wrote the letter to father . . . they stacked their arms and colors and "vamoosed the ranch."
1859 Reid, Samuel, *Scouting Expedition*, p. 47: On we vamosed, over high rocky hills and immense level plains.
1888 Custer, E. B., *Tenting on the Plains*, vol. I, p. 32: I got that far when the eyes of the old galoots started out of their heads, and they vamoosed the ranche.

Millar, J. G., *Breath and Veldt*, p. 175: The hunter was voted
a fraud . . . and . . . told to vamoose . . .

1903 O. Henry, *Heart of the West*, p. 125: "Vamoose, quick,"
she ordered peremptorily, "you coon!"

1912? Cozzens, S. W., *The Young Trail Hunters*, p. 19: We
mounted our ponies, old Jerry called out in a cheery tone,
"Vamose!"

1928 Seabury, David, *Growing Into Life*, p. 221: I had already
vamoosed once myself from the farm, and I shall never forget
mother's face when I came limping in the next morning.

vanilla See the *New English Dictionary*.

vaquero English modifications **vacquero, baquero, buckaroo,
buckeroo** (*Spanish*, va: ké: ro:; *English*, və kέr o:, bə kέr: ro:,
bə ke:r o:, *also* bə kə rú:). A cowboy. The word comes from the
Spanish *vaca* with the common Spanish suffix *ero* which usually
signifies "one engaged in" or "one who does" as for instance
zapatero—one who makes *zapatos* (shoes); *carnecero*—one who
sells *carne* (meat). *Vaquero* is commonly used in the border territory and has been popularized throughout the United States
by its use in adventure stories and other similar writings. Although *vaquero* is used when designating cowboys in general it
means more particularly Mexican cowboys, especially where
cowboys of both American and Mexican nationality are under
discussion. The variation *buckeroo* is common both in written
and spoken form.

1894 Harte, Francis Bret, *The Mystery of the Hacienda*, p. 215:
I shall have my vaqueros and rancheros to look after the crops
and the cattle . . .

1902 Atherton, Gertrude, *The Splendid Idle Forties*, p. 4: They
beat the sides of their mounts with their tender hands in imi-
tation of the vaqueros.

1925 Scarborough, Dorothy, *The Wind*, p. 1: Civilization has
changed them . . . as the vacqueros changes . . . the wild
horses . . .

1926 Branch, Douglas *The Cowboy and His Interpreters*, p. 51:
Until after the Civil War there was little call to improve on the
desultory system of the Mexican *vaquero*, who rode out on the
range with a branding-iron strapped to his saddle . . . *Ibid.*,
p. 166. "Calf roping—Nevada Buckaroo."

1928 James, Will, *Lone Cowboy*, p. 265: On the other side . . .
the riders, called *buckeroos*, used single-cinch . . . saddles.
1930 Lyman, George D., *John Marsh, Pioneer*, p. 206: . . . Noriega was afraid to live there alone and most of the time maintained ten vaqueros—and never less than seven—to protect
him.

vara (*Spanish* vá: ra:; *English*, vár ə) A unit of linear measure-
ment approximately 33 inches, or 836 millimeters, in length. The
term *vara* in Spanish means "bar" or "stick" and is applied to
all measuring sticks whether or not they be of the official *vara*
length. The common lineal measuring stick in Mexico is one meter long. A store or other organization dispensing goods to the
public is required to keep and, at least theoretically, to use a *vara*
that has been inspected by a government official for accuracy
and approved by him. The word is heard occasionally among the
older citizens in the border region but is not common among
the younger citizenry. It is encountered often in the writings
of the earlier colonization period.
1836 Latrobe, Charles Joseph, *The Rambler in Mexico*, p. 95:
The great adit . . . lies 242 varas below the mouth of the
shaft.
1886 McLane, Hiram H., *Irene Viesca*, p. 20: The dwelling was
placed . . . but a few varas from the stream.
1901 Powell, Lyman P., *Historic Towns of Western States*, p.
454: The Indians paid an annual tribute of a vara of cotton
cloth and a fanega of corn per family in return for their teaching and "civilization."
1927 Denis, A. J., *Spanish Alta California*, p. 32: Elks were
seen whose horns measured three varas across.

vega (*Spanish*, vé: ga:; *English*, *the same and* ví: gə) An open
tract of ground; a plain, especially one moist and fertile.

venta English modification **vent** (*Spanish*, ve:n ta:; *English*,
vent). The duplicate brand or mark put on an already branded
animal to indicate that it has been sold. As a verb it is the act
of putting on a *vent* brand. The *vent* is usually placed on the same
side of the animal as the original brand. If the latter has been
placed on the hip the *vent* brand is burned on the shoulder or ribs
and vice versa. If an animal changes ownership several times and
the brand of each successive owner is put on and *vented*, the ani-

mal's side portrays an array of brand figures; as many as ten is not impossible. The *vent* brand takes the place of a bill of sale or *papel de venta*. Its chief usefulness is found where the number of animals is large or where identification on the open range is desirable. It is a relatively simple matter to determine ownership by this system of brand cancellation. And a *vent* brand is never lost. The person whose brand appears uncancelled is presumably, and in most instances actually, the owner.

1888 Bancroft, H. H., *California Pastoral*, p. 572: All horses found in the possession of anyone without the *venta* . . . should be restored to the owners.

1912 Hough, Emerson, *The Story of the Cowboy*, p. 113: Here was the original of the bill of sale, and also of the counterbrand or the "vent brand," as it is known on the upper ranges . . .

1922 Rollins, Philip Ashton, *The Cowboy and His Interpreters*, p. 236: . . . the brute might be given . . . the vent brand . . . which was the seller's admission of the fact of sale . . .

vicuña South American borrowing.

vigilante English modification, **vigy** (*Spanish* vi: hi: lá:n te:; *English*, vɪdz ɪ lǽn ti:) A member of a vigilance committee, i.e., a volunteer committee of citizens for the oversight and protection of any interest, especially one organized to suppress and punish crime summarily, or when the processes of law seem inadequate.

1862 *Rocky Mountain News*, Denver, May 31 The vigys pointed to an empty saddle and gave him just ten minutes to skedaddle.

1912 Hough, Emerson, *The Story of the Cowboy*, p. 283: In this campaign the vigilantes killed between sixty and eighty of the rustlers.

1929 *New York Times*, Aug. 25: Kansas Vigilantes Organize to Stop Bold Thefts of Wheat.

1929 *New York Times:* Armed 'Vigilantes' Seek Bandit Trio.

viva (*Spanish*, ví: va:; *English the same*) An exclamation meaning literally "let live" or "long live." It is used in Spanish in the sense of "long live." *Viva Madero*, for example, is equivalent to "long live Madero." The word is also used as a general exclamation of approval either of an individual or of his words on the occasion of a public address. *Viva* is quite generally used when referring in English to the sort of exclamation described. The Italian *viva* it would seem was borrowed independently.

1836 Parker, ————, *A Trip to the West and Texas*, p. 276: By and by there will be a reading of the Declaration of Independence and an address punctured by vives . . .

1844 Kendall, George Wilkins, *Narrative of the Texan Santa Fe Expedition*, p. 311: Instantly the air was filled with *vivas*, and in ten minutes we received a visit from the governor's secretary.

1923 Smith, Wallace, *The Little Tigress*, p. 74: I wonder if he still *vivas* for Madero?

wrangler One who watches over the *remuda* of horses and *wrangles*, i.e., gathers them in for use. The term is also applied to regular herding of stock although not so commonly. *Wrangler* cannot be traced unequivocably to American-Spanish origin but in the absence of trustworthy evidence to the contrary it is listed here. The statement of Charles F. Lummis is not to be taken unguardedly when he maintains that *"caballerango* is a pure Mexicanism. It meant the man in charge of the spare riding ponies of an expedition. *Caballo*, every cowboy knew, was horse; so, translating half the word and corrupting the rest, we got 'horse-wrangler.' " In support of this theory it is worth noting that the form "cavy-wrango" does occur but is rare as compared with *wrangler* or "horse-wrangler" both of which are indeed common.

1925 James, Will, *The Drifting Cowboy*, p. 80: I had a wrango horse tied up . . . and I see where I have to saddle him up and get to work again. *Ibid.*, The cavy-wrango had brought the horses in, and they were all there to pick from one another day's riding.

yerba (*Spanish*, jeːr baː; *English*, jɛr bə *and* jr bə) Literally an herb; a weed; a plant. The word is not used often alone but does occur in a number of botanical names with a modifier. Examples are *yerba buena, yerba santa* (*Eriodictyon tomentosum*), *yerba mansa* (*Anemopsis californica*); translated "good plant," "holy plant," "gentle plant." The word will probably never attain a position in the language beyond its present technical status.

yerba salada (*Spanish*, jéːr baː saː laː ðaː) "Evening primrose (*Œnothera trichocalyx*. A low, strong, rather spreading plant with large, rather narrow, grayish green leaves and very large fragrant flowers, white (pink when faded) with sulphur-yellow centres, opening at night. Blooms in mid- and late spring."

you betcha que si. A facetious colloquial expression of approval.

yucca See Webster's *New International Dictionary*.

zacate English modification **sacate** (*Spanish*, sa: ká: te:; *English*, sɔ kǽ ti:) "Wild hay," i.e., grass harvested from swales, mesas, etc., where it grows naturally and without cultivation to suitable height for cutting with a mowing machine. Grama grass seems to be the favorite variety for wild hay. But the best of *zacate* is considered far inferior to alfalfa as feed for animals. It serves as a substitute for alfalfa.

zacaton English modification **sacaton** (*Spanish*, sa: ka: tó:n; *English* sǽk ɔ to:n) Literally, a large *zacate* or grass. *Zacaton* is applied to a particular kind of grass probably (*Epicamper rigens*) that grows in tussocks or "hills" along river bottoms and other lower land where the soil does not become excessively dry. This grass is usually referred to as "*zacaton* grass" or "basket grass." Sacaton, a town in Arizona, derives its name from *zacaton*.
1863 Fergusson, D., *Report to Congress*, p. 16: "Sacaton" indicates water near surface.

zarape English modifications **sarape sarepe, serape** (*Spanish*, sa: rá: pe:; *English*, sɔ rǽ pi:) A blanket-like wrap used by men to throw about the shoulders and body. The *zarape* is worn extensively by the people of Mexico and other Spanish-speaking countries. *Zarape* is not entirely synonymous with *poncho* but the two words are used interchangeably. In some sections of Mexico the *zarape* has a hole cut in the center, as does the *poncho*, through which the head is inserted. The *zarape* serves as overcoat, as bedding, or as hand luggage for the travelling Mexican of the middle and lower classes. It is an important item in the *charo* outfit. No little pride is taken in its quality and beauty of color.
1836 Latrobe, Charles Joseph, *The Rambler in Mexico*, p. 47: Our costume was a marvellous mixture of European and Mexican; the serape, the sombrero with its silver band, the scarlet sash, and jacket of the latter having been adopted, while the residue of the male outfit was European.

1844 Gregg, Josiah, *Commerce of the Prairies*, p. 209: An additional value is set upon the fine sarape on account of its being fashionable substitute for a cloak.

1847 Ruxton, George F., *Adventures in Mexico and the Rocky Mountains*. In spite of my dress and common sarape, I was soon singled out. *Ibid.*, p. 21: . . . Castillo had thrust his head through the slit in his serape . . .

1902 Atherton, Gertrude, *The Splendid Idle Forties*. As he rode, he tore off his serape and flung it to the ground . . .

1912 Lawrence, David H., *The Mozo*, p. 73: He bargained for flowers and for a *sarape* which he didn't get . . .

1926 Cather, Willa, *Death Comes for the Archbishop*, p. 130: These he gathered in his serape and carried to the rear wall of the cavern . . .

zequia See ACEQUIA.

ADDENDUM

temporal (*Spanish*, teːm poː raːl; *English*, tem pə rál) The Spanish meaning is "temporary" or "temporal" but the word is applied to a field or to cultivated land which depends on rainfall and not on irrigation for its moisture. In other words a dry-farm.

APPENDICES

I. WORDS OF AMERICAN INDIAN ORIGIN

Spanish or English adaptations of American Indian words, chiefly Nahuatl, in use by speakers of English in the Southwest. Spanish and English forms of these words are in bold-faced type.

apache *probably from* apachu
atole attoli
avocado *and* **alligator pear** aguacate *or* aguacatl
chicle chictli, tzictli
chile chilli
chocolate chocolatl
claco *or* **tlaco** tlacoualoni
coyote coyotl
gachupin *a composite of* cactli, *and* catsopin
jacal xacalli
mecate mecatl
mescal mexcolli
mesquite mizquitl, *a composite of* mexque *and* cuahuitl
metate metatl

mole molli
nopal nopalli
ocote ocotillo ocotl
petate petatl
peyote peyotl
pinole pinolli
sacate *or* **zacate** zacatl
sarape *or* **zarape** tzalape (tzalanpepechtli *modified to* tzalanpechtli *thence to* tzalapech *and to* tzalape)
sotol
tamale *or* **tamal** tamalli
tecolote tecolotl
tegua tewa
tobacco taboca (Guarani)
tomato *or* **tomate** jitomate, xictomatl

II. SPANISH PLACE NAMES[1] IN THE UNITED STATES[2]

Alabama

Alfalfa	Creola	Lavaca
Bermuda	Cuba	Lilita
Bexar	Delmar	Manila
Buena Vista	Gordo	Mexboro
Calera	Havana	Mexia
Chavies	Joquin	Palos
Chepultepec	Lasca	Perdido

[1] For a discussion of place names see page 16.

[2] This list is taken from *Leonard's Guide*, ninth edition, and does not include names of counties, rivers, lakes, mountains, valleys, or of streets, roads, passes, etc.

Perdido Beach
Perote

Saco
Texas

Valhermoso Springs
Vina

Arizona

Agua Caliente
Aguila
Ajo
Alhambra
Alto
Amado
Apache
Arivaca
Bolada
Bonita
Camp Verde
Canyon Diablo
Casa Grande
Cascabel
Chino Valley
Cibola
Concho
Cordes

Cortaro
Don Luis
Dos Cabezas
Ganado
Geronimo
Gila (Xila)
Laguna
Madera Canyon
Marana
Maricopa
Mesa
Mescal
Naco
Navajo
Nogales
Nutrioso
Palo Alto

Palomas
Palo Verde
Pantano
Pima
Portal
Quijotoa
Rillito
Sacaton
Sahuarita
San Carlos
San Simon
Sombrero Butte
Sonora
Tacna
Tonalea
Tonto Basin
Venezia

Arkansas

Alto
Armada
Bella Vista
Bexar
Bonanza
Cabanal
Chula
Delmar

Diaz
El Dorado
Elk Ranch
El Paso
Jacinto
Lavaca
Luna Landing
Mesa

Montana
Moro
Paraloma
Salado
Saltillo
Toledo
Toltec
Tomato

California

Acampo
Adelanto
Agua Caliente
Alameda
Alamo
Alcatraz

Alma
Alta
Altadena
Alta Loma
Altaville
Alturas

Alvarado
Arroyo Grande
Atascadero
Avila
Bautista
Bernal

Blanco
Boca
Bodega
Bodega Roads
Bolinas
Bonita
Borego
Buena Park
Cabazon
Cajon
Calabasas
Caliente
Calor
Camanche
Camarillo
Camino
Campo
Campo Seco
Camp Sierra
Canyon
Carpinteria
Casa Blanca
Casitos Springs
Castella
Cazadero
Ceres
Chico
Chino
Chowchilla
Chualar
Chula Vista
Cima
Cisco
Colma
Concepcion
Conejo
Coronado
Corral De Tierra
Corte Madera
Costa Mesa
Coyote

Cresta Blanca
Crucero
Del Loma
Del Mar
Del Monte
Del Paso Heights
Del Rey
De Luz
De Sabla
Descanso
Diablo
Dos Palos
Dos Rios
Duarte
Dulzura
El Cajon
El Centro
El Cerrito
El Dorado
El Granada
El Mirage
El Modeno
El Monte
El Nido
El Portal
El Prado
El Rio
El Segundo
El Toro
El Verano
Elverta
Encanto
Encinitas
Escalon
Escondido
Esmerelda
Esparto
Fallon
Famoso
Fortuna
French Corral

Fresno
Fruto
Gaviota
Goleta
Gonzales
Granada
Grenada
Guadalupe
Hermosa Beach
Hernandez
Hondo
Hornitos
Ignacio
Indio
Jacumba
Laguna Beach
Lagunitas
La Habra
La Honda
La Jolla
La Manda Park
La Mesa
La Mirada
La Panza
La Porte
Las Plumas
Laton
Linda Vista
Llanada
Llano
Loma Linda
Loma Mar
Loma Portal
Lomita
Lomita Park
Lorenzo
Los Alamitos
Los Alamos
Los Altos
Los Angeles
Los Baños

Los Gatos
Los Molinos
Los Nietos
Los Olivos
Lucia
Madrone
Malaga
Manteca
Manton
Manzanar
Marina
Mariposa
Martinez
Mar Vista
Melones
Mendocino
Mendota
Merced
Mesa Grande
Milpitas
Mina
Mira Loma
Miramar
Miramonte
Miranda
Mocalno
Modesto
Moneta
Mono Lake
Monrovia
Montalvo
Montara
Montebello
Montecito
Monterey
Monte Vista
Moreno
Morro Bay
Navarro
Navelencia
Novato

Nuevo
Oceano
Olancha
Omo Ranch
Oro Grande
Oro Loma
Orosi
Pacheco
Paicines
Pala
Palermo
Palo Alto
Palo Cedro
Paloma
Palos Verdes
Palo Verde
Paraiso Springs
Pasadena
Paso Robles
Pescadero
Petrolia
Pico
Pinole
Placentia
Platina
Point Arena
Point Loma
Point Reyes
Pomona
Pondosa
Port Costa
Port San Luis
Portero
Pozo
Prado
Pueblo
Puente
Pulga
Ramona
Rancho Santa Fe
Reseda

Redondo Beach
Represa
Requa
Rio Bonito
Rio Campo
Rio Dell
Rionido
Rio Oso
Rio Vista
Rivera
Rodeo
Sacramento
Salada Beach
Salida
Salinas
San Andreas
San Anselmo
San Ardo
San Benito
San Bernardino
San Carlos
San Clements
San Diego
San Fernando
San Francisco
San Gabriel
San Geronimo
San Gregorio
San Jacinto
San Joaquin
San Jose
San Juan Bautista
San Juan Capistrano
San Leandro
San Lorenzo
San Lucas
San Luis Obispo
San Luis Rey
San Marcos
San Marino
San Martin

San Mateo
San Onofre
San Pablo
San Pedro
San Quentin
San Rafael
San Ramon
Santa Ana
Santa Anita
Santa Barbara
Santa Clara
Santa Cruz
Santa Fe Springs
Santa Margarita
Santa Maria
Santa Paula
Santa Rosa
Santa Susana
Santa Ynez
Santa Ysabel
San Ysidro

Sausalito
Sepulveda
Sierra
Sierra City
Sierraville
Solana Beach
Soledad
Sonoma
Sonora
Sorrento
Tamales
Tamalpais
Tecate
Tecopa
Temecula
Termo
Tia Juana
Tiburon
Tolenas
Tres Pinos
Trigo

Trinidad
Triunfo
Trona
Tulare
Vacaville
Vallejo
Vallicita
Val Verde
Valyermo
Venado
Ventura
Verdugo City
Vidal
Villa Grande
Vista
Yermo
Yolanda
Yolo
Yerba Linda
Zamora

Colorado

Aguilar
Alamo
Alamosa
Alma
Antonito
Arboles
Aroya
Arriba
Arvada
Barela
Blanca
Bonanza
Boncarbo
Boyero
Buena Vista
Cahone
Campo
Canon City

Capulin
Cebolla
Chama
Colona
Como
Conejos
Cortez
Cuchara Camps
Cumbres
Delcarbon
Delegua
Del Norte
Dolores
Durango
Eldora
El Moro
Escalante Forks
Espinoza

Frisco
Galatea
Garcia
Granada
Huerfano
Jaroso
La Boca
La Garita
La Jara
La Junta
Laplata
La Veta
La Veta Pass
Leal
Limon
Loma
Manzanola
Mesa Verde

Mesita
Mogota
Molina
Monte Vista
Montezuma
Morapos
Mosca
Naturita
Niñaview
Ojo
Ortiz
Pagosa Junction
Piedra

Piñon
Poncha Springs
Portal
Primero
Pueblo
Redmesa
Rico
Rioblanco
Rosita
Saguache
Salida
San Acacio
San Luis

San Pablo
Sapinero
Sedalia
Solar
Sonora
Tercio
Termina
Timpas
Trinchera
Trinidad
Valdez
Yampa

Florida

Altamonte Springs
Alturas
Alva
Anastasia
Andalusia
Arredondo
Aventina
Azucar
Bocagrande
Boca Raton
Bonita Springs
Buena Vista
Capitola
Captiva
Cocoa
Cocoa Beach
Cordova
Coronado Beach
Cortez
Española
Estero
Esto

Fernandina
Florida City
Floridatown
Florosa
Fort Barrancas
Gasparilla
Gomez
Gonzalez
Hernando
Hibernia
Industria
Islamorada
Key Largo
Key West
Lacota
Lake Jovita
Largo
Lecanto
Limona
Manavista
Marco
Mayo

Ortega
Oviedo
Pasadena
Pedro
Ponce De Leon
Ponce Park
Progresso
Punta Gorda
Punta Rassa
Rio
San Blas
San Carlos
San Mateo
Santa Fe
Santa Rosa
Santo
Sorrento
Uleta
Umatilla
Valparaiso
Villa Tasso
Vista

Georgia

Alma
Altamaha

Alto
Campania

Canoe
Desoto

Eldora
Eldorado
Eldorendo
Loco
Martinez
Montezuma
Montivedio

Pavo
Resaca
Rincon
Talona
Texas
Toledo

Unadilla
Uvalde
Valambrosa
Valona
Villa Rica
Waco

Idaho

Acequia
Almo
Corral

Lago
Mesa
Orofino

Orogrande
Plano
Santa

Illinois

Alma
Alto Pass
Andalusia
Argenta
Avena
Basco
Bogota
Bolivia
Buena Vista
Camargo
Cerror Gordo
Chasco
Chili
Cordova

Cuba
De Soto
Eldorado
Elmira
El Paso
Frisco
Gila
Hidalgo
Lima
Manito
Media
Metamora
Modesto
Montezuma

Moro
Nevada
Paloma
Palos Park
Petrolia
Plano
Reno
Rio
Sandoval
Tampico
Texas City
Toledo
Toluca
Tonica

Indiana

Alto
Alton
Amo
Buena Vista
Chili
Cuzco

Florida
Lagro
Lapaz
Metamora
Mexico
Monterey

Montezuma
Nevada
Saltillo
San Jacinto
Santa Fe
Waco

Iowa

Alta
Alta Vista
Buena Vista

Canoe
Castana
De Soto

Durango
Eldorado
Fonda

Key West
Lima
Monterey
Montezuma

Nevada
Palo
Paralta
Peru

Plano
Rubio
Toledo

Kansas

Alamota
Alma
Alta
Alta Vista
Antonino
Arma
Bonita
Capaldo

Cimarron
Cuba
De Soto
Eudora
Granada
Kanorado
Lerado
Linda

Mayo
Montana
Montezuma
Palco
Ramona
Salina

Kentucky

Alhambra
Allegre
Benito
Buena Vista
Callaboose
Camargo
Canoe
Comargo

Cordova
Cuba
Hidalgo
Linda
Matanzas
Mexico
Miranda
Sacramento

Seco
Silva
Sonora
Teresita
Texas
Tobacco
Uno
Waco

Louisiana

Alfalfa
Alto
Alton
Ama
Arizona
Bolivar
Capitan
Cargas
Creole

Delcambre
Delombre
Esto
Frisco
Gonzales
Luna
Lunita
Mansura
Mayo

Mora
Nuñez
Rio
Rita
Segura
Serena
Sorrento
Tunica
Maine

Michigan

Alamo
Alma
Alto
Armada
Bravo

Caro
Eldorado
Escanaba
Luna Pier
Mio

Monterey
Palo
Ramona
Unadilla

Minnesota

Almora
Altura
Alvarado
Carlos
Fernando

Glendorado
Granada
Havanna
Keywest
Monterey

Montevideo
Mora
Palo
St. Rosa
Santiago

Mississippi

Alligator
De Soto
Doloroso
Eldorado

Gitano
Jacinto
Mesa
Molino

Quito
Sabino
Saltillo
Soso

Missouri

Alma
Altamont
Amazonia
Antonia
Bolivar
Caverna
Conception
De Soto
Eldorado Springs
Florida
Fortuna
Frisco
Manila

Mano
Mendota
Mexico
Molino
Nevada
Palopinto
Panama
Passo
Plano
Plaza
Pomona
Reno
Saco

Salcedo
San Antonio
Santa Fe
Santa Rosa
Santiago
Sereno
Silva
Solo
Vinita Park
Vista
Waco
Yucatan
Zora

Montana

Alma
Alzada
Amazon
Argenta
Chico
Comanche
Como

Cordova
Fresno
Laredo
Lima
Loma
Marias
Merino

Mona
Monida
Navajo
Pablo
Ranchcreek
Saco
Vida

Nebraska

Alma
Arizona
Chalco
Cordova

Desoto
Eldorado
Lavaca

Loma
Orafino
Sacramento

Nevada

Alamo
Caliente
Cobre

Cortez
Las Vegas

Mesquite
Orovada

New Mexico

Abeytas
Agua Fria
Alameda
Alamo
Alamogordo
Albuquerque
Algodones
Alire
Alma
Alto
Amalia
Amistad
Anal
Ancho
Animas
Anton Chico
Apache Creek
Aragon
Archuleta
Armijo
Arroyesco
Arroyo Hondo
Atarque
Augustine
Belen
Berino
Blanco
Bodega
Bosque
Buena Vista
Bueyeros
Caballo
Cabezon
Cambray
Cameron

Canjilon
Cañones
Capitan
Capulin
Carrizozo
Casa Blanca
Cebolla
Cerrillos
Cerro
Chacon
Chama
Chamberino
Chamisal
Chamita
Chaperito
Chico
Chijuilla
Chilili
Chimayo
Chupadero
Cienega
Cimarron
Cobre
Colonias
Contreras
Cordova
Corona
Correo
Costilla
Coyote
Crystal
Cuba
Cubero
Cuchillo
Cuervo

Cundiyo
Cunico
Dereno
Domingo
Dominguez
Doña Ana
Dora
Dulce
Duoro
El Morro
El Paso Gap
El Porvenir
El Rito
El Valle
Embudo
Encino
Escabosa
Escondida
Española
Estancia
Fierro
Flora Vista
Florida
Galisteo
Gallegos
Gallina
Gamerco
Garita
Gascon
Gavilan
Gila
Glenrio
Glorieta
Gran Quivira
Guadalupe

Guadalupita
Hachita
Hermosa
Hernandez
Hilario
Hondo
Inez
Isleta
Jarales
Jemes
Jemez Springs
La Cueva
Laguna
La Jara
Lajoya
La Luz
La Madera
La Mesa
Laplata
La Puente
Largo
Las Cruces
Las Palomas
Las Tablas
Las Vegas
La Union
Liendre
Los Cerrillos
Los Chavez
Los Lunas
Lucero
Magdalena
Malaga
Mangas
Manuelito
Manzano
Marcia
Marquez
Mescalero
Mesilla
Mesilla Park

Mesquite
Miera
Milagro
Mimbres
Mogollon
Montezuma
Montoya
Mora
Mosquero
Negra
New Laguna
Nogal
Ocate
Ochoa
Ojo Caliente
Ojo Feliz
Ojo Sarco
Optimo
Orogrande
Oscuro
Paguate
Pajarito
Palma
Palvadera
Pasamonte
Pastura
Pecos
Pedernal
Peñablanca
Peñasco
Perea
Petaca
Picacho
Pilar
Piñon
Pinos Altos
Pintada
Placitas
Portales
Progresso
Puertocito

Puerto de Luna
Quemado
Questa
Ramon
Raton
Rayo
Rencona
Ribera
Rincon
Rio Grande
Rio Pueblo
Rociada
Rodarte
Rodeo
Romeroville
Ruidoso
Sabinoso
San Acacia
San Antonio
Sanchez
Sandia Park
Sandoval
San Felipe
San Fidel
San Geronimo
San Jon
San Jose
San Lorenzo
San Marcial
San Mateo
San Miguel
San Patricio
San Rafael
Santa Cruz
Santa Fe
Santa Rita
Santa Rosa
San Ysidro
Sapello
Seboyeta
Seneca

Señorito
Serafina
Servilleta
Socorro
Sofia
Solano
Taos
Tapia
Tecolotenos
Tererro
Tierra Amarilla
Torreon

Trampas
Trechado
Trementina
Tres Lagunas
Tres Piedras
Tres Ritos
Truchas
Trujillo
Tularosa
Tusas
Vadito

Vado
Valdez
Valedon
Valencia
Vallecitos
Valmora
Veguita
Velarde
Vermejo Park
Villanueva
Volcano

New York

Alma
Boliver
Chili
Churubusco
Cuba
Florida

Fonda
Leon
Lima
Mariposa
Mexico
Monterey

Montezuma
Panama
Rio
Santa Clara
Sonora

North Dakota

Alamo
Cuba
Emerado
Fonda
Fortuna

Grano
Havana
Juanita
Mona

Ojata
Plaza
Ruso
Silva

Ohio

Agosta
Alma
Boneta
Cavallo
Chili
Chillicothe
Desoto
Eldorado
Florida
Havana

Isleta
Lima
Limaville
Metamora
Mexico
Monterey
Montezuma
Morral
Pedro

Peru
Rio Grande
Saltillo
Santa Fe
Sonora
Texas
Tobasco
Toboso
Toledo

Oklahoma

Alfalfa
Alma
Amorita
Apache
Blanco
Camargo
Ceres
Cerrogordo
Cestos

Clarita
Cogar
Comanche
Concho
Cruce
Eldorado
El Reno
Frisco

Goza
Harjo
Leon
Lima
Loco
Optima
Salina
Santa Fe

Oregon

Alma
Bonanza
Bonita
Canyon City
Canyonville
Chico

Delmar
Estacada
Glenada
Grande Ronde
Juntura
Montavilla

Moro
Salado
Santa Clara
Toledo
Vida
Vistillas

Pennsylvania

Andalusia
Anita
Arroyo
Blanco
Bolivar
Buena Vista
Chinchilla
El Dorado
Fontana

Frisco
La Jose
Lima
Lopez
Manito
Matamoras
Mesta
Mont Alto

Primos
Sacramento
Salina
Salona
Saltillo
Saluvia
Sonora
Villa Maria

South Dakota

Pedro

Peno

Tennessee

Alamo
Almaville
Altamont
Alto
Bogota
Cerro Gordo

Cordova
Cuba
Del Rio
De Soto
Elpardo

Lascassas
Quito
Saltillo
Santa Fe
Tobaccoport

Texas

Acala
Agua Dulce
Agua Nueva
Aguilares
Alamo
Alamo Alto
Alcino
Aledo
Aleman
Algerita
Alhambra
Alma
Almeda
Alta Loma
Altavista
Alto
Altonia
Alvarado
Amarillo
Anahuac
Apolonia
Argenta
Atascosa
Bandera
Barbarosa
Benavides
Blanco
Blanconia
Bogata
Bolivar
Bonanza
Bonita
Boquillas
Bosqueville
Brazos
Bronco
Buenavista
Calaveras
Camp San Saba
Camp Verde

Candelaria
Cañutillo
Canyon
Caranchua
Carlos
Carmona
Caro
Carrizo Springs
Carta Valley
Casa Piedra
Cayote
Chapman Ranch
Charco
Chico
Chicota
Chillicothe
Chita
Cibolo
Colorado
Comal
Como
Concepcion
Concho
Crestonio
Cuero
Cuevitas
Del Rio
De Soto
Dinero
Durango
El Bernardo
El Campo
Eldorado
Encinal
Encino
Estacado
Frijole
Frio Town
Geronimo
Glen Rio

Goliad
Golindo
Guadalupe
Guajillo
Guerra
Hacienda
Helotes
Hidalgo
Hondo
Isla
Itasca
Izoro
Jacobia
Kyote
La Blanca
La Feria
Lagarto
Laguna
La Joya
Lamesa
Lampasas
La Paloma
Laredo
La Reforma
Lariat
Lasara
Latexo
La Tuna
La Villa
Levita
Llano
Lobo
Loco
Lolita
Lometa
Lopeno
Los Angeles
Los Ebanos
Los Fresnos
Los Indios

Los Saenz
Lozano
Madera Springs
Madero
Mambrino
Martinez
Matador
Matagorda
Mendota
Mendoza
Mercedes
Mesa
Mesquite
Mexia
Mico
Mirando City
Monaville
Montalba
Monteola
Morales
Navarro
Navasota
Navidad
Nevada
Nopal
Nubia
Olivia
Olmito
Palacios
Palito Blanco
Paloduro
Palo Pinto
Pampa
Pasadena
Patilo
Patonia
Patroon
Pecos
Pedigo
Percilla
Placedo

Placedo Junction
Plano
Ponta
Port Lavaca
Presidio
Primera
Progreso
Pueblo
Puerto Rico
Pyote
Ramirez
Ramirito
Ranchland
Randado
Realitos
Refugio
Ricardo
Rio Frio
Rio Grande
Rio Hondo
Riomedina
Riovista
Rita Santa
Roma
Ruidosa
Sabanno
Sabinal
Salado
Salineno
Saltillo
San Angelo
San Antonio
San Augustine
San Benito
Sandia
San Diego
Sandoval
San Elizario
San Felipe
San Gabriel

San Jacinto
San Jose
San Juan
San Leon
San Manuel
San Marcos
San Patricio
San Perlita
San Saba
Santa Anna
Santa Cruz
Santa Elena
Santa Maria
Santa Monica
Santa Rosa
Santo
San Ygnacio
Saragosa
Saron
Sebastian
Sejita
Sion
Socorro
South Bosque
Stampede
Talco
Tascosa
Tierra Alta
Tira
Toledo
Tolosa
Tornillo
Trevino
Trinidad
Uvalde
Vega
Viboras
Vista
Voca
Ysleta

Utah

Bonita	Mona	Salduro
Callao	Pinto	Salina
Escalante	Pintura	Spring Canyon
Frisco		

Washington

Alameda	Manzanita	Redondo
Alfalfa	Mesa	Rosalia
Almira	Mill Ranch	Rosario
Carbonado	Monte Cristo	Roza
Covada	Mora	San de Fuca
Delrio	Oroville	Silvana
Jovita	Oso	Tampico
Juanita	Pateros	Toledo
Malo	Plaza	Vega
Manito		

Wyoming

Alcova	Canyon	Ranchester
Altamont	Canyon Ranche	Toltec
Arminto	Mona	Uva
Arvada	Pedro	

III. BULLFIGHT TERMS

alguacil A police, or municipal, officer of the bull ring.

arrastre The dragging out of the bulls or horses killed in the arena.

banderilla A dart or stick about two feet long provided with a metal prong or hook which is stuck into the neck of the bull to stir him to angry action. The instrument derives its name from the colored bannerettes which it usually bears. *Banderillas* are fixed in the animal's neck in pairs.

banderillero A member of the bullfighting personnel whose function it is to affix the flagged darts (*banderillas*) in the neck of the bull.

barrera A barrier about five feet high separating the arena from the grandstand.

brindis The short formal toast or speech delivered by the matador to the presiding officer just before the killing *suerte*.

capa A cloak.

capote A cloak worn by the matador.

chulo An assistant in the bull ring.

cornado From *cornar*, to horn. Horned.

corrida A bullfight performance; also *corrida de toros*.

cuadrilla The troop of bullfighters; i.e., picadores, *banderilleros*, and matador.

espada A sword used for killing the bull in the final scene. The matador is also known as the *espada*.

estocada The stroke with the sword or *estoque*.

estoque A long, narrow sword used by the matador to dispatch the bull.

faja A scarf worn about the waist by bullfighters.

garrocha An iron-tipped pike, usually three pronged, used by the *picador* (the horseman).

hoi! hoi! Ejaculation made by the fighter to attract the bull's attention.

lidia From *lidiar*, to fight. The act of bullfighting.

matador From *matar*, to kill. One who kills. Of the bull ring's dramatis personae, the *matador* plays the leading role (excepting, of course, the bull itself).

mono sabio Literally "wise monkey." Ring attendant or *mozo* who performs various menial tasks.

montera The decorated hat or head covering worn by a bullfighter.

muleta The rod, and red cloth blind attached to it, carried by the *matador* in his left hand.

paseo de las cuadrillas The grand entry of the fighters into the ring at the opening of the bullfight.

penco A broken-down horse; a nag, or jade.

picador From *picar*, to stick in or prick. The bullfighter on horseback who uses a *garrocha* or pike to prod the bull.

plaza de toros A bull park or bull ring.

puntilla A thin dagger.

suerte A "turn" or sort of "innings" at provoking the bull; thus a *suerte* by the picadores, then a *suerte* by the *banderilleros*, etc.

tauromaquia The art of fighting bulls according to traditional and definite rules.

torero A bullfighter; synonymous with *espada* and *matador*.

toril The pen in which bulls are kept before entering the ring.

IV. EXAMPLES OF BILINGUALISM

The letters given below illustrate the extent to which Americans along the border who have a ready command of Spanish may use Spanish expressions in informal correspondence. It is quite possible that at times the Spanish serves to maintain informality. At other times the Spanish seems to be used for effectiveness. *Hermanito*, for instance, near the end of the first letter could scarcely be replaced adequately by any word in English. *A que hijo tan tres piedras*! is an idiomatic Spanish phrase hard to match in English. The bilinguist, or semi-bilinguist, when writing informally, often finds at his ready disposal such expressions. Apparently he takes advantage of them in preference to searching his vocabulary for suitable English equivalents.

1

Dear . . .

If this letter is delayed any longer it will soon be as slow as your last one was. I can plainly see why you delayed so long now though. We are very eager to *saber tus planes ahora. Vas a venir aqui el ano que viene?* . . . and a dozen other questions which you *sabes muy bien que deseamos saber.*

We are contemplating going to the U . . . of . . . the coming year. They have an outstanding department there and I am quite sure of a fellowship. I am trying to close an agreement which will permit me to do research work for them this summer, *pero Quien sabe?*

Before I forget about it, just a few words about Junior. *A que hijo tan tres piedras! Ayer cumplio nueve meses y pesa veinte y cuatro libras, tiene neuve dientes, sabe decir el* "bye, bye," *y sabe andar cogiendo las sillas y hasta sabe decir* "da da," *lo que quiere decir* Daddy. *Ha dormido afuera todo el invierno; aun cuando fueron doce grados bajo el zero. Ay como le gustan los legumbres naranjas, atole, y hasta el* Cod liver oil. *Quiere bañarse al sol todos los dias, y como esta aprendiendo tocar el piano! Hay muchas otras cosas que merecen decirse en su favor pero basta con estas.*

Tu hermanito T . . . was victorious . . . He defeated his opponent by two hundred votes . . .

Rey manda muchas saludas a J . . . y quiere que ella le escriba unas cuantas palabras si es que le da gana. Esperamos que no delatan tanto en escribir.

Quedamos como siempre,

2

Dear . . .

I daren't imagine how long it has been since you wrote me *una cartita buena* . . . But it was not so long that I do not remember it with appreciation.

Since then *he tenido experiencias varias y ahora, como le ha dicho mi "dulce" sin duda, estoy con la mama por unos cuantos dias.* The collecting is going right along. The other steps will be simple enough, except perhaps the assembling which will cost our . . . corporation about *un mil* or *dos. Que sin virquenzas son aqui . . .*

Ah, *que hijo tienes, de veras.* He would make three like ours . . . From several we have heard that he is a prize winner in every way, *hasta la voz y todo.*

I am interested in your plans for studying. You may also know that we are rather disappointed that you did not come here. The fellowship however, is a great consideration. With your ambitions set so high now I'd like to call *una junta para saber el porque y como. Tenga cuidado con estos socios tuyos en el departamento, que tienen ideas modernas . . . No olvides el papá Juanito y las enseñanzas de la juventud! Es decir . . .* He hablado con los tres y me dejan con el "quien sabe"?*.

Now the chief purpose of this letter is to wish you *buen viaje y buena fortuna* and to hope that before long *nos vemos. Recuerdos a la familia, y por favor manda la mia pronto.*

Como siempre,

3

Mi querido amigo y familia:

Me parece que una cartita tuya has been calling for an answer for a long time. I don't know whether you will still be at this address or not, *pero veremos.*

Leimos en el "News" *que has recibido un nombramiento . . .* That is *muy tres piedras y te felicitamos bastante.* Are you going to be able to take a *viaje a la tierra prometida*? I had a very good trip there this, or last Summer. Went on a real hunting trip and got two deer and *algunos* trouts. Ah *que* fish suppers *tuvimos tan buenas.* I reached here in time for the second term of Summer school.

We are getting along very well. They have a very good department here. I should like to have gone to—but the department there is *muy debil.* They have let all their best men go elsewhere.—

Y la niña como esta? Ya sabe decir Papa? Hay como hacen la vida interesante, verdad? No podriamos vivir sin el hijo. Es que ha vuelto tu esposa? Que piensas del new *Presidente en Mejico? Una sorpresa que no?*

Pues ojala que el Santa Claus *te visita con bolsas llenas. Saludos a todos los amigos que me conozcan.*

"*Hasta la vuelta*"

SELECT BIBLIOGRAPHY

DICTIONARIES

Alemany, Jose, Diccionario Enciclopedico Ilustrado. Barcelona, 1927.

Bartlett, John R., Dictionary of Americanisms. Boston, 1877.

Century Dictionary, The. 6 vols., New York, 1889.

Farmer, John S., Dictionary of Americanisms. London, 1889.

Larousse, Pierre, Pequeño Larousse Ilustrado. Paris, 1917.

Maitland, James, American Slang Dictionary. Chicago, 1891.

Murray, James A. H., The New English Dictionary. Oxford, 1888.

Real Academia Española, Diccionario Manual y Ilustrado de la Lengua Española. Madrid, 1927.

Salvá y Perez, Vicente, Diccionario de la Lengua Castellana. Madrid, 1837.

Skeat, Walter William, Etymological Dictionary of the English Language. Oxford, 1888.

Stanford Dictionary of Anglicized Words and Phrases, The, ed. by C. A. M. Fennell. Cambridge, 1892.

Webster's New International Dictionary. Springfield, 1932.

GLOSSARIES, WORD LISTS, AND LANGUAGE STUDIES

Alvarez, Victoriano Salado, Mejico Peregrino. Mexico, 1924.

Bancroft, H. H., California Pastoral. San Francisco, 1888.

Bierschwale, Margaret, English of the Texas Range. Master's Thesis, Columbia, 1920.

Blackmar, F. W., Spanish American Words.

Castillo, Ricardo de, Mejicanismos.

Chapin, F. A., Spanish Words That Have Become Westernisms. 1925.

De Vere, M. Schele, Americanisms; the English of the New World. New York, 1872.

Espinosa, A. M., Palabras Españolas y Inglesas.

——— Speech Mixture in New Mexico (From "The Pacific Ocean in History" by Stephens and Bolton, New York, 1917.

——— Studies in New Mexican Spanish (Thesis, Ph.D., Chicago, 1909.

Frazier, Allegra, English Usage and the Schools in Arizona (Master's Thesis, Columbia, 1919.)

Garcia, Don Joaquin, Mexicanismos. 1905 (1899).

Granada, Daniel, El Americanismo en los Vocabularios Españoles y Portugueses. 1919.

Hills, E. C., New Mexican Spanish (Publication M.L.A., 1906)

Hispanic Notes and Monographs (Essays, studies and brief biographies issued by the Hispanic Society of America)

Minsheu, John, Guide into Tongues. London, 1625.

Read, William Alexander, Louisiana Place-Names of Indian Origin. Baton Rouge, La., 1927.

Rubio, Dario, La Anarquia del Lenguage en la America Española. Mexico, 1925.

Scott, F. N., Pronunciation of Spanish American Words. 1891.

Socrates, Hyacinth, Southwestern Slang. (In *Overland Monthly*, vol. 3, San Francisco, 1869.)

Thornton, R. H., An American Glossary. Philadelphia, 1912.

Tucker, Gilbert M., American English. New York, 1921.

Vizetelley, and DeBekker, A Desk-Book of Idioms and Idiomatic Phrases in English Speech and Literature. New York, 1923.

Miscellaneous

Bancroft, H. H., History of Arizona and New Mexico. San Francisco, 1888.

Bartlett, J. A., Personal Narrative of Explorations in Texas . . . 1854.

Benedict, H. Y., and J. A. Lomax, Book of Texas. 1916.

Blackmar, F. W., Spanish Institutions of the Southwest. Baltimore, 1891.

Bourne, E. G., Spain in America. New York and London, 1904.

Bradley, G. D., Winning the Southwest. Chicago, 1912.

Chapman, Arthur, The Pony Express. New York, 1932.

Chase, J. Smeaton, California Desert Trails. Boston and New York, 1916.

Cody, William Frederick, Heroes of the Plains. 1891.

Coues, Elliott, Expeditions of Zebulon M. Pike. 3 vols., New York, 1895.

Denis, A. J., Spanish Alta California. New York, 1927.

Dobie, J. Frank, A. Vaquero of the Brush Country. Dallas, Texas, 1928.

Duffus, R. L., The Santa Fe Trail. New York, 1930.

Emory, Lieut-Col. W. H., Notes of a Military Reconnoissance. Washington, 1848.

Encyclopaedia Britannica, 14th ed. London & New York, 1929.

Fremont, J. C., Report of the Exploring Expedition to the Rocky Mountains . . . Washington, 1843–1844.

Garrison, G. P., Western Extension 1841–1850; the American Nation: a History. New York & London, 1906.

Ghent, W. H., The Early Far West. New York, 1931.

Goodwin, Cardinal, The Trans-Mississippi West, 1803–1853. New York, London, 1928.

Gregg, Josiah, Commerce of the Prairies. 2 vols., New York, 1845.

Gruening, Ernest, Mexico and Its Heritage. New York, 1928.

Handbook of American Indians. Washington, 1910. (Bulletin 30, Bureau of American Ethnology.)

Inman, Henry, The Old Santa Fe Trail. New York, 1897.

Kendall, G. W., Narrative of the Texan Santa Fe Expedition. 2 vols., New York, 1844.

Lyman, George D., John Marsh, Pioneer. New York, 1930.

McBride, George M., The Land Systems of Mexico. New York, 1923.

McCaleb, W. F., The Aaron Burr Conspiracy. New York, 1903.

McLean, Robert Norris, That Mexican! New York, London, etc., 1928.